AF506295

The

McCallum

Saga

"Tahquitz, canyon of spirits,"
oil by John W. Hilton. Ed Ainsworth collection.

The McCallum Saga

The Story of the Founding of Palm Springs

By Katherine Ainsworth

1973

THE PALM SPRINGS DESERT MUSEUM

Printed in the United States of America by Grant Dahlstrom/The Castle Press, Pasadena, California.

Foreword

The Palm Springs Desert Museum considers it a special privilege to publish The McCallum Saga which presents a remarkable story of the McCallum family and of other early settlers, as well as of the founding of Palm Springs. It reveals an extraordinary era of pioneering in California shared by John Guthrie McCallum, lawyer, State Senator, editor, State Constitutional leader, and early land developer, and by his family, including particularly his surviving daughter, the late Pearl (Mrs. Austin G.) McManus. Her family brought her to the desert as a child in 1884, and she devoted most of the years of her long life until her demise in 1966 to her father's dream of achieving a beautiful and productive desert community.

It is very fortunate that the skillful and painstaking services of Mrs. Katherine Ainsworth could be secured for the extensive research and writing of this important chapter of California history not heretofore so fully presented.

In the achievement of the superb new facilities now under construction, the Palm Springs Desert Museum also is proud that its Natural History Wing is to be known as The McCallum Wing and is made possible through a major challenge grant by the trustees of The McCallum Desert Foundation established by the late Pearl McManus in honor of her father.

Contents

PART ONE

Pilgrimage to Greatness

PART TWO

The Land of the Afternoon

PART THREE
The Steadfast Dream

The Foreshadowing

The shade from this venerable fig tree provided the first shelter for the McCallum family until their adobe home was built.

JOHN GUTHRIE McCALLUM

Courtesy Palm Springs Desert Museum.

EARILY the two dust-covered men reined the tired, heaving
horses to a halt as their wagon rounded a bend and came to a rise in the
rutted tracks midst the sand and boulders across which they had jolted
for so many miles.

From this crest the two men looked out upon a wide stretch of the
mysterious Colorado Desert — dreaded cauldron it had been proclaimed
by those who feared its scorching heat. The swarthier of the two men
stretched an arm and pointed out to his friend the long, rolling reaches
of sand dunes flowing from the base of a lofty mountain. Then, turning
slightly, his finger centered upon clusters of tall palms, sentinels of
the canyons and the oasis which was their goal for the day.

Will Pablo, Indian guide and interpreter, was eager for his friend
to reach the healing waters of the oasis. He urged the exhausted horses
to press ahead. The surrey approached the waters, and the other man —
tall, full-bearded John Guthrie McCallum — gazed about in wonder. He
saw great beauty in the changing, glowing sunlight as it was reflected
upon the rounded breasts of the sand dunes and each desert plant. He
was astonished to see the myriad varieties of these plants and the pro-
fusion of desert growth, when his first cursory glance saw what appeared
to be but vast empty wastes of harsh sun-bleached land.

As the wagon drew up to the delightful mineral water and a few
brown-faced gentle Indians shyly came to extend a welcome, the sun
suddenly, without any warning that the day was drawing to a close
despite the early hour, plummeted behind the tall mountain peak. The
entire area was cloaked in shadow and the long afternoon began. It was,
thought the visitor, as though the mountain standing in such exalted
arrogance relented of its pride and bent forward to envelop them in its
embrace and cloak them in its cooling shade.

The sonorous words of Tennyson's narrative poem, *The Lotos-Eaters*,
came rushing back as he sat looking upward at the peaks now brushed by
the rosy tints of the setting sun. He recalled the poem-story of those

weary wanderers, The Lotos-Eaters, and repeated the lines in a hushed voice: "In the afternoon they came unto a land / In which it seemed always afternoon."

He thought the words most appropriate and ever afterwards thought of this spot as being the "Land of the Afternoon." In the poem Tennyson had described a land where the air was languid, palm trees waved in the breeze, and the people were dusky-hued and gentle. Again the man spoke aloud as he recalled the closing line of the poem which seemed to be especially applicable: "We will no longer roam."

John Guthrie McCallum felt an immediate affinity for the welcoming oasis. He knew instantly that this Palm Valley, as he called it in his mind, with the warmth and fragrant air and the healing waters was the place to which he must bring his family. Into this Palm Valley they would come.

And so it was that Palm Springs, as it would eventually become known, the gayest and sunniest spa on earth, was born of a double sorrow.

This settlement on the Colorado Desert, huddling at the foot of towering Mt. San Jacinto, began in the first place out of the anxiety of a widowed Indiana mother for her two sons in faraway San Francisco on the Pacific Shores at the time of the Gold Rush. It was to be culminated years later, by the desperate illness of that same woman's grandson and the events growing out of it.

San Gorgonio Pass, Carl Eytel.
Courtesy Southwest Museum.

The McCallum Saga

McCALLUM ADOBE.

Watercolor painted in 1892. Presented to Patricia Moorten by Pearl McCallum McManus as a gift. A rare painting showing the house in its entirety.

Part One
Pilgrimage Toward Greatness

Sketch by Carl Eytel. Courtesy Southwest Museum.

I.

The Pilgrimage Begins

Typical of the first steamboats on the Ohio River is this sketch drawn by Donna Cole, nationally known artist, for the Vevay Reveille-Enterprise Souvenir Edition. These boats were designed with flat-bottom hulls to enable them to ride the water currents ranging from fifteen inches to five feet of water.

Ellen McCallum, John Guthrie McCallum's mother. Courtesy Palm Springs Desert Museum.

THE STORY OF PALM SPRINGS, California, began with the delivery of a letter to a widowed mother living in a small hamlet in Indiana.

The year was 1852.

The name of that village was Vevay in Switzerland County.

Switzerland County, Indiana, on the banks of the brooding Ohio River which wound its way through towns with stately old homes, was founded in 1801 by a group of Swiss immigrants. They called the county seat Vevay (pronounced Vee-Vee) and planted vineyards in the rich yellow clay soil. These industrious Swiss became famous for their special wine.

It was not too long before wine-making in this region gave way to agriculture. A group of hardy, frugal Scotch families began a settlement on ''Long Run'' about 1817-18. They soon discovered that a bushel of potatoes would buy a gallon of wine and was far faster and easier to produce!

3

"Among those Scottish families were Neil McCallum, Duncan McCallum, John McCallum, Donald Cowan, the Malcomsons, John Anderson and perhaps one or two other families not now recollected. They were what are known as 'Seven(th) Day Baptists.' It was rather novel to the citizens, to travel up 'Long Run' on Saturday and see none of those people stirring about, and then passing on Sunday, to see every one able to do any work out in the clearing chopping, piling and burning brush and rolling logs." So wrote Perret Dufour in his account *Swiss Settlement of Switzerland County.*

Dufour continued, "The first steamboats of any considerable size that were navigating the Ohio River were built about the year 1819 to 1821. *The Velocipede, General Green, Ploughboy, Highland Laddie* and *Eliza* are the steamers of the early days now recollected by the writer. In 1823 the writer was two days and two nights on the trip from Vevay to Cin-

4

Mouth of the Licking River,
across from Cincinnati, 1840.

cinnati on the *Highland Laddie*, a small boat owned by Duncan Mc-Callum, one of the early Scotch settlers on 'Long Run.' "

Was this Duncan McCallum the father of John Guthrie McCallum who was to found Palm Springs many years later?

Fragmentary as the evidence is, there are sufficient clues available upon which we can rely and which tempts one to make such a conclusion. Firstly, there was the repeated statement of J. G. McCallum himself. He was fond of telling that his father built and operated one of the first steamboats upon the Ohio River. In the year 1878 a biographical sketch of him was to appear in print which stated, "He (McCallum) is of American descent from revolutionary stock on his mother's side, and of Scotch descent on that of his father, who owned and operated one of the first steamboats on the Ohio."

The 1820 Census records, listed in Switzerland County, Indiana:

5

Aerial view of present-day Vevay.
Louisville Courier-Journal
photograph.

"McCollum, Duncan — foreign born, farmer — Dependents: 1 w. male, age 16-25 (probably himself), 1 w. female, (wife) age 16-25, 2 w. males under 10."

If this is our family the two boys under ten might be the brothers who eventually went off to California, and at this time, John Guthrie McCallum and his two sisters had not been born. The difference in spelling of the name was commonplace in those days.

John Guthrie McCallum was born in Vevay, Indiana, on August 10, 1826. According to the Indiana Gazetteer published that same year the town was "situated on the north bank of the Ohio River, 100 miles by water below Cincinnati, 18 above Madison, and 95 south-east from Indianapolis. It contains," continued the gazetteer, "about 100 handsome brick and frame dwelling houses, 400 inhabitants, 7 stores, 3 taverns, 3 lawyers, 3 physicians, and a printing office; there are also several extensive vineyards in its immediate vicinity. . . ." One of these taverns was the Swiss Inn, built in 1823. It was the main meeting place and attraction for visitors to the small community and is still standing to this day.

The Indiana Land Entries v. 1, Cincinnati District, compiled by Margaret R. Waters shows the following land purchases from the Federal government by Duncan McCallum:

> Page 69 Southeast, Section 18, township 2N, range 3W of the first Principal Meridian, 12-11-1816 Northeast 31, same, 11-30-1819. Page 132 Southwest 30, 2N, 2W of first Principal Meridian, 6-28-1815.

The first two pieces of land are in Craig township, Switzerland County, and the third in Jefferson township, Switzerland County.

From the Records of the U. S. Census for Indiana for the year 1850 considerable information about the McCallum Family once again may be deduced. We find:

House No.	Family No.	Name	Age	Sex	Oc.	Place of Birth
		Ellen McCallum	52	F		Pen.
85	85	Jane McCallum	25	F		O.
		John G. McCallum	24	M	Lawyer	Ind.
		Elizabeth McCallum	20	F		O.

From the above, one may assume that the father, Duncan, was dead, the two older sons had gone to the California Gold Fields, John G. was already practicing law, and the two sisters' birthplaces being listed as Ohio, revealed that the family had traveled from one state to another, probably on the steamer, *Highland Laddie.*

Vevay, in those days, must have been a place of enchantment for a young imaginative lad. On the wooded hills were vestiges of the ancient lookout stations used by the Indians before the white men came. Little boys could roam over these hills and hide in these mysterious places. Always there was the river for fishing, swimming and dreaming of far off places to where the steamers plied their way. The frequent trips on the father's *Highland Laddie* to Cincinnati must have been exciting.

John McCallum attended school winters and during the hot summer days read every book he could lay his hands upon. Mostly he read the books around the house, and especially those about McCallum More, the head of the clan of McCallum. John's relatives, like many other loyal Scotsmen, claimed kinship with this brave leader. Sir Walter Scott in his romantic, historical novel *The Heart of Midlothian* wrote: "When McCallum More's heart does not warm to the Tartan, it will be as cold as death can make it."

Vevay could boast of having the first brick house built in Indiana! It was constructed by George Ash. Photograph from the Vevay Reveille-Enterprise, *the oldest weekly newspaper in Indiana, dating from 1816.*

The carefree days of childhood were to be of short duration for John McCallum. His father died when the lad was six years old, leaving what he thought was a sufficient amount for his family's comfort; but, after years of litigation, this competency was all lost, and the family was left to struggle on the modest farm. To help eke out an existence a steam saw mill was erected upon this piece of property. The children had to help operate this, so John went to work on the engine when he was about eight years old. He learned the trade of engineer, but having no aptitude for this line of work, he was never very successful at it.

Young John McCallum continued at his studies at the country school house in Vevay, and when he had completed the elementary grades he attended the County Seminary. When he was older, he obtained employment as an engineer and frugally managed to save enough money to go to Cincinnati to begin studying law. Finally he attended the Law Department of Indiana University and obtained his Bachelor of Law Degree from this institution in 1848. Soon after, he was licensed and began the practice of law in Indiana.

One of the stately homes in Vevay. Swiss pioneer home of John Francis Dufour, member of the Vevay, Indiana, founding family. Vevay Reveille-Enterprise photograph.

The following year Indiana, along with the entire nation, was astonished to learn of the marvelous discovery of gold in California. The gold fever struck the two older McCallum boys and they, with hundreds of others who dreamed of quick riches to be had for the taking, hurried off to that far place to strike it rich.

On February 25, 1851, the steamer *Ohio* with Captain Haley in command sailed into San Francisco harbor. On its passenger list were two young men, D. McCallum and M. McCallum, who immediately upon debarking seemed to vanish. Days and months passed without a word being received from the two adventurers.

John McCallum, unswayed by the excitement of get-rich-quick schemes, steadfastly continued with his law practice in Indiana until the worried mother received a letter.

The letter, which had been in transit for several weeks before it reached Vevay, was written by a family friend. It told of the epidemic which raged through the Gold Country and had struck down one of her sons.

The distraught mother, unable to leave home responsibilities, turned to John. She implored him to make the long journey to California to find his brothers and to urge them to return home. The young attorney closed out his law practice and yielding to his mother's pleadings, started the long journey around the Horn to locate his brothers in California.

Ships abandoned in San Francisco harbor when the crews deserted and dashed off to the gold fields, along with such men as the two McCallum brothers who arrived on the S.S. Ohio *in California, February 25, 1851. Courtesy Title Insurance and Trust Company, Los Angeles.*

2.

Years of Testing: Days of Glory

When the young McCallum brothers arrived in San Francisco in 1851 they found scenes such as this on Montgomery Street near Washington Street.

JOHN MCCALLUM arrived in San Francisco in May of 1854. He immediately sought out the friend who wrote the letter to mother McCallum telling of the serious illness of her older son.

One look at the expression of sorrow upon the friend's face was enough to warn John. As gently as possible, the friend told him of the death of his two brothers. Reeling with shock John undertook the sad duty of writing the tragic word back to his anxious mother. His long trip had been futile. The brothers had succumbed shortly before his ship sailed into San Francisco harbor.

Yet, despite the burden of such great sorrow, John McCallum, filled with a young man's eagerness for adventure, immediately was captured by the roaring glamour of San Francisco life. Even more, he fell so in love with the California countryside that he decided to remain. Stimulating as life appeared to be in San Francisco, he believed that the real opportunities for the future were to be found in the tumultuous mining regions of El Dorado County.

He took his few possessions and went into the hilly regions of Hangtown and began practicing his profession of law. This rugged community, originally called Old Dry Diggins during the early mining days, was later given the dubious name of Hangtown when there occurred several swift and effective reprisals by means of a rope and a convenient tree limb for the culprits. Its name was officially changed to Placerville in 1850 when it became the capital of the northern province of the Mother Lode.

Young John McCallum found there were enough constant disputes in this area over mining claims and land titles to keep an attorney busy. In addition, he tried his hand at mining, but meeting with scant success, quickly lost interest in getting rich by such uncertain means. He became acquainted with the people and entered into the affairs of the community.

The more he conversed with the men of the town the more he became aware that the turmoil of a nation rapidly undergoing the threat of dissolution over the slavery question had reached the far reaches of that mining country as it had elsewhere. The very air was filled with political bombast and rancor. John McCallum soon began to take an increasingly active part and became more involved until politics were to become his greatest concern for the ensuing thirty years.

As ADVENTUROUS and sometimes hardened men rushed to California mining towns in search of gold, equally tough men went into the state's political scene in search of power. Violence, lawlessness, and a tendency toward mob action ruled these men for the most part. Not all men coming to California sought gold: some came with the announced intention of gaining political power. Two of these were David C. Broderick, who proclaimed to the Democratic faction before coming west in 1850 that he would return as U. S. Senator from California, and William M. Gwin, leader of the pro-slavery California Democrats. The power struggle between these two so split the Democratic Party that the newly formed American Party was able to gain eminence.

The American or Know-Nothing Party, as it soon became known, was nationally consolidated in 1852 out of several secret bodies and was first organized in California in May 1854. The old Whig Party had died out and the new party was composed of both Whigs and Democrats, some of whom had deserted the old parties and hoped to ride into office and power in the new party. It also attracted to membership other men of a more idealistic bent who genuinely believed in the reform element of the American Party. It was a secret organization and its members sworn to answer that they "knew nothing" if questioned about the party's functions and membership. Nationally the party was hostile to Catholics because it assumed them to be under the control of a foreign power. It was also antagonistic toward German and Irish immigrants, deeming them to be free thinking and radical refugees. In California there was considerable denunciation of the Chinese, while anti-Catholicism was played down due to the preponderance of Spanish speaking Catholics in the state.

On August 7, 1855, the Know-Nothings held a convention in the Methodist Episcopal Church in Sacramento. They adopted a platform which had as its main points:

Declared for the Union and U. S. Constitution
Favored universal religious tolerance
Purity of the ballot box
Registration laws

THE AMERICAN OR KNOW-NOTHING PARTY

David C. Broderick, a prominent leader of the California Democratic Party in the 1850's.

The Know-Nothings, on the national level, accused Irish and German immigrants of stealing American elections, and of being controlled by foreign governments.

William M. Gwin, leader of pro-slavery Democrats and U.S. Senator from California for nine years.

Americans only to hold political office
Opposed the union of church and state
Opposed vigorously fraud and corruption in high places.

John McCallum, present at that convention, heartily endorsed the policies of reform so evident in the party platform. When the opposing Democrats held their next convention and had as their first transaction of business the exclusion of any member known to be part of or in sympathy with the Know-Nothing Party, it became evident that some means must be found to bring before the citizens the message of the American Party. McCallum had anticipated this need as early as in the spring preceding this meeting. It seemed to him that the press was the only way this could be done.

He looked around and found just what he was seeking.

A NEW STAGE OF ACTION

NEWSPAPERS had proliferated throughout many of the small mining communities until they were so numerous that as one historian put it, "The press seemed to be a lichen that flourished among the rocks. Printed in six different languages, they represented eight religious denominations and seven political parties, and devoted themselves to the interests of religion, politics, morals, law, medicine, commerce, agriculture, news and slander." Editors of these papers came and went as the tides of fortunes rose and fell. It was, therefore, not surprising when politically minded John McCallum actively entered the journalistic field.

In the nearby mountain community of Georgetown, site of some of the richest gold strikes, he found a J. Wing Oliver, who as proprietor and editor had first issued the *Georgetown Weekly News* on Oct. 19, 1854. On Feb. 1, 1855, John Platt took over ownership, with Oliver carrying on as editor. On May 23, 1855, J. G. McCallum bought into the firm and became co-proprietor and editor of the *Weekly News*.

J. Wing Oliver, in the issue of the *Georgetown Weekly* dated May 24, 1855, wrote his farewell editorial which ended by his writing, "In taking our leave we would announce your future editor, J. G. McCallum Esq. He is just the person which this station requires; use him well and you will secure the services of an able and honorable man."

Under the new ownership, the *Georgetown Weekly* dated May 31, 1855, carried the masthead listing J. G. McCallum as editor. In the lead editorial he wrote, "We now enter upon this new stage of action. In politics the *News* will be independent."

Opposite page. Georgetown Weekly News *of May 31, 1855. First issue under McCallum ownership.*

GEORGETOWN WEEKLY NEWS.

VOL. 1.   GEORGETOWN, EL DORADO COUNTY, CAL., MAY 31, 1855.   NO. 33.

A Parent's Prayer.

BY REV. L. WASHINGTON.

The following lines were published a few years
since—the article is one of uncommon beauty and
excellence, and will find a ready and warm response from every Christian parent:

At this hushed hour, when all my children sleep,
Here in my presence, gracious God, I kneel,
And while the tears of gratitude I weep,
Would pour the prayer which gratitude must feel.
Paternal love! Oh set thy holy seal
On those soft hearts, which thou to me has sent,
Repel temptation, guard their better weal,
Be thy pure spirit to their frailty lent,
And lead them in the path their infant Savior
went.

I ask not for them eminence or wealth,
For these, in Wisdom's view, are trifling toys,
But occupation, competence and health,
Thy love, thy presence, and the lasting joys
That flow therefrom; the passion which employs
The breasts of holy men, and that to which
Thou, to the humblest heart, a charm alloys—
This is the better boon, Oh God, I ask of thee.

This world, I know, is but a narrow bridge,
And treacherous waters roar and foam below;
With feeble feet we walk the wooden ridge,
Which creaks and shakes beneath us as we go!
Some fall by accident, and thousands throw
Their bodies headlong in the hungry stream;
Some sink by secret means, and never know
The hand which struck them in their transient
dream,
Till wisdom wakes in death, and in despair
they scream.

If these soft feet, which now these feathers
press,
Are doomed the paths of ruin soon to tread,
If vice, concealed in her unspotted dress,
Is soon to turn her polluted bed—
If thy foreseeing eye discerns a thread
Of vile guilt impelling on their doom,
Oh spare them not—in mercy strike them dead,
Prepare for them an early welcome-tomb;
Not far eternal blight; let my false blossoms
bloom.

But if some useful path before them lie,
Where they may walk obedient to thy laws,
Though never basking in ambition's eye,
And pamper'd never with the world's applause,
Active, yet humble, virtuous too, the cause
Of virtue in the dwellings where they dwell,
Still following where thy perfect spirit draws,
Release them there from the bands of hell—
If thus 'tis life, then let them longer live, 'tis
well.

And teach me Power Supreme, in their green
days,
With meekest skill thy lessons to impart;
To shun the harlot, and to show the maze
Through which her honied accents reach the
heart;
Help them to learn, without the bitter smart
Of sad experience, vigor to deny,
From trickery, falsehood, knavery, may they
start,
As from a hidden snake, from women, wine,
From all the guilty scenes with which such
scenes combine.

How soft they sleep; what innocent repose
Rests in their eyes, from older sorrows free,
Sweet babes, the curtain I would not unclose,
Which wraps the future from your minds and me;
But Heavenly Father, leaving them with thee—
Whether on high or low may be their lot,
Or early death, or life await them—be
Their Guardian, Saviour, Guide, and bless the
spot
Where they shall live or die; till death forsake
them not.

Though persecution's arches o'er them spread,
Or sickness undermine, consuming slow,
Though they should lead to the their Saviour
led,
And to deep poverty be doomed to know.
Whatever throw shalt order, let them go.
I gave them up to thee, they are not mine,
And I could call the sweetest winds to blow,
To bear them from me, to the pole or line.
In distant lands to plant thy gospel's bleeding
shrine.

When as the scroll these heavens shall pass
away,
When the cold grave shall offer up its trust,
When Jesus shall burn, and the last dreadful
day
Restores the spirit to its scattered dust,
Then, thou most merciful, as well as just,
Let not my eye, when elements are tossed
In wide confusion, see that darkest, worst
Of painful sights, that ever parent crossed—
Hear my sad, earnest prayer, and let not mine
be lost.

Post Office Regulations under the New Law.

As much interest is felt, and many inquiries are daily made, relative to the late Act
of Congress making very important changes
in the Post Office Laws, we publish the following from the instructions of the Postmaster General. They are copied from the
Times and *Transcript* of the 24th inst:

Books not weighing over four pounds
may be sent in the mail, prepaid, at one
cent an ounce any distance in the United
States under three thousand miles, and
at two cents an ounce over three thousand
miles, provided, they are put up without a
cover or wrapper, or in a cover or wrapper
open at the ends or sides, so that their character may be determined without removing the wrapper. If not pre-paid, the postage under three thousand miles is one cent
and a half, and over three thousand miles
in the United States three cents and a half.

Letters enclosed in stamp envelopes may
be carried out of the mail, provided such
stamps are equal in value, and amounts to
the rates of postage to which such letters
would be liable if sent in the mail; and provided, also, that the envelopes are duly sealed, &c.

A letter bearing a stamp, cut or separated from a stamped envelope, cannot be sent
through the mail as a prepaid letter. Stamps
so cut or separated from stamp envelopes
lose their legal value. Stamped envelopes,
as well as postage stamps on prepaid letters,
should be cancelled immediately on the letters being placed in the post-office.

Contractors and mail carriers may carry
newspapers out of the mails, for sale or distribution among regular subscribers; but
when papers are placed in a post-office for
delivery, postage must be charged and col-
lected. Contractors and other persons may
also convey books, pamphlets, magazines
and newspapers (not intended for immediate
distribution) done up in packages as mer-
chandise, and addressed to some bona fide
agent or dealer.

Publishers of newspapers may, without
subjecting them to extra postage fold within their regular issues a supplement, provided the weight of the whole does not exceed one and a half ounces within the State
where printed, or three ounces when sent
out of the State. But in all cases, the added matter must be a genuine supplement
or appendage to the newspaper in question,
and of the same essential character, conveying intelligence of passing events of general
interest.

Money and other valuable matters sent
by mail, are at the risk of the owner. Da-
guerreotypes, when sent in the mail, should
be rated and charged with letter postage by
weight.

Payment of postage on newspapers, periodicals and magazines, quarterly or yearly in advance, may be made either at the
office mailing or office of delivery.

It is a violation of law to enclose or con-
ceal a letter or other thing, except bills
and receipts for subscriptions, or to make
any memorandum in writing, or to print
any work of communication after its publication upon any newspaper, pamphlet, magazine or other printed matter. In all such
cases legal letter postage should be demanded, and if the person addressed should re-
fuse to pay such letter postage the package should be returned to the "Postmaster
from whose office it came" to prosecute the
sender for the penalty of $5; and all trans-
ient printed matter should be distinctly post-
marked at the mailing office.

Postmasters are allowed one cent for the
delivery of each free letter, except such as
come to themselves, and two mails each on
newspapers (to subscribers) not chargeable
with postage.

Letters mailed in the cars can be prepaid
only by using postage stamps or stamped
envelopes; and when not thus prepaid, it is
the duty of Postmasters to treat all such
letters as unpaid although marked "paid"
on some agent being permitted to receive
pre-payment in money.

Circulars, advertisements, and business
cards, not weighing over three ounces, sent
any distance in the United States, are chargeable with one cent postage each when pre-
paid, and two cents each when not pre-paid.
The same rates apply when sent in packages, unless the package be sealed, so as to
prevent the contents from being ascertain-
ed. If sealed, they are chargeable with letter postage by weight.

Properly franked mail matter, or mail
matter addressed to a person enjoying the
franking privilege, is entitled to be carried
free in the mail when "forwarded" to the
person elsewhere as well as in transporta-
tion simply to the office to which originally
addressed.

Postmasters receiving letters referring to
business not connected with the Department, but designed to promote private interest without payment of postage, must
return said letters to the parties sending
them under a new envelope charged with letter postage.

Bona fide subscribers to weekly newspapers can receive the same free of postage,
if they reside in the county in which the paper is printed and published, even if the
office to which the paper is sent is without
the county, provided, it is the office at which
they regularly receive their mail matter.

Postage cannot be pre-paid on regular
newspapers or periodicals for a less term
than one quarter; and in all cases postage
must be paid on such matter at the com-
mencement of the quarter.

Bills of lading and unsealed letters rela-
ting exclusively to the whole or any part
of the cargo of a vessel or steamboat, may
be sent on such vessel or steamboat outside
of the mail, unless they are placed in an
envelope with other matters. In the latter
case, the whole package is subject to letter
postage.

Under no circumstances can a Postmaster open a letter not addressed to himself.

Ship letters, as they cannot be pre-paid,
and are not supposed to be embraced in the
new Act, will continue to be dispatched a-
greeably to the provisions of the fifteenth
section of the Act of March 3, 1825.

The Americanization of Nicaragua.

INTERESTING CORRESPONDENCE.

We find the following very interesting
correspondence in the New York *Tribune*
of the 20th ult. It perhaps gives more reliable information upon the subject than
what has heretofore appeared in the public
prints:

Mr. Corwine to Col. Kinney.

NEW YORK, April 16, 1855.

Col. H. L. KINNEY—Dear Sir: I have
learned, from the public journals and otherwise, that you are connected with an enterprise or Association having in view certain
schemes with regard to Central America, or
some part of it. Would you be kind enough
to inform me in general of the object of this
Association, if you are connected with it,
and of its character and plans?

I do not ask from mere curiosity, but with
a desire to obtain information that may
guide me in some contemplated movements
of my own;

In the first place, I would like to know if
the Company, if there be one, is the "Central American Company" with which your
name has been connected, or is it a new one
on another basis.

I should be inclined, perhaps, to take an
interest, if desired, in an enterprise which
might be legally and safely engaged in, and
which promises a reasonable return.

I should wish, however, to be assured that
there was no such objection possible to be
made to it as that of "filibustering," and
that everything contemplated was legal and
safe, as well as likely to be remunerative.

If your convenience and interest permit
an answer to my inquiries, it would much
oblige, Very respectfully, your
friend and ob'n't serv't.
AMOS S. CORWINE.

Col. Kinney to Mr. Corwine.

NEW YORK, April 17, 1855.

DEAR SIR: I am very happy to reply to
the inquiries contained in your favor of the
16th inst.

An Association of gentlemen has been
formed in this City, under the name of the
"Nicaragua Land and Mining Company,"
the object of which is to settle upon and improve some lands granted by the Nicaragua
Government, and others purchased of citizens of that Republic, and to work the
mines that may be found thereon, which are
supposed to be very valuable—to cultivate
some of the lands, and to cut mahogany and
Nicaragua wood, for export, &c.

It is true, we hope to establish freight and
passenger boats on the river and lake, to
mail some villages and hotels for the ac-
commodation of travelers, and, in fine, to
settle and clear up the country, and bring
its productions into market.

This Association has no connection
with the "Central American Company,"
whose interests are all in the Mosquito
Territory, and who have an entirely separate organization.

A considerable portion of the lands has
been obtained from Mr. Fabens, our present
Consul at San Juan, who has made large
purchases from individuals, and who is interested with us.

I am confident that the enterprise will be
a very profitable one, and it is liable to no
objections such as you refer to. Our grants
are good and sanctioned by the laws of the
Government of Nicaragua, under whose authority we expect to hold our lands, and we
hope to be of material service to that country by developing its resources, cutting
canals, making roads, and establishing commercial relations with Europe and the United States.

The vegetable productions of the country
are very valuable, comprising tobacco,
cocoa, Nicaragua wood, mahogany, &c.,
and the India-rubber trees in the greatest
abundance.

The mineral resources are known to be
extensely rich in gold and silver, and coal,
which last will be of very great importance
and the beds of which lie extremely convenient and accessible.

I should be very glad to have you take
an interest in our enterprise, and will readily afford you any other information in my
power.

If industry and perseverance can reclaim
a country and repay exertion, we hope to
show something worth while within two
years or less. Yours very truly,
H. L. KINNEY.

A LARGE NUGGET.—An immense lump
of gold which has been on exhibition at a
Banking House in San Francisco, has recently been assayed. The *Alta* says:—

"The weight of pure gold extracted was
511 ounces 37 dwts. Its value in specie
was $89,012, and netted the fortunate own-
er $8,829 29. Rather a pretty little for-
tune for short hard times, and picked up in
one piece. What a pity the 'mines are giving out!'"

RAIL ROAD.—The *Town Talk* states that
the clipper ship Winged Racer, now daily
due, is reported to have on board the entire
portable machinery for the Sacramento
Valley Railroad. The freight, it is reported, will cost the company over $100,000.

The London Times on the American Party.

The Boston *Journal*, by the last steamer,
copies the following as the most important
portion of the article in the London *Times*
on the Know Nothing or American party.
It has attracted considerable attention in the
East. The "Thunderer" discourses as
follows:—

"We have read with great interest a
State paper, which appears to us to be drawn
up with ability and moderation, on behalf
of the Know Nothings, or, as they profess
to call themselves, the American party, in
the United States. This party has already
obtained a decisive ascendancy in the Northern States of the Union, and it is extremely probable that it will name the successor
of President Pierce at the next Presidential
election. But the principle on which the
party is formed is of far greater importance
than any personal consequences it may produce, for this principle may lead to permanent results in the policy of the Union.—
The American party, places itself in opposition to the rival claims of the old political
leaders, and it boasts that its organization
has been completed entirely without their
assistance.

The object of its founders has been to
preserve their design from the assaults of
other parties until they could rely on their
own strength; and for this purpose, they
state, curiously enough, that "their organization is more or less secret in action, and
almost altogether secret in the source from
which it derives its counsel and design."—
Yet, in spite of this mystery, which would
seem so little adapted to the political habits of the United States, the party has un-
questionably gained ground with singular
rapidity. It must therefore represent an
opinion shared by large masses of the American people. Its main object is declared to
be to re-assert the original purpose of the
Union, to revive the national spirit of the
country, to crush those factions which have
converted party warfare into a mere struggle for the power of dispensing patron-
age, and above all, to resist the increase
of foreign influences in the United States.

This last motive is more especially the
Know Nothing party. They state that not
less than half a million strangers are driven
annually by poverty or misrule to swell
the population of the United States; and
that although this acquisition of labor is in
some respects useful to the community, yet
that these immigrants are ignorant of the
institutions, the laws, and even the language
of the country, and animated by a spirit very
different from that of American citizens.—
These persons are, however, very speedily
invested with the franchise and the exercise
of political power.

This immigration "furnishes what many,
without much exaggeration of phrase, be
called the distinct estate in our republic.—
Its ever-swelling tide is visible in every community. It is banded into combinations
more or less apart from our long-known and
familiar masses of native citizens, by ties of
foreign kindred, by unforgotten and ever-
cherished nationalities, and by sympathies
alien to the spirit which alone sustains our
peculiar, temperate and complicated system
of freedom. Worse than this, it has caught
the notice and stimulated the craft of selfish
political aspirants and demagogues, who
have too easily found it a pliant resource
for party use, and who have cajoled, flatter-
ed and seduced it into the rank of partisan
strife, and thus imparted to it a consequence and an influence most powerful to
aid a perverse ambition, but utterly power-
less to accomplish any honest end for which
the highest prerogatives of citizenship were
originally designed." To this we may add,
that it exercises an undue and almost exclusive influence over the American press, that
it is always endeavoring to embroil the U.
States, for its own sinister purposes, with
the European powers, and that it is led by
the renegades, the sympathizers and the an-
nexationists of every cause who have sought
a refuge beyond the Atantic.

But the views of the American party do
not stop here. They observe that a very
large portion of this annual emigration be-
longs to the Church of Rome—a body regarded with distrust by the greater number
of the American people, professing at least
a moral allegiance to a foreign and absolute
power, and organized in a peculiar manner
for the promotion of Roman Catholic objects at the expense of those very liberties
which these persons exercise and enjoy.—
The American party, therefore, proclaims
that it takes its stand against the political
action of the Roman Catholic Church in the
United States, not from intolerance of the
doctrines of that faith, but from a conviction that the tendency of that church is to
embody its adherent in a party the objects
of which are at variance with the institutions and national spirit of the American
people.

These declarations are to a great extent
new in the history of the United States.—
Hitherto, unlimited facilities and encouragement have been held out to immigration,
and the political parties in the community
have professed absolute indifference to the
religious faith of their members. Experience seems to have convinced at least one
considerable section of the American community that these privileges cannot always
be as liberally conceded as they have hitherto been; and it is obvious that the principles of this new party are mainly directed
against the extraordinary increase of Irish
element among the American population, both as aliens and as Papists. On
many other topics the manifesto preserves a
discreet and significant silence, probably because, although the Know Nothings are

cordially united on some points, that union
does not extend to all. Thus, the vital
question of slavery is left unnoticed, because
in Massachusetts, for instance, the Know
Nothings have declared for emancipation,
while in other States they support the Fu-
gitive Slave Law. Again, the annexation
of Cuba and other territories is not alluded
to, probably because every extension of territory inhabited by men of the Spanish race
and the Roman Catholic faith must tend to
weaken the national American character of
the Union.

If these are the established principles of
the Know Nothing party, we cannot but
regard them with considerable sympathy.
We have ever watched with sincere admiration the progress of the United States, as
long as it is directed to those legitimate objects which are to be found within the magnificent territories of the Union. A less
favorable opinion of their policy and condition has only been formed and expressed in
Europe when public opinion in the United
States was misled by factious agitators, or
misdirected to objects incompatible with the
rights of others. The strength of the Union
and the peace of the world would be protected and secured by a policy which pro-
fesses to concentrate the strength of the
American people on American objects.—
The language of the new party appears to
us to be patriotic and wise, and far more
nearly akin to the true principles of the
founders of the commonwealth than the
scandalous attempts of the modern democrats to court popularity at the expense of
honesty and honor. The Know Nothings
owe their existence to a reaction against
the follies and excesses of Kossuth meetings,
of Irish journalism, of the Romish priests,
and of Mr. Pierce's ministers; and it is not
improbable that they will succeed in con-
stituting the next government of the United
States, as they have already returned a majority to the new Congress."

The Artesian Well.

One of the most extraordinary things in
Paris—or, indeed, in the world, is the arte-
sian well of Grenelle. It was begun in
1834, and finished after several forced sus-
pensions about the year 1841. It is bored
in the center of the Court of Abbatoir,
goes 1,700 feet into the bowels of the earth,
and the column of water, nine inches in diameter, rises in a copper tube 112 feet above
the surface. From this elevation it de-
scends by means of another tube to the
ground, and is conducted to the reservoir at
the Pantheon, whence it is distributed for
the use of the inhabitants. The temperature
of the water is constantly 80° Fahrenheit.
It holds several salts in solution, among the
rest, (which colors glass submitted to its
action) and is highly charged with carbon-
ic acid gas. Now, what is most interesting
about this well, is, that the facts developed
by it, it being the deepest yet bored, have
served to explode the old doctrine that such
wells were mere examples of a jet of water
having its head on some mountain or high
table land, passing under ground and spring-
ing through the outlet up to the height of
its head.

The force that drives a column of water
up to an elevation of 1,800 feet, with
such rapidity as to supply 3,400,000 gallons
in 24 hours; the force that shows itself to
be variable sometimes comparatively quiet,
at others almost terrible in its violence, is
thought to be volcanic, and to result from
expansion within the inner crust of the
earth—to be, in fact, a sort of explosive
escape from an artificial valve in the immense steam boiler on whose surface we
live.

When the well was first opened, and before the water was carried to its present
height, vast quantities of mud came out,
from which the height of the column now
clarifies it. But for a while the residents in
the city were greatly alarmed, thinking that
the ground on which they lived was being
gradually undermined by the action of the
water, and that some day they would be en-
gulfed. This notion has now ceased to alarm
them, as it is evident that the augur has
pierced through the rocky exterior into the
very interior, the soft central mass of the
earth, whence the detritus that frightened
the Parisians proceeded, and not, as they ig-
norantly imagined, from just beneath their
houses.

SIMPLICITY OF DRESS.—Prentice, the editor of the Louisville *Journal*, speaks thus
to his readers: "Those who think that, in
order to dress well it is necessary to dress
extravagantly and gaudily, make a great
mistake. Nothing so well becomes true
feminine beauty as simplicity. We have
seen many a remarkably fine person robbed
of its fine effect by being over dressed.—
Nothing is more unbecoming than overload-
ed beauty. The simplicity of the classic
taste is seen in old statues and pictures
painted by men of very superior artistic genius. In Athens, the ladies were not gaudily, but simply arrayed, and we doubt
whether any ladies ever excited more admiration. So also the noble old Roman
matrons, who kept up forms were prized
on delightedly by men weary of them, were
always very plainly dressed. Fashion often
puts the lines of the butterfly, but fashion is not a classic goddess.

FAMINE PRICES.—At last accounts the
best flour was selling in New York at thir-
teen dollars and fifty cents per barrel, potatoes $2 per bushel, at wholesale, and at re-
tail fifty per cent. higher. Beef command-
ed twenty cents per pound, and choice
steaks thirty-seven and a half cents. Without an unusually great crop is raised the
present summer, prices next winter will be
worse than they are now.

Hangtown (later Placerville) during the early 1850's. The infamous "hanging tree" is at the left of the Empire Building in the upper center of this picture.

Then, farther along in the editorial McCallum made it very clear that the new regime of the paper did not "sympathize with the present organization in this county, which has assumed the name of Democratic Club."

Proof that McCallum was in the political arena to stay was indicated by a small announcement down in one of the advertising columns of the June 7 issue of the *News*. Under the heading in bold capital letters "REMOVAL," the notice went on to announce, "McCallum and George have removed their Law Office to the corner of Church and Placer Streets (Georgetown) where one or both may always be found."

He had moved to the center of the scene of political action.

Immediately, the entire tone of the paper changed. Originally published as a Whig paper, McCallum made it the organ of the American Party. He ran long articles favorably reporting on the activities of the newly formed Party, while at the same time running other articles lambasting the shenanigans of the Democratic Party. The inclinations of the new editor were clearly revealed.

John McCallum developed into a skilled orator and spoke at many meetings for the American Party. His wit, wisdom and urbane manner of speaking delighted the audiences and the large city newspapers began printing articles about his speeches. He continued his support of the party in his *Weekly*.

Ardently believing in the moral reform element of the Americans, he ran the party platform in its entirety on the front page of July 26, 1855.

GEORGETOWN NEWS.

WEDNESDAY, SEPT. 5, 1855.

Mr. Octavien Hoogs is our authorized agent for the Georgetown News at San Francisco. He may be found at 97 Merchant street.

Kirk Brothers are our Agents in Sacramento, at the Post Office Literary Depot, next door to the Post Office.

American Nominations.

For Governor,

J. Neely Johnson,

OF SACRAMENTO.

For Lieut. Governor,

ROBERT M. ANDERSON,

OF EL DORADO.

For Justice of the Supreme Court, (Long Term,)

HUGH C. MURRAY,

OF SOLANO.

For Justice of the Supreme Court, (for unexpired term of Hon. A. Wells, dec'd.)

DAVID S. TERRY,

OF SAN JOAQUIN.

For Controller of State,

GEORGE W. WHITMAN,

OF TUOLUMNE.

For Treasurer of State,

HENRY BATES,

OF SHASTA.

For Attorney General,

W. S. WALLACE,

OF SANTA CLARA.

For Surveyor General,

JOHN H. BREWSTER.

OF SONOMA.

For State Printer,

GEN. JAMES ALLEN.

OF YUBA.

For State Prison Directors,

E. WILSON, of San Francisco.
F. S. McKENZIE, of Trinity.
ALEX. BELL, of Los Angeles.

American Ticket--El Dorado County.

For Senators.

J. G. McCALLUM,
DR. H. M. FISK.

For Assembly,

JAS. E. BOWE.	S. T. GAGE.
T. D. HEISKELL,	JAS. D. WHITE,
J. BORLAND.	L. S. WELCH.
W. H. TAYLOR.	J. W. OLIVER.

Americans Beware!
BOGUS TICKETS!!

A Telegraphic despatch was received on last Monday at this office, exposing a gross fraud which it is intended to perpetrate on Wednesday. It states that a large number of bogus tickets were being printed at the office of the Democrat at Placerville. These tickets will resemble the American ticket in almost every respect, but on close inspection it will be found that the name of one or more of the regular American Candidates will be left out and the names of the Phalanx Candidates for the same offices substituted. BEWARE OF THEM.— By this fraud it is admitted that on a fair vote our ticket must succeed, therefore fraud is resorted to. Compare the ticket with the ticket as published in the Placerville American, Empire County Argus, Georgetown News and the posters containing the American nominations.

The Cause.

From every precinct in the county we have most cheering accounts of the progress of American principles. It is confidently believed that the American ticket will not only triumph, but by such a majority as to entitle the Empire County to be styled the Banner County of the State.

At Diamond Springs, where in consequence of the dissolution of a small Council the Phalanxers imagined that the American ticket would lose many votes, we have the best assurance that the effect has been to rouse up every true American to put on the armor; and whereas heretofore the Americans that were lukewarm and too indifferent, the recent action of those who have acted traitorously to the cause, has had the most beneficial effect, and it is now understood that the American ticket will receive one hundred more votes than before the lopping off the so-called Silver Lake Council. At El Dorado (Mud Springs.) the effect has been similar, and we are assured that the cause will triumph at that precinct by a tremendous majority. At Placerville the Americans have it all their way. Those

The "Democrat" Again.

After giving notice for a week previous the last number of the Placerville paper devotes something over a column this paper. It undertakes to prove that the representations about the recent County Convention were true, because one Chamberlain had represented that such nominations were made by trading and wire working. As to Mr. C.'s statement on the subject, we refer the Democrat to the abundant testimony of his neighbors as to the position he occupied before the convention, and also the fact that the individual alluded to was not a delegate in that convention, as our neighbor erroneously states. The other witness is one C. B. Patterson, and as to his credibility and peculiar position before that convention.— We also refer to the abundant testimony of his neighbors at Diamond Springs. This is the whole evidence produced, which our neighbor thinks is more reliable than that of one who is a nominee of that of one who is a nominee of that convention, because of the interest of the latter. But it ought to be remembered that the latter is corroborated by nearly the entire delegation, while the witnesses relied on by our cotemporary, who are entirely uncorroborated, could not be taken as sufficient to prove any assertion, even though there was no testimony on the other side. But in this case it is abundant. We dismiss the subject. Our neighbor has been deceived, and he ought to chastise those that have made him look so ridiculous.

Political County Corresponeduce of the Georgetown News.—The Canvass.

NEGRO HILL, Aug. 29, 1855.

A number of the candidates on the American Ticket met the people of this place this evening. About one hundred and fifty persons were present. D. K. Newell, Esq,, addressed the meeting in an able and eloquent speech of about one hour. Some of the candidates for the Assembly also addressed the meeting with a few appropriate remarks. After this, Mr. French, (I believe the same person who was so obstropulous in the Phalanx county convention) also spoke. of course for the Phalanxers.— He was annihilated, however, by Mr. A. P. Catlin, who chanced to be present. He, like Mr. Newell, is not a regular member of the American party, but gives all his influence in favor of its success. Depend upon it we will do our whole duty at Negro Hill.   SAM.

For the Georgetown News.

BOTTLE HILL, Sept. 2d, 1855.

Mr. EDITOR—*Sir:*—I have but a few words to say to you at this time. In regard to mining, it is generally dull. Some tunnels are paying well, on the Divide between the North and Middle Forks of the

Georgetown Weekly News *of September 5, 1855, showing entire slate of American or Know-Nothing candidates.*

About a month later, on September 5, he printed the complete slate of state nominees for his party, listing his own name for State Senator.

Further political news, allegedly coming from news correspondents from various mining towns, was printed on the same editorial page. Accounts of triumphant speech-making by McCallum and other representatives of that party were listed.

On August 31, 1855, the *Georgetown News* reported the Hon. Messrs. Newell and McCallum addressed the people of Yankee Bar with about 150 present, some coming from Maine Bar, which was about half a mile away. "The speeches were well received and the candidates had the assurance that a large majority will be given for the American and State and County ticket."

McCallum, as candidate for State Senator for the American Party, also spoke at Volcanoville on Sept. 2, 1855. "Judging from the expression given by the large assembly at least two thirds were actively engaged in the support of the American ticket. The meeting resulted in much good to the American cause."

Good news for the Party was also received from Georgetown, Negro Hill, Bottle Hill, El Dorango (Mud Springs), Silver Lake, as well as the community of Murderer's Bar and other mining camps where McCallum addressed the assemblages.

At the bottom of one of the columns on the page, McCallum evidently could not resist an impish note. He wrote seven lines under the heading "WATERMELON: We feel grateful towards Mr. Jordan of the "Mountain Vegetable Wagon" for that delicious watermelon left by him at our office the other day. It is said that "Jordan is a hard road to travel," but we assure our readers that Jordan's watermelons are not *hard* to take."

On September 5 the paper had an article with the scare-head of "AMERICANS BEWARE" which went on to warn that the Democrats were printing "Bogus Tickets." These were printed to resemble closely the American Party ballot, but were in truth "Gross Frauds," the names of the opposition candidates being inserted in the places of the actual nominees.

Despite such vigorous opposition, when the Know-Nothings presented their ballot to the electorate the entire slate was unanimously swept into office.

Jubilantly the *Georgetown Weekly* of Sept. 13, 1855, ran a notice calling the faithful to come to a celebration. The notice had undoubtedly been penned by McCallum:

"AMERICAN RALLY

A mass meeting of Americans and all friendly to their cause, has been appointed for

SATURDAY EVENING

the 15th of Sept.

AT GEORGETOWN

to celebrate in appropriate manner the great American victory gained at the late election. Speeches will be made, guns fired, and a good time generally. Let all who rejoice at the late victory attend.

By order of the Committee"

The little newspaper had served its purpose and was under John McCallum's guidance a dominant influence in obtaining such a triumph for the American Party. On October 11, 1855, he wrote an editorial announcing the end of his connection with the paper. Two advertisements also appeared in the same issue. One announced the dissolution, by mutual consent, of the newspaper partnership of McCallum and Oliver. The other notice told of the dissolution, also by mutual consent, of the legal partnership between J. G. McCallum and W. A. George.

McCallum was ready to undertake his responsibilities in the State Capital at Sacramento.

John Neely Johnson, fourth elected governor of California and friend of J. G. McCallum. Courtesy Pasadena Public Library.

NEW CHALLENGES

THE SEVENTH session of the California State Legislature met at Sacramento on January 7, 1856. It adjourned April 21, 1856, and was entirely in the control of the American or Know-Nothing Party. It had as Governor, J. Neely Johnson; State Senator, J. G. McCallum; President Pro tempore, State Senator Delos R. Ashley; and Speaker of the Assembly, James T. Farleys; all faithful members of the brotherhood.

The newly elected governor, John Neely Johnson, age 28, appointed John Guthrie McCallum, age 26, to the Federal Relations, the Judiciary and the Finance Standing Committees.

California of the 1850s was for young men.

THE CHANGING POLITICAL SCENE

ON MARCH 12, 1856, there appeared in a Sacramento newspaper a statement which was to prove prophetic for that presidential year:

"In the approaching election, it is highly probable that we may witness the appearance of a new party in the political field — a party as yet unknown in the history of California, and one of the principles of which it has been the determined effort of all politicians to suppress and avoid."

17

John Charles Frémont at forty-three was in 1856 the youngest man to run for the presidency.

This was in reference to the Republican Party, founded two years before in Ripon, Wisconsin, and named for Jefferson's old Republican faction. It was primarily created to resist the Kansas-Nebraska Act of 1854 which reopened the further expansion of slavery in the various states.

This question of slavery was an especially dangerous issue in California.

A Republican movement would force every politician to declare himself on the subject of slavery at a time when it was crucial for California to remain free from controversies, so thought the Know-Nothings.

At their semi-annual convention of the state council meeting in Sacramento on May 13, 1856, they resolved that:

> "The Republican movement in this state is regarded by this council as mischievous and treasonable. That the American Party will oppose with all its power, the success of said Republican movement, and we pledge ourselves to each other to wage an uncompromising war upon it."

AMERICAN PARTY CONVENTION

ON SEPTEMBER 2, 1856, the Know-Nothing state nominating convention was held in the Congregational Church on Sixth Street in Sacramento to select their choices for the national governmental offices. On the second day of the meeting permanent officers were selected with J. G. McCallum of El Dorado County as president.

The final resolution of the convention was virtually their platform:

> "That the American Party, being essentially a reform party, they pledge themselves in laboring to elect Fillmore and Donnelson, the nominees of the convention; to lend their energies in the aid of the great essential reform movements of the day — the Pacific Railroad, the purity of the ballot box, the elevation of none but pure men to positions as local officers, and that we recognize all persons advocating the election of Fillmore and Donnelson as co-laborers with us in the glorious cause of union and regeneration."

THE ELECTION OF 1856

MEANWHILE, the nascent weakling of a Republican Party also decided to participate on the national scene and nominated as their presidential candidate the once popular Senator John Charles Frémont who had proven disappointingly inadequate in this office. The Democrats, alarmed at the strength of the American Party and the growth of the newly organized Republicans, united and forgot their difference in their

18

determination to win this election. They had as their candidate, James Buchanan.

The election taking place on Tuesday, Nov. 4, 1856, resulted in a triumphant victory for the Democrats both nationally and statewide. They gained complete control of the California State legislature.

There were but nine of the eleven Know-Nothing Party held over in the Senate, their terms not expiring until the following year. Among these holdovers was J. G. McCallum. During the 1857, 8th session of the State Legislature, Governor Neely Johnson assigned McCallum to the following Senate Standing Committees: Judiciary, State Prison, Contingent Expenses of the Senate, Engrossed Bills and the Committee on Public Morals.

It was under the sponsorship of the last committee that John McCallum tried repeatedly to obtain the passage of a "Sunday Law." The citizens of Placerville presented him with a signed petition praying for the passage of such a law and this he presented to the Senate where it was referred back to the Committee on Public Morals.

John McCallum, along with many other citizens of the mining region, was deeply concerned about the relaxed, easy morals which were carried over from the rambunctious mining days. Murder was as common as were arson and theft. Houses of prostitution flourished openly. McCallum believed that these houses of ill fame along with saloons were contributing much to the lawlessness and dissoluteness of the citizens. He also knew that a certain element in the community profited in the operation of both businesses.

Republican Song of 1856.

Gambling became one of the main recreations during the Gold Rush period. A faro game as illustrated in Harper's Weekly, *October, 1857.*

His efforts to have this "Sunday Law" passed failed. It is interesting to note that the long fight John McCallum waged on behalf of the public morals was to be continued by others of the same mind. A Red Light Abatement Act, declaring houses of prostitution to be public nuisances, was to be defeated in 1911, and then passed in the session of 1913.

The mining town region, for the most part, ignored this law and it was not until the mid-1900s that the houses of prostitution in Jackson, Placerville and other gold mining regions would be locked up and put out of business.

It made little or no difference what Governor Johnson recommended as the state legislature, composed largely of the opposing party of Democrats, was not disposed to pay any attention to him or his committees. The American or Know-Nothing bubble had burst. The members of the secret party had been swept from control of the state government into a position of relative unimportance. Their one year of glory had ended.

The youthful exuberance and lack of political know-how of most of the members of the party and the fact that it failed to present a concrete plan for action caused them to be almost totally ineffective.

It is difficult to understand the appeal such an organization held for a man of the character of John Guthrie McCallum. He was known to be an altruistic, gentle, somewhat visionary man of such noble demeanor that his friends and colleagues bestowed upon him the affectionate and honorary title of "Judge" without his ever having served on the bench.

Perhaps the following quotation from the definitive article by Peyton Hurt in the California Historical Society Quarterly of March, 1930, entitled, "The Rise and Fall of the Know-Nothings in California," would help to clarify the reasons why men of McCallum's ilk took interest in the party:

"The secret character of the order was a strong attraction to many men. The secret meetings, the possession of secret ritual, signs, passwords, grips and the secret membership of the Know-Nothings were a lure which drew thousands of Californians to its councils. In the rough pioneer life of the '50s, the thrill of participating in the acts of such an organization, and in attending its formal meetings, filled a wide gap in the social life of the average member. To combine politics with such a romantic association was an excellent method of attracting and controlling large numbers of voters — at least until the charm of mystery had worn away, replaced by the clash of the personal ambitions of various cliques within the Order. Membership cost nothing, there were no dues, and it is little wonder that large numbers of the men of California flocked to the secret Know-Nothing councils, seeking diversion in this new type of political organization.

"But there was another reason for the rapid growth of the Know-Nothings in California. This secret order arrived at an opportune time in California politics. Political corruption in both state and local offices had grown so shocking in its faithlessness to public trust that the better citizens were anxious to turn to anything which promised to overthrow the existing regime. Thus, the reform element welcomed the formation of the Know-Nothing councils, hoping that they might purify California politics. This secret political machine was considered as a possible solution of a bad political situation."

The American Party or Know-Nothings of California never were part and parcel with the principles of the national nativistic and anti-Catholic leanings of the national party. While its political life was of short duration, "the Know-Nothings of California served as a temporary party bridging the gap between the breakup of old parties and the rise of Republicans, with the accompanying realignment of political parties taking sides on the slavery controversy."

The meteoric career of this political organization is unequaled in California history. The Know-Nothing Order rose within a year to include in its ranks a majority of the voters of the state, but was unable to live beyond its single year in power. The peculiar combination of circumstances which led to its success did not last long, and the decline of the Know-Nothing Party was as rapid as its ascent to power.

His STINT as State Senator coming to an end, John McCallum turned once again to his legal practice. He continued to be in demand as a speaker all the while he was gaining increased prestige as a brilliant attorney. It was during the year 1857 that he was admitted to practice before the State Supreme Court.

The next two years evidently were spent in his law practice and it is not until late in 1859 that the records show him again entering the political action scene.

RETURN TO
PRIVATE LIFE

3.
The Railroad Era in California

JOHN MCCALLUM's political views remained closely aligned with those of the Union-American Party which ultimately ceased to exist after 1860. He then sought a similar conservative political affiliation with a strong reform element and turned to the Union-Republican Party which was rapidly growing in influence.

The sixteenth plank in the Republican platform of the Republican National Convention, which had nominated Lincoln for president, declared that a railroad to the Pacific Ocean was imperative and that the Federal government ought to "render immediate and efficient aid in its construction." From the very first mention of a transcontinental railroad John McCallum became its staunch advocate. He was among those Americans in California who felt extremely remote from the other people of the nation and who believed that if the country was to be preserved, a railroad linking all parts together was mandatory.

Throughout the Gold Rush days and all of the 1850s the intensification of the national bitterness and divisiveness over the slavery issue was accompanied by the bitterly contested railroad project. The Southerners feared that a northern route for the proposed railroad would lead to the creation of future "free" states, and that a southern route, which did not have to cross the great barriers of the Rocky Mountains and the Sierra Nevadas, could be developed much cheaper than any other. The Northern sympathizers were equally adamant in their opposition to the railroad which could lead to the expansion of slavery. Members of Congress caught in this sectional fray, could only agree on a provision enabling surveys to be made of all the possible routes. These surveys, published in 1855 and consisting of 15 large volumes, merely concluded, as all knew, that five different transcontinental routes were feasible.

Young Theodore D. Judah, called by some "Crazy Judah" because of his obsession with the building of the transcontinental road, had gathered facts and statistics and was presenting them across the nation to

Theodore D. Judah, called by many "Crazy Judah," who conceived the idea of a transcontinental railroad and interested the "Big Four" in building it.

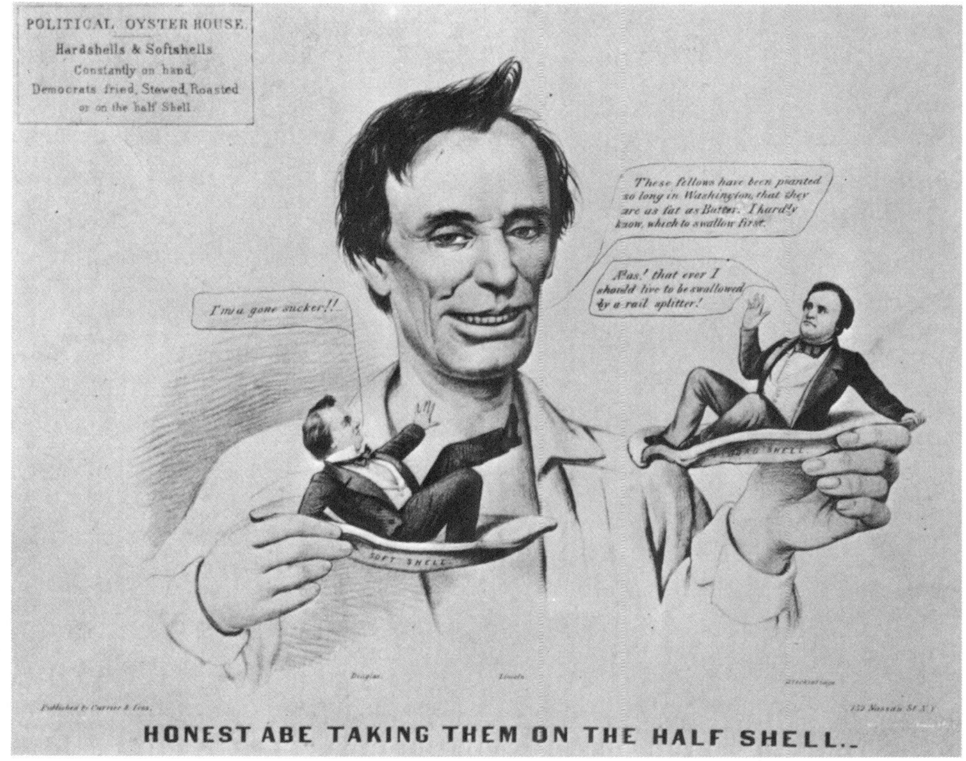

Republican campaign cartoon of 1860 shows Lincoln ready to gulp his Soft Shell and Hard Shell Democratic opponents.

anyone who would listen to him. He had built the Sacramento Valley railroad which was formally opened on Feb. 22, 1856. After listening to Judah and dismayed by the laggard actions of the national government, the California legislature on April 5, 1859, adopted a concurrent resolution calling for a railroad convention to promote the interest and protection of California, Oregon, and Washington, and called for delegates equal in number to the members of the legislatures of each territory and state.

The convention met in Assembly Hall at San Francisco with 100 present. John G. McCallum, as one of the delegates, drew up the final resolution of the session. Although the work of the Pacific Railroad Convention of 1859 resulted in no further direct formal action, nevertheless, it had an important effect upon public opinion, and the McCallum resolution favoring the central route became in many respects the progenitor of the Pacific Railroad Act which passed Congress in 1862. It also spelled out the right and expediency of legislative control of all monopolies deriving their authority from the Legislature, including railroads, gas and water companies. It was but a reiteration of the stand he had taken years ago as a member of the California State Senate.

23

YOUNG JUDAH carried the word of the California Railroad Convention back to Washington where Lincoln finally signed the Pacific Railroad Act in 1862. The president strongly believed the railroad to be a military necessity and a strengthening bond helping to hold the far West in the Union. Furthermore, it would facilitate the flow of gold from California and Nevada into the national coffers.

This act was to be amended two years later to make its terms more generous to the railroads. The "big four," Mark Hopkins, Collis P. Huntington, Leland Stanford, and Charles Crocker emerged as the strong-armed controllers of the Central Pacific Corporation which was to build eastward from Sacramento. The Union Pacific, a corporation chartered by Congress, was to build westward from Omaha, Nebraska, the federal government furnishing extensive loans and land grants to both of these companies.

United States public lands were granted to the railroad companies in alternate sections, checkerboard fashion on both sides of the right of way. Under an Act of 1864 the Central Pacific and the Union Pacific were given ten alternate sections on each side of the line. This meant that half of the land along the way was in the control of the railroad.

Leland Stanford, one of the Big Four, was elected governor of California in September 1861 and took office in January, 1862. Immediately it became evident to John McCallum and other conservative men that Stanford would have no scruples in advancing his own interests. When in 1863 he succeeded in inducing the State to add further subsidies benefiting the railroads in addition to those promised by the federal government, McCallum's apprehensions grew.

He would live to see the day when 11,585,393 acres or 11.4 percent of the state's lands would rest in the hands of the Big Four.

4.
The Fateful Decade of the 1860s

ONE EVENING during the year 1861 John McCallum was in San Francisco and attended a concert at the Freeman home. The lovely young sister of his host was the artist. John was enchanted by the fragile loveliness of this young woman and charmed by the sweetness of her lilting voice. He courted and won the heart and hand of beautiful little Emily Freeman.

Emily, of the large deep-set eyes and bobbing curls, was to bear him four sons and two daughters. The first son died in infancy and was buried in a grave in the Placerville cemetery. Gently reared and never in robust health (blinding migraine headaches tormented her entire life), Emily followed John through the heights of fame down into the depths of sorrow and misfortune. Nothing much is known about her and she remains to this day virtually a shadowy creature.

Throughout the days of courtship and marriage John McCallum still retained his interest in politics — especially the national scene.

When the Republicans passed over their best-known party men and nominated Abraham Lincoln of Illinois for president, the nation was irretrievably split despite his impassioned "House Divided" speech. Lincoln's election set the nightmare of dissolution in motion. South Carolina was the first state to leave the union. Seven seceded southern states met in Montgomery, Alabama, on February 8, 1861, to form the Confederate States of America.

In California the group of former Know-Nothings sincerely wished to save the Union from "any and every attempt to destroy and weaken its bonds." They met in convention and John McCallum ably assisted in the formation of a new Union Party.

The National Union Party, "representing the loyalty of the land," opened its nominating convention at Baltimore on June 7, 1864. Lincoln and Johnson were nominated. Two nights later in Platt's Hall in San Francisco a "union ratification" meeting was held for the Lincoln-Johnson ticket. Salutes were fired in honor of the event. The nominations were

Emily Freeman McCallum (Mrs. John Guthrie McCallum). Courtesy Palm Springs Desert Museum.

Pro-Union political rally. San Francisco, 1861.

Union Ticket, 1864, with McCallum as an elector. Courtesy Huntington Library, San Marino.

entirely acceptable to the Union men of California, who were to a man enthusiastic admirers of Abraham Lincoln.

The State Republican Committee called for a nominating convention to be held in Sacramento the following August. At this meeting J. G. McCallum was elected temporary chairman of the convention on the first ballot by a vote of 199 to 170 for his nearest competitor. The following day, August 31, he was elected permanent president. The convention came to a close with McCallum and Samuel Brannan being nominated without opposition for presidential electors at large.

The election was held on Tuesday, Nov. 8, 1864, and the official canvass of the vote on December 8th. Brannan received 62,053 votes as elector for Lincoln and McCallum 62,120. The Union electors met in the Senate Chamber of the state capitol on Dec. 7 and cast the vote of the state for Lincoln and Johnson. McCallum was appointed messenger to convey the return to Washington.

When McCallum carried the electoral vote to Washington, he was admitted to practice before the Supreme Court of the United States. He remained to witness Lincoln's second inauguration and, it is reported, experienced the horrors of the night of the president's assassination in

Ford's Theater. John McCallum was one of a delegation which went to pay respects at the bier of the nation's fallen idol. Lincoln's death was a very personal sorrow to McCallum.

It must have been difficult, indeed, for John McCallum to tear himself away from his home at this time. Only his tremendous admiration for President Lincoln could have caused him to leave his delicate wife so soon after the birth of their second child.

John Guthrie McCallum, Jr., was born on Dec. 22, 1864, to his parents' great joy. Other children were to come, but it would always be Johnny who was the lodestar of his parents' lives.

Concerning her father's abiding admiration and loyalty to Abraham Lincoln, his daughter Pearl said many years later in a printed interview:

"The Great Emancipator was a powerful inspiration to my father . . . he followed a similar pattern that Lincoln had set for himself . . . Lincoln had many enemies in government who scoffed at him and did not believe he was of the stature history would reveal. My father was one of his greatest admirers and staunchest supporters, and saw in him one of the great figures of history."

Leslie's weekly shows how Booth sneaked up on Lincoln and fired from behind. Mrs. Lincoln sits beside the President. At right are their two guests, Major Rathbone and his fiancée.

Lincoln memorial services in San Francisco.

Lincoln's last photograph, taken April 9, 1865. Four years of war had cut deep lines of sorrow upon his face.

Andrew Johnson who succeeded Lincoln as president.

THE CIVIL WAR made an awesome impact upon the entire nation and resulted in many changes. This crushing of the party when it soon became evident that President Lincoln's successor, Johnson, was urging the return of the seceded southern states into the Union, caused McCallum and others of the loyal Union Party to be aroused to action. They looked upon the conduct of these states in seceding from the Union and setting up their own country as being treasonable and seditious. Furthermore, for the President to advocate the return of these states was, they thought, a direct intrusion of the Executive branch into the prerogatives of the legislative branch of the government. A protest meeting of the Union Party faithfuls who objected to "Executive dictation" the "schemes of designing politicians," and the "machinations of traitors" was advertised for Friday evening, March 2, 1866, at 7:30 P.M. in Agriculture Hall, Sacramento.

A salute was fired by the Sacramento Light Artillery before the Pavilion, bonfires were lighted, and bands blared out patriotic tunes as ladies filed in to be seated in the 500 chairs provided for their comfort. It was reported that a crowd of over 3,000 assembled that night. Several men spoke before J. G. McCallum rose to take the stand to "captivate the crowd from the very start of his speech."

"It was my fortune, Mr. President and fellow citizens to be near our martyred chief when he fell, and one of the delegation which visited the body a day or two after the assassination. I saw him dead. I saw that calm, humane and benevolent expression upon his countenance which dwelt there while he lived, and I thought of the language of the master poet — language in regard to another ruler who fell, also by assassination:

'After life's fitful fever he sleeps well.
Treason has done its worst;
Nor steel, nor poison,
Malice domestic, foreign levy,
Nothing can touch him further.'

I thought, too, of those memorable words in his last Inaugural address — which read like an extract from the Sermon on the Mount — as I heard him pronounce them before 50,000 people then present, before his country and the world: "Let us finish the work we have begun, and care for him who has bourne the battle, and for the widow and the orphan." I call upon you tonight, fellow citizens, in his language: "Let us go on and finish the work we have begun. [Applause] It is not finished; we need not believe that while we live the contest between slavery and liberty, right and wrong, will ever be finished. We must strive on to the end for the great principles which we won upon the battle fields of the republic. We see the loss of half a million lives and three thousand millions of treasure, and more too, for if all the sighs the war has cost were united, they would rise to the fury of the whirlwind; if all the groans were united in one peal they would sound like the mutterings of the thunder. When we remember these things who will not say the victory won in the field — not only of Union but of Liberty in its most comprehensive sense — must be secured. [Applause] This contest must go on."

McCallum continued to speak along these lines, with outbursts of applause from the appreciative listeners interrupting him. Once he said, "I suppose my time is about up," and the words were met with shouts of "Go on! Go on!" He closed his speech with another quotation from Abraham Lincoln and returned to his seat on the speaker's platform, according to the newspaper accounts, to "Cheers and applause."

At its state convention the next year the Republicans nominated J. G. McCallum for the office of Secretary of State. On July 26, McCallum published a card declining the nomination for this office.

EVIDENTLY deciding that Sacramento was nearer to the heart of the political action, John McCallum moved his family and his law office to the State Capital sometime during 1868. At first his law offices were at 45 Fourth Street, and his residence on G Street between 10th and 11th. It was during this same year that the Union Party met, the State Central Committee was selected, and the executive committee of nine included the name of J. G. McCallum. The California Union Party chose U. S. Grant as their candidate for president and Schuyler Colfax as his running mate.

At the Republican convention of the second district, convening at Sacramento, J. G. McCallum along with four other nominees lost the nod for Congressman to A. A. Sargent. McCallum came in fourth when the votes were counted.

Undismayed by this defeat, McCallum, ever loyal to the party, spoke on behalf of the Grant-Colfax team ten times during 1868, each speech being reported at length in the *Alta California* newspaper. His obvious relish for the give and take of rough-and-tumble political speechmaking is apparent in the excerpts from the detailed reporting on June 5, 1868, of the talk he gave in San Francisco.

A CHANGE OF SCENE

President Ulysses S. Grant, shortly after he became President. He never swore, hated politics and political talk, and loathed military parades and martial music.

Young McCallum probably looked upon such a scene when his offices were located on J Street in Sacramento.

A vast crowd assembled with many Democrats and Southern sympathizers present, who threatened to rebel again if Grant and Colfax were elected. McCallum, aware of this hostile element, geared his comments towards them. In these few excerpts from his speech, comments from the crowd are enclosed in brackets.

"Mr. Chairman and Fellow Citizens of San Francisco:

". . . . Four years ago I remember having attended a ratification meeting in this city when there was involved in the mighty contest then pending, not only liberty, but the very existence of the Nation. Liberty, as ever in the contest of the past, is still involved; for as was expressed some years ago by our martyred President . . . . there is a conflict ever enduring between freedom and slavery. I do not deem this contest, however, as similar to the last, further than so far as it involves liberty . . .

"It will be observed in this that I pay but little attention to the idle threats of the Democratic Party. I pay no attention to the threats adopted in their recent state convention that if we succeed in electing our President by votes which they might not think proper they would not submit and they would rebel again. [Laughter and a voice, "That's all right."]

"Those threatening gentlemen belong to that class to which the first secessionist belonged, and the first secessionist, fellow citizens, was the devil himself. [Laughter and applause]

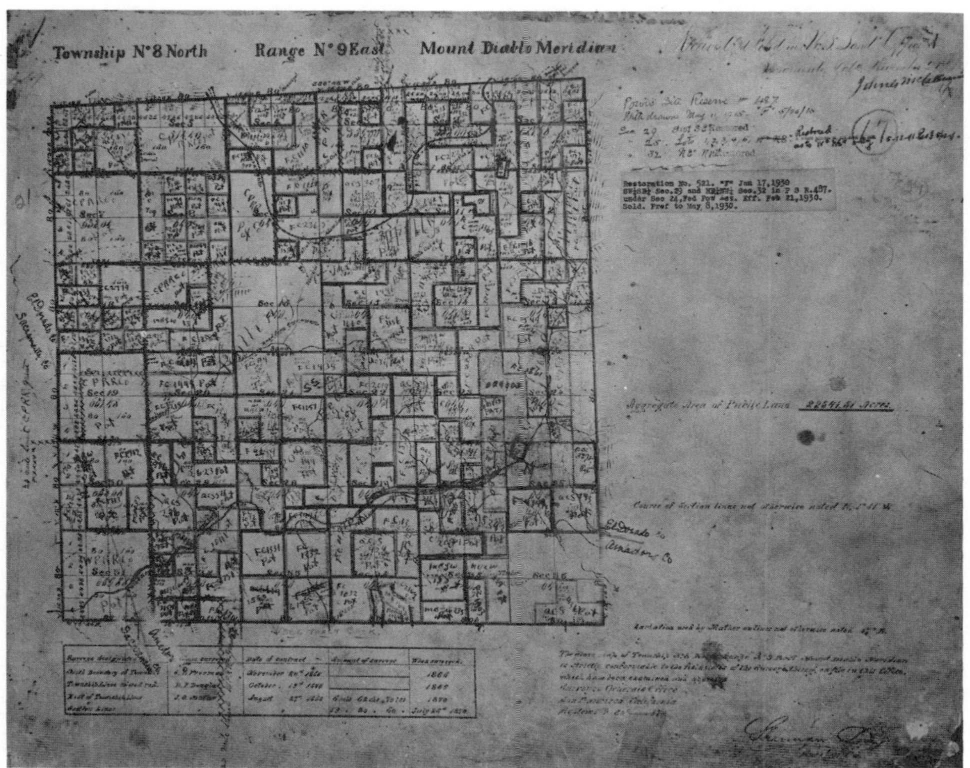

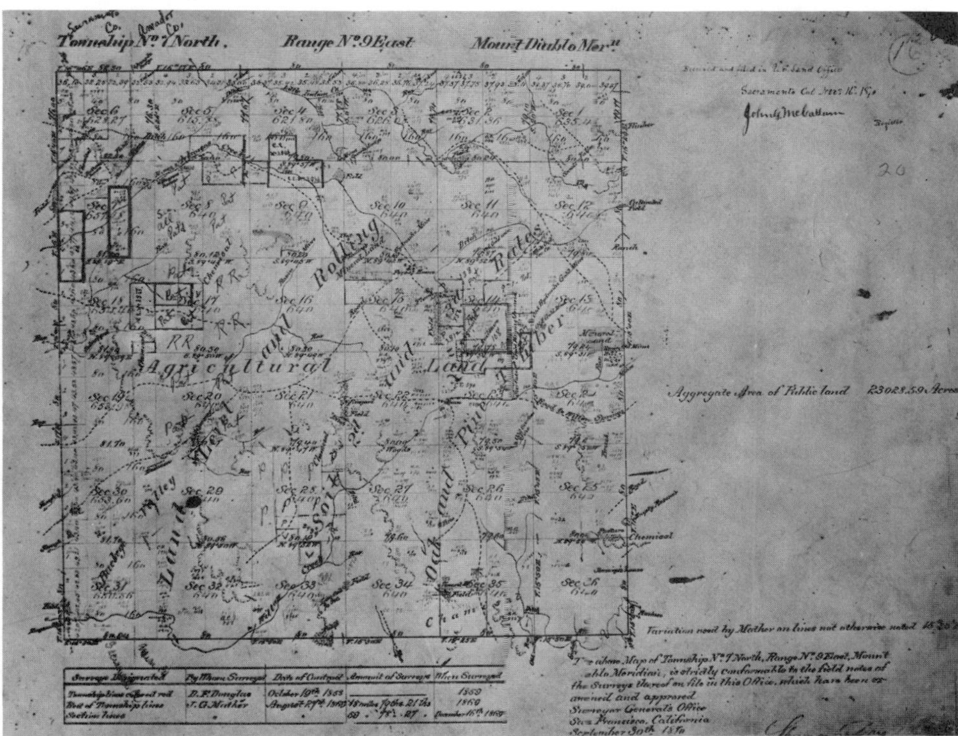

Land plots filed November 16, 1870, by John G. McCallum while serving as U.S. Government Land Register in Sacramento. Note his signature in upper right corner.

"When they talk about nominating some Republican like Chase, or Charles Francis Adams . . . . there is some presentiment of some great change. What do these signs portend unless some great disaster is about to happen to the Democratic Party. [Applause] In November, next, it will sink to rise no more. I propose, fellow citizens, that we bury it, and with its head downward and its heels upward, so that if it ever crawls out again it may crawl out on the other side [great laughter] perhaps in China, and if it does let that party and the Chinamen fight it out there." [Renewed laughter and great applause]

This long speech continued in the same vein to the delight of McCallum's admirers and to the jeers and catcalls of the opposition. To his enjoyment, his speeches during this campaign met with the same vigorous response everywhere he spoke.

The responsibilities of a growing family (his son Wallace having been born Sept. 18, 1866, in Placerville) made it necessary for John McCallum to undertake additional means of making a livelihood. He was appointed Register U. S. Land Office, at the same time continuing with his law practice. He moved his offices to 117 J Street between J and 19th Streets.

The first daughter, May, was born on Oct. 19, 1869.

McCallum moved his law office in 1872 to the Odd Fellows building at J and 18th Streets, and the following year to 121 K Street. By this time he had relinquished the duties of Register and concerned himself solely with his law practice.

Sacramento, 1868.

5·

The Depression of the Seventies

The nation-wide depression caused financial panic as shown in this scene of the San Francisco Stock Exchange.
Illustrated London News.

THE STATE of California plunged into what has become known as the "terrible seventies." John McCallum, along with virtually everybody, felt the effects of the financial depression and during the years 1873-74 became, along with his legal practice, a "general land agent."

"By a cruel paradox, the completion of the first transcontinental railroad not only failed to bring California the expected surge of prosperity, but marked instead the beginning of a deep and general depression that continued through the whole next decade. A frustrated and embittered populace blamed its disappointments and sufferings on the railroad and on the Chinese. Thus the difficulties of a long period of economic distress were aggravated by racial antagonism and political upheaval," so wrote Walton Bean in his *California, an Interpretive History*.

Instead of the anticipated "land boom," real estate prices declined. The railroad, it was true, brought in thousands of people, but mostly these were seeking quick prosperity and very few could afford to buy land at

The "Big Four." Southern Pacific
Company photographs.
Charles Crocker.

Mark Hopkins.

The first overland trains reached
the Oakland station at Seventh
and Broadway on November 8,
1869, thus connecting this city
with the rest of the nation.

high prices. When the panic of 1873 struck the national economy as a whole, it intensified the depression that had begun in California a few years earlier.

It was during this time that John McCallum closed his office in Sacramento and moved his family to Oakland. He settled them at 1115 Jackson Street, and for about two years, practiced law across the bay in San Francisco. In Oakland as in Sacramento his restless nature was revealed by his constant moving. McCallum moved his law practice from San Francisco into Room 9 in the Union Bank Building in Oakland, but kept the same family residence at the Jackson Street address. He remained in these offices during the year of the Constitutional Convention of 1879, but later that same year moved his residence into the Nicholl House, a

Trains meeting the Southern Pacific ferry at the Oakland wharf, 1871.

Collis P. Huntington.

Leland Stanford.

hotel on the northeast corner of Washington and Ninth Streets run by John H. Nicholl. As advertised in the Oakland *Times*, the rates for the Nicholl House were: "suites from $20 to $30 per day; singles $8 to $15, and weekly or daily rates were also available."

Judge McCallum, as more and more of his friends were honoring him with this affectionate title, enlarged his law office when he moved to rooms 11 and 12 at 859 Broadway, and the family residence was at 354 East 14th Street. The next year he kept the same office, but moved the family out to Alameda, where there were handsome large houses and luxuriant gardens near the bay.

McCallum continued speaking out against the greed of the huge railroad combination. The great pioneer railroad builders, Crocker, Huntington, Hopkins and Stanford, saw in Oakland an ideal terminal for their Central Pacific Railroad, a connecting link with their first transcontinental railroad. First they had obtained a monopoly on the waterfront of

The railroad monopoly grew so powerful cartoonists began lampooning it. This "Curse of California" cartoon appeared in The Wasp, *a San Francisco weekly magazine of August 19, 1882.*

that city. Likewise, despite a bitter fight, they had gained a foothold on the waterfront of San Francisco and taken political control of that city which would take decades to overcome, so strong was their domination.

While they were completing their stranglehold on the bay, the Big Four were also making plans to capture the rest of the state. McCallum watched in dismay as the Big Four began in 1870 to construct a line into Southern California and to gobble land grants throughout the San Joaquin Valley. After first enticing small farmers into the San Joaquin, the railroad offhandedly, but with the consent of the courts, then was successful in depriving these small landowners of their ranches.

To understand completely the rapaciousness of the railroad magnets we turn again to quote from Walton Bean, "the railroad's power to make or break almost anyone engaged in agriculture, mining, manufacture, or commerce, through its discriminatory freight rates, was effectively used in interrelation with the development of its control over politics. California's government, as well as its economy, became a prisoner of 'the railroad.'"

The reform element in the state looked with increasing alarm at the blatant furthering of selfish interest of the Big Four. John McCallum was among those persons expressing objection, vigorously and all too effectively. He could not have known the drastic effect the railroad combine would one day have upon his entire life.

The old and the new, from Frank Leslie's Illustrated Newspaper.

6.

The Irrepressible Conflict

Denis Kearney, arousing a group of the Workingman's Party on the top of Nob Hill, San Francisco, the night of October 29, 1877.

GREAT as was his yearning to slip quietly into private life with his family and law practice, Judge McCallum soon found the distressing conditions prevalent throughout the state precluded any such idea.

The general distrust of the people of California for the railroads intensified; the widespread hatred of the Chinese laborers increased; the radical Marxist labor element grew with surprising vigor. The latter became known as the Workingmen's Party and was under the rough and tumble leadership of Denis Kearney. Kearney was a member of the "pick handle brigade" which engaged in pillage and arson, and after meeting in vacant lots, this group also became known as the "sand lot" party.

Added to the general unrest and dissension in the state were the increasingly vociferous demands from the people for a new State Constitution. The call for a new Constitutional Convention was finally approved by the voters in the state elections on Sept. 5, 1877. By the following April the State Legislature adopted an enabling act setting the election of delegates to the convention.

The radical Workingmen's Party had become organized well enough to nominate a full ticket of delegates in every part of the state. This show of strength so alarmed the conservative elements of both Democrats and Republicans who grew fearful that the communists would gain control of the state, that they momentarily set aside party differences and fused under the label of "Non-partisan."

Judge McCallum, observing that all he held dear was being placed in jeopardy by the so-called Marxists, was easily persuaded once again to lend his considerable prestige to the conservative causes.

The election for delegates to the Constitutional Convention was held on Wednesday, June 19th, and the "Non-partisan" ticket for delegates at large was elected. The name of John G. McCallum was listed on the official roster of delegates as being of the "Non-partisan Party, representing Alameda County," and with his former political affiliation as that of "Independent Republican and profession as lawyer." In the book giving *Biographical Sketches of the Delegates to the Convention to Frame a New Constitution for the State of California, 1878*, published by Waldron and Vivian, it was stated:

> "Mr. McCallum has usually preferred private life, having declined several nominations for important offices, such as he has accepted invariably leading to election. As a public officer, speaker, and sometime editor, the Delegate from Alameda has taken such earnest part in the leading questions of the times as have made him well known throughout the State, whilst his education and brains make him capable to assist prominently in the Amendment of the Constitution."

The delegates to the Constitutional Convention assembled in Sacramento on September 28, 1878. By occupation 39 were farmers; 8 were merchants; 57 were lawyers and mostly conservatives; while the others were scattered over a wide range of occupations indicating the diverse skilled trades of the San Francisco workingmen. The conservative delegates included some of the shrewdest lawyers and politicians in the state, and could have controlled the convention were it not for the fact that some of the agrarians joined with the workingmen on reform issues.

The convention got underway with a warning from the Stockton *Independent* newspaper which proclaimed, "The organic law of the state must not be changed to meet the view of the communist reformers."

The conservatives were of the same opinion.

John McCallum immediately assumed one of the dominant leadership roles of the convention. The work he accomplished during the long strenuous sessions of the convention was to be among his finer efforts and would mark the culmination of his political career.

In the index of the official account of the *Debates and Proceedings of the Constitutional Convention Convened at the City of Sacramento, Saturday, Sept. 28, 1878*, the name of John G. McCallum was listed 101 times.

As soon as the preliminaries of the convention were out of the way, the chairman made his committee appointments. McCallum found himself appointed to the Legislative, the Right of Suffrage, and the City, County and Township Organization standing committees. While working diligently to carry out the responsibilities of these appointments, McCallum also spoke out repeatedly upon important issues. His first speech before the delegation came on October 30 when he defended the U. S. Constitution as being the paramount power in the land. He spoke to tremendous applause and received considerable commendation for his patriotic speech.

Within but three days into the work of the convention, Judge McCallum took the floor and introduced a proposed amendment defining and declaring the right of the state to regulate and limit the rates to be charged for freights and fares of the railways, and for gas and water, the rates of other services and commodities by corporations, and making the exercise of that right mandatory. Later in the session he spoke out against the combination of common carriers. Once again the railroads received the full benefit of his indignation. "I am one of those who believe that there is now an irrepressible conflict between monopoly powers and popular rights," he pronounced.

Continuing with his speech, McCallum claimed that in making laws the state legislature had acted solely in favor of the railways and had "violated a great public trust." Persisting along these same lines he stated, "I am perfectly aware that in taking this position I am taking a position, not as gentlemen seem to think, on the strong side, but in a great sense the weak side. If there is any great power in this state over all other powers, political or otherwise, it is that great corporation called the Central Pacific Railway Company. It has controlled absolutely the politics of the state for 15 years. Why it has more power than Mohamet. When the Central Pacific orders mountains to come to them, they come."

"The New Constitution Expected to Save the State." The sole newspaper to support the new constitution of 1879 was the San Francisco Chronicle. Courtesy Pasadena Public Library.

Later, in another session, he spoke strongly against increases of rates being set by a railroad commission and expressed the opinion that rates were already too high. He went on to stress that there "must be a definite, clear, expression of the constitutional right of the people to regulate, not only railroad corporations . . . but all corporations coming under the general head of furnishing articles, or rendering services for public use, that in all cases, without exception, the charges for articles furnished and services performed, shall be specifically regulated by law."

On the appointment of Railroad Commissioners, he gave his views: "I am not satisfied to elect for four years these commissions — to hold office for four years — so that, in case the railroad companies should get control of a majority of them, we will not have to wait for four years to get rid of them." He had previously suggested that the terms of office for the railroad commissioners be staggered to 2-3-4 years with one member being elected at each general election every two years, "In order that

40

"Conservatives Feared the New Constitution." One of the many newspaper cartoons which denounced the new constitution of 1879. Courtesy Pasadena Public Library.

there may be frequent changes, and bring this power nearer home to the people."

Other large corporations came under his scrutiny and again he spoke to the assembly stating, "Other great monopolies also should be state regulated by commissions or otherwise . . . I have not the slightest degree of prejudice against corporations. They were necessary to the development of the country, and should be encouraged. Let them incorporate as they please, but let them not be exempt from taxation." He also spoke to the subject of directors of corporations being legally liable for actions taken by the corporations as a whole and favored legislation to bring this into effect.

McCallum ran the gamut of his interests. He proposed amendments which would bring about speedier court action in municipal courts. The law cases, under this amendment, would have to be tried within a specific time period or be re-submitted. He then spoke on behalf of mechanics liens and introduced an amendment to enable mechanics, artisans and labor and material men to obtain liens upon structures for which they had supplied labor or materials and not received compensation.

Perhaps the most striking example of the moral fiber of John Guthrie McCallum was revealed when a large segment of those present at the Convention advocated the return to corporal punishment for criminals. Inflexible moralist that he was, and as deeply concerned as he was over the rampant and rising crime rate at the time, McCallum's deep humanitarian feelings were repelled by the prospect of such a return to the brutality and disciplinary practices of the dark ages. He leaped to his feet and spoke in soaring words against such a proposition stating, "The way of the transgressor is hard and for the protection of society perhaps it should be even harder than it is now. I think the argument of the gentlemen who are in favor of the restoring of corporal punishment has proved that proposition, but I cannot admit that they have proved the way to make it harder is by returning to the dark ages."

He then went on to advocate punishment by hard labor, and sterner discipline and then ended his talk by saying, "I have heard it said that the worst thing you can do to a man is to hang him. I deny it. The worst thing you can do is publicly whip him and then turn him loose upon society. You had better hang him in the first instance."

The speech met with thunderous applause from his fellow delegates and the measure was promptly dropped.

Twice during the long weeks of strenuous work of the convention, Judge McCallum apologized to the chair for the brevity of some of his comments upon important issues because of poor health. The one time when fatigue and illness showed in his demeanor was when in response to some critical comment from another delegate, McCallum responded with acerbity, "Legislatures have been known in the past as 'Legislatures of a thousand privileged questions' and 'the legislature of a thousand drinks.' I hope this convention may not be known as the convention of a thousand discourtesies."

The convention was in session nearly six months and adjourned March 3, 1879. The delegates produced the longest written constitution in the world. It achieved very little net improvement over the first state Constitution, and eventually led to virtually no reforms.

Practically no one was entirely pleased with the convention's lengthy

Oakland, California, as it was in 1879, the year Pearl McCallum was there. Courtesy Pasadena Public Library.

product. The Conservatives denounced it as communistic and vicious. The Workingmen's Party was angered because it accomplished so little directly concerned with labor problems. The strongest approval came from the farm areas where the Grangers hoped for reduction in railway freight rates and lower taxes. Banks, railroads, manufacturing firms, mining companies, and water and gas companies launched a vigorous campaign against the adoption of the new Constitution.

Governor Irwin proclaimed an election for May 7, 1879, to allow voters either to ratify or reject the document. The Constitution was ratified and became the state's fundamental law in January, 1880.

The San Francisco *Chronicle* was practically the single newspaper favoring the new constitution and advocated the formation of a new political party in its support. On May 17 a conference was held in San Francisco with J. G. McCallum among those present and lending his support. At this meeting, it was decided to extend an invitation to all citizens to assemble in every election precinct in the state on Saturday, May 24, to form "new Constitution" clubs.

THE AFTERMATH OF THE CONVENTION

SEVERAL leaders of the Democratic, Republican and the Workingmen's Party joined with the Conservative in the New Constitution Party which caused but a brief flurry in the political scene. Bitterness continued for some time and so acrimonious grew the sentiment for and against the new Constitution that two shootings resulted.

Weary and half sick as he was, John McCallum met with other members of the Republican State Committee in San Francisco two days after the close of the Constitutional Convention. It was resolved to call a state convention to meet at Sacramento on June 17. At this meeting concern over the continued iniquitous railroad domination of the entire state absorbed the thinking of those assembled.

In the party platform, which was largely involved with reforms, a pledge for prospective railroad commissioners was spelled out. Each candidate of the Republican Party was obliged to pledge himself to taking this oath:

> "I do solemnly pledge my sacred honor that I will, if elected a railroad commissioner faithfully support, without any modification or change the following order: Ordered that the rate of fares and freights on all railroads between points within this state which have received national aid, shall from and after the 1st day of February, 1880 be fixed at three-fourths the usual rates demanded and received on the 1st day of June, 1870. I further solemnly pledge myself, that during my term of office, I will never vote for any increase rate of charge for any railroad service, but that any charge voted for by me after February 1, 1880, shall be a reduction."

Judge John G. McCallum permitted his name to be placed in nomination for Railroad Commissioner at this time.

He was defeated in the September elections.

McCallum was, from that moment, a marked man.

TROUBLED TIMES

THE Constitutional Convention over and done with, McCallum could return to his badly neglected personal affairs. During the year of 1879 his second daughter and last child had been born. They named her Pearl, and she was exactly eighteen years younger than their oldest child, Johnny. Shortly after Pearl's birth, the family moved to San Francisco. It was then that the Judge received a visitor in his law office.

Legend has it that this was a representative of the railroads named Gen. David D. Colton. This pouter pigeon of a little man was financial director of the powerful Big Four. Colton, it is said, made McCallum a lucrative offer to join the staff of the railroad. The Judge indignantly showed him the door and literally ejected him from the office.

The Big Four, evidently tiring of McCallum's successful handling of cases involving unfair freight charges, had decided to buy him off. In the ensuing days, one by one, McCallum's law clients, many of them of years standing, came to him and shamefacedly confessed they could no longer withstand pressures that were being put upon them by the railroad. They were being forced into withdrawing their business from his practice.

The Southern Pacific Railroad goliath moved relentlessly against John McCallum. When he persisted in his efforts to thwart their grasping, ruthless methods of overcharging, the persecution was doubled. It was only by selling some of the San Francisco property he had wisely bought at modest prices and then sold under inflated conditions, that the McCallum family was able to exist.

Unfortunately, the historical and official records of this period of San Francisco were all subsequently destroyed in the earthquake fire of 1906. However, the account of the attacks made upon McCallum by the railroads was related by his daughter Pearl to author Ruth Eleanor McKee who retold them in but a slightly fictionalized version in the novel *Christopher Strange* written in 1946.

There is also a most poignant account in the novel of the typhoid epidemic which struck San Francisco in 1881. The four older children were stricken and for a while their lives endangered by this sickness. The infant Pearl was the only child to escape. All of the children seemed to respond to treatment and quickly recovered except the oldest boy Johnny. For a while they believed he was not going to survive through the epidemic. Then, an onslaught of pneumonia immediately following the typhoid so weakened the boy that he lapsed into tuberculosis. The family was fortunate to have a doctor whose specialty was tuberculosis and who was modern enough in medical theory to insist upon rest and warm, dry climate rather than the popular concept of high altitudes, cold weather and strenuous exercise which caused many persons to hemorrhage to death.

When the doctor told him that Johnny must be taken to a more salubrious climate, the distraught father immediately decided to forego the

Pearl McCallum at two and a half years. The family was still residing in Oakland.

45

satisfaction of continuing his fight against the railroads and the struggle to maintain his legal practice against such tremendous odds. Determined to devote his future and his remaining fortune to the restoration of his beloved son's health, the Judge began closing out his languishing law practice. To the anxious mother and father there was no question over the necessity for making the change. Their son was critically ill. The only problem was in deciding where would they find the dry warm climate in which Johnny could regain his health and where the Judge could find the means of starting his life again.

Fortunately, a friend made this important decision for them.

7.

The Road Turns

On July 17, 1883, the Hon. John F. Miller, United States Senator from California, sent a telegram to the Hon. H. M. Teller, U. S. Secretary of the Interior, which stated:

> "Hon. John G. McCallum, Six Thirty-seven Kearny of San Francisco is best man for Indian Agent, Mission Agency.
>
> *(signed)* Jno. F. Miller"

Later that same day the Senator dispatched a letter to the Secretary setting forth in detail the reasons for this nomination:

> "Lavergue, Napa, California.

"Hon. H. M. Teller,
My dear Sir:

"I received your telegram in respect to the Mission Agency and began at once to cast about for an honest capable man who would take the place at the small salary. Hon. John McCallum of San Francisco is as honest a man as any now living and he is a man of fine ability. He is not doing much now and I found him

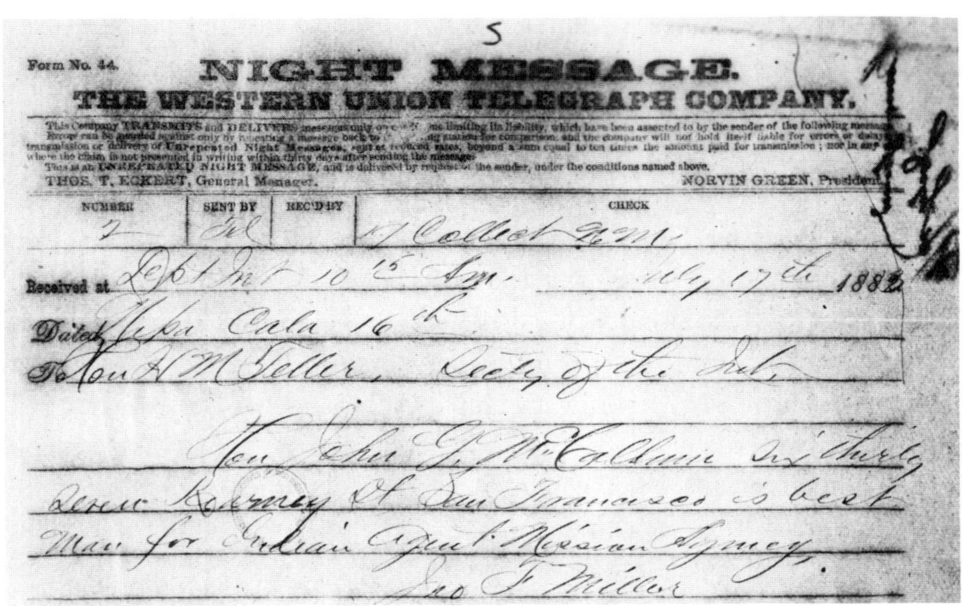

Senator Miller's telegram suggesting John G. McCallum as Indian Agent. Records of the Office of the Secretary of the Interior, Appointment Division.

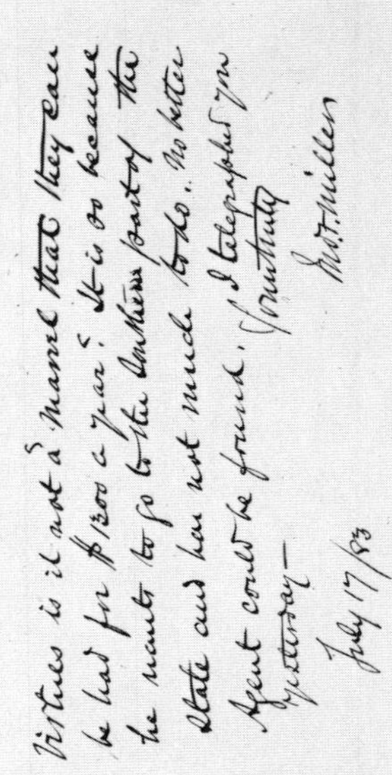

Senator Miller's letter of recommendation for John G. McCallum as Indian Agent. Records of the Office of the Secretary of the Interior, Appointment Division.

willing to take the place. I told him the salary was $1500 and now I find it is $1300. Still I think he will accept. You can rely upon him with perfect faith. He is a good lawyer, a good natured kind-hearted man, truthful, sensible and of high character. He was a member of our last Constitutional Convention and was one of the best members. With all these virtues is it not a marvel that they can be had for $1300 per year? It is because he wants to go to the Southern part of the State and has not much to do. No better Agent could be found. I telegraphed you yesterday.

Yours truly,
(*signed*) Jno. F. Miller

July 17, 1883"

Eight days later, Judge McCallum received a welcomed notice from Washington, D. C. requesting that he submit to the office of Indian Affairs his "official bond with certificate of the United States Attorney in San Francisco and the oath of office, plus affidavits of two sureties, required by law" before being appointed Indian Agent. These he hurriedly obtained and rushed back to headquarters on Aug. 13. In his perturbation, he inadvertantly neglected to date the documents and the entire procedure had to be repeated.

On Sept. 1, 1883, he again sent the required documents to Washington with a letter of transmittal. His anxiety over the critical state of his son's health and the necessity for quick action in making the move to a milder climate can be deduced from the closing sentence of the letter,

"I respectfully request that my commission when issued be directed to me at San Bernardino and, if proper, that I then be notified by telegram, at my expense, addressed to me *here*, of the mailing of the commission.

Very Respy,
Your obdt. servt.
John G. McCallum"

After eleven long days of anxious waiting lapsed without his receiving word of the appointment, McCallum turned again to his friend, the Senator, who sent the following telegram:

"To Hon. H. Price, Commissioner of Indian Affairs, Washington.
Have McCallum Agent commission forwarded reply McCallum here.

(*signed*) John F. Miller, U. S. Senator."

The records of the Bureau of Indian Affairs in the National Archives in Washington, D. C. show that John G. McCallum received an interim commission as Agent for the Mission Indians on June 19, 1883, which had been duly signed by President Chester A. Arthur.

He was not to receive the permanent four-year appointment until the following December 29, 1883, when his re-submitted bond had been received and preliminary procedures approved.

By the time the first official document arrived Judge McCallum had already taken the turn in the road to what he sincerely believed would bring about a beneficent change for him and his family. He had moved his family to the south.

San Bernardino, at the time of the arrival of the McCallum family, had a county-wide population of 7,786. The city, founded by Mormons, had wide streets, neat well-built houses and trim gardens, and was surrounded by small farms, most of which had been abandoned when Brigham Young issued the call for the faithful Mormons to return to Salt Lake City. At night the city was illuminated by gas lights installed the previous year.

The McCallums arrived in time to witness several exciting civic celebrations. A splendid event took place when the first telephone service was installed between the Transcontinental Hotel at Colton and Starke's Hostelry at San Bernardino — a distance of some six miles. Excited

Letter of acceptance from John G. McCallum.

49

crowds gathered to enjoy the inaugural ceremonies and to listen to the band concert at which a Miss Buford sang.

During 1883 the "most complete theater building on the West Coast, outside of San Francisco" was built by the Messrs. Waters and Brinkmeyer.

All in all, San Bernardino with its dry climate and civic industriousness, offered much to the downcast family with their ailing son.

There was but one drawback.

Once again Judge McCallum found himself in the midst of an atmosphere seething with antagonism towards the omnivorous maw of the railroad company which had helped to hasten his departure from San Francisco. Following its usual practice of extortion from cities through which it wished to build its lines, the Southern Pacific demanded exorbitant sums from the city of San Bernardino. This city resisted and so, as a punitive measure, the railroad had bypassed it and built its division point a few miles away, thus creating the new town of Colton, named after the widely disliked little representative of the system who had made the odious offer to Judge McCallum that fateful day in the northern city.

The doughty merchants of San Bernardino in resisting the pressures of the Southern Pacific found that their goods coming from the east could be shipped to Anaheim Landing by steamer and then hauled from there by mule team cheaper than they could be brought to Colton by rail. This "mule line" was patronized and the trains ignored until the railroad was forced to meet the competition and reduce its rates and extend the line into San Bernardino in 1883. There was great rejoicing when the first train rolled into the city. Later that same year the California Southern Railway completed a line running from San Diego through the San Bernardino Valley, thus connecting the desert with the sea.

Still weary from years of constant wrangling with the railroad, Judge McCallum refrained from participating in this local fracas. As soon as his family was comfortably settled, he plunged eagerly into the work as U. S. Agent for the Mission Indians.

Chester A. Arthur

President of the United States of America,

TO ALL TO WHOM THESE PRESENTS SHALL COME, GREETING:

Know ye that, reposing special trust and confidence in the integrity, diligence, and discretion of *John G. McCallum* of *San Francisco California* I have nominated, and, by and with the advice and consent of the Senate, do appoint him to be

Agent for the Indians of the Mission Agency in California

and do authorize and empower him to execute and fulfill the duties of that office according to law: **And** to have and to hold the said office, with all the rights and emoluments thereunto legally appertaining, unto him, the said *John G. McCallum* during the term of four years from the *20th* day of *December 1883* unless this commission be sooner revoked by the President of the United States for the time being.

In testimony whereof I have caused these letters to be made Patent, and the Seal of the Department of the Interior to be hereunto affixed.

Given under my hand, at the City of Washington, the *twenty-ninth* day of *December* in the year of our Lord one thousand eight hundred and *eighty-three*, and of the Independence of the UNITED STATES OF AMERICA the one hundred and *eighth*

Chester A. Arthur

By the President:

H. M. Teller
Secretary of the Interior.

Certificate signed by President Arthur appointing John G. McCallum as Indian Agent for the Mission Indians.

8.

McCallum as Indian Agent

THE GROUPS of Indians over whom Judge McCallum assumed authority
were designated as the Missions, so named originally by the Padres when
the natives clustered around the first Missions. These Indians actually
were of different tribes each with a different dialect.

"They were divided roughly into Serranos, totalling about 390; Coa-
chillas (later called the Cahuillas), 793; San Luis Reyes, 1,142; and the
Diegueños, 745; totalling in all approximately 3,070 Indians, two thirds
of whom lived in San Diego County." A small number dwelt in Los Angeles County and nearly all the remainder dwelt in San Bernardino
County.

The Indians lived in about twenty villages, generally on reservations,
the nearest being 30 miles distant and the farthest over 120 miles from
the Agency office. To inspect all the reservations the Agent for the Mission Indians traveled over 250 miles on horseback over exceedingly
rough terrain and frequently into areas where no roads were to be found.

President Grant, on May 15, 1876, signed into law a decree setting
aside land for nine small reservations for the Mission Indians. It was not
until 1877 that a Mission Indian Agency was created. Reverend S. S.
Lawson was appointed Indian Agent and had his headquarters in San
Bernardino.

One of these small reservations was known as Potrero Ajeno and
among the leading families were the Morongos and the Pablos. Captain
John Morongo served Agent Lawson as aid and interpreter. Because of
the language barrier this interpreter also drove the Agent wherever the
roads permitted and assisted him in speaking with the Indians. Mc-
Callum assigned these duties to Will Pablo who became not only his aid
but his fast friend.

The Judge was shocked to discover how inadequately the Agency was
staffed. Besides himself, there was but one other man — a doctor named
Dr. Albert Thompson. There were no medical facilities such as a hos-

Washingtonia filifera

Chief Cabezon, last of the old
Cahuilla warriors, and his captains.
Seated second from the left is
Will Pablo, friend of Judge
McCallum. Courtesy
Title Insurance and Trust
Company, Los Angeles.

pital and the doctor was expected to handle all the medical needs of the
Indians and serve as Agency clerk as well. For all this work the doctor
received $1000 per year and was paying another person out of his own
pocket to do the clerical work for him. Judge McCallum in an effort to
relieve the overburdened doctor, put in one of his sons (undoubtedly
Harry since Johnny was too ill and Wallace was away most of the time
studying) to do some of the clerk's duties.

McCallum quickly set to work and soon developed a deep concern
over and genuine affection for his Indian charges. He coined a phrase
which was to become his credo: "If there is any doubt, the benefit must
go to the Indians." He had scarcely begun familiarizing himself with
the Agency work when tragedy again struck.

Johnny continued to fail in health. He began coughing up blood again
. . . The move to San Bernardino had not wrought the benefits prayed for
by his parents.

In despair Judge McCallum turned to Will Pablo.

The Indian, understanding his friend's anguish, told him of a hidden
oasis not too many miles away where there was perpetual sunshine, the
air was always fresh and sweet, and where healing waters bubbled from
the warm sandy earth.

Scene in Palm Canyon.

John McCallum did not hesitate in starting out to find this desert place of such promise. With Will Pablo as his driver, they set out one day in a two horse-drawn surrey to drive the miles across the desert. The road was but two rutted tracks meandering over boulders and sand until it finally came to where it wound around the base of a lofty mountain.

Ahead and around them McCallum saw only the arid, sun-baked boulder-strewn sand until finally Will Pablo halted the sweat-soaked horses on a rise. From this elevation a full, breath-taking view spread out before their eyes.

Speaking of this moment in her father's life, his daughter Pearl, over half a century later would comment, "From where he stood on this high spot he surveyed the entire desert scene, beginning with the Little San Bernardino, or the Shadow Mountains, on the north, to the great sand dunes that the Indians called the 'Devil's Playground.' On the east and south were the painted desert hills surrounding the present Salton Sea or ancient Cahuilla Lake, and to the south the Santa Rosas back of the present-day Smoke Tree Ranch. Completing the circle to the southwest and west was the wild Palm Canyon, towering up to mighty San Jacinto, almost eleven thousand feet. The vista was painted bright with sunlight, making the desert hues even more intense.

"As this man of vision — my father — stood on that ridge, he landscape-pictured this area with its dry, healing climate, as the answer to his prayers that his son might be healed. And in this new land he also saw, from the sunshine, rich soil and abundant life-giving waters that flowed from the canyons, a vast future development not only for abundant crops, but for the earliest fruits in the world."

*   *   *

After the friendly welcome from the gentle brownfaced natives who were gathered about the delightful waters of the oasis, John McCallum explored the valley down which cool water coursed from the mountain peaks. He wandered in the shade of the lofty palms with their fronds hanging down and through which soft breezes whispered and made a lulling, swishing sound. Always the sonorous words of Tennyson's poem *The Lotos-Eaters* ran through his mind and the ending phrase throbbed in his head: "We will no longer roam."

Were all the restless years of constant moving from one place to another but a preparation for his readiness to embrace this Eden so readily, he kept wondering? Judge McCallum instantly knew, and with an abiding conviction, that this Land of the Afternoon, as the poet had mentioned in the poem, was where he must purchase a plot as quickly as possible upon which he could build a home and start life anew.

He found the piece of land, purchased it, and thus became the first white settler in what was one day to be world renowned as Palm Springs.

"Native palms."

Cahuilla Indian basket, Carl Eytel.
Courtesy Southwest Museum.

Part Two

The Land of the Afternoon

CAPTAIN JUAN BAUTISTA DE ANZA

Captain Juan Bautista de Anza, who crossed the desert but missed the palm springs, and went on to open a land route from northern Sonora to Monterey and to found San Francisco, after naming the towering San Jacinto peak he saw from a distance. Courtesy Title Insurance and Trust Company, Los Angeles.

9.
Those Who Came Before

WHILE all honors must go to John Guthrie McCallum for being the first white settler in the valley of the palm-shaded oasis, he was not the first white man to pass that way.

For centuries the valley lay scorched by the summer sun and caressed by gentle warmth in winter. Geological evidence reveals that once there was a large inland tropical sea around which grew these swaying palms. The exact origin of these stately trees is not known, and they were to receive their botanical name in 1879 when a German horticulturist named Herman Wendland saw in a Belgium hothouse young trees growing from seed brought from the United States. He named them in honor of George Washington and called them Washingtonia filifera.

The native palms of California are all of the fan type. It has been estimated that over 11,000 of these palms are on the California desert. The trees gave shelter and provided food for the Indians who gathered around the bubbling springs.

These Cahuilla Indians roamed about gathering seed and foraging for food, weaving reed baskets, and luxuriating in the warm spring waters during the winter months. As the days grew unbearably hot

Mt. San Jacinto,
named by de Anza.

from the summer sun, the Indians left the desert sands and climbed the
trails up the steep mountainside following the plentiful game and returning to the valley floor with the coming of cooler days.

George Wharton James in his book *California, Romantic and Beautiful* portrayed these Indians as being:

> "A brave, hardy, rugged lot of aborigines using the wonderful and scareful
> spring of hot water at Palm Springs as their health resort, gathering their big-
> pitted native dates from the palms of Palm Canyon, collecting their acorns from
> the mountain slopes and making their mush, flour, bread, tortillas, drink and
> candy from the beans found on the mesquite trees which dotted the desert's
> face on every side."

The area which has become known as Palm Springs existing as it
does approximately 470 feet above sea level has an annual average
temperature range of about 55.3 degrees and a summer range from 101
to a maximum of 120 degrees. Because of the cloud-free skies and lack
of water vapor in the atmosphere the temperature ranges between day
and night sometimes are quite drastic. The Indians well knew that in a
desert region of such extremes one could freeze as well as bake. It was

60

not unusual for them to awaken of a winter morning to find an ice crust on the rim of a pool beneath a wild palm. The occasional cold, actually, was dreaded far more than the blistering heat of the sun. So, in their wandering, they prized these hot springs more than any other earthly possession. They became the most popular gathering place in the entire desert.

It was but a chance decision which kept this area from discovery as early as 1774 when Captain Juan Bautista de Anza led a band of soldiers and colonizers across the desert in the attempt to open up a route across the Gila and the Colorado Rivers to the seacoast of California. Accompanied by two priests who kept a careful diary of the journey, an Indian guide, and a few soldiers, with 65 head of cattle and 140 horses, Anza's party suffered terribly crossing the sand dunes west of Yuma to Yuba Springs. It was there he made his decision to go by way of Borrego Valley and Coyote Canyon, thus delaying the discovery of Palm Springs for nearly a century.

However, the courageous Anza left his mark upon the region. The haughty, craggy 10,805 foot mountain peak, (the most swiftly rising eminence of any to be found in America) was plainly seen from the place where he paused. It is claimed that Anza, viewing with awe, named the mountain San Jacinto after Saint Hyacinth, a Silesian nobleman who became a monk and was noted for his intellectual superiority and piety.

Anza traveled twice across the desert sands and each time missed the ancient Indian water hole as did Capt. Pedro Fages in 1772 and 1782 when he marched up and down the Carrizo Wash, a few miles to the west. It is a matter of recorded history that during the years 1826 to

The way the pioneers crossed the desert, Carl Eytel.
Courtesy Southwest Museum.

1846 many other venturesome men traversed the desert, but there is
no mention on record of their having been at the oasis. General Stephen
Watts Kearny, leading the Army of the West to San Diego in 1846, came
near and but narrowly missed the oasis when marching from Carrizo
to Vallecito.

The diarists of the Mormon Battalion, January 1847, were the first to
start the actual documentation of the water hole. While Kearny evidently followed Carrizo Wash across the desert, Colonel Cooke had in
his company of 400 soldiers several mountain men and Indian guides,
who undoubtedly knew of the place and took the trail past the oasis.

On January 17, 1847, Colonel Cooke wrote, "The road was very deep
with sand and the forenoon very hot, but the teams reached the Palm
Springs between twelve and one o'clock; and there being no grass, I
determined to continue the march to Vallecito."

During the Gold Rush days of 1849 many thousands of emigrants
trudged into California over the Yuma Crossing. The old desert trail so
familiar to mountain men and gold seekers and plain travelers throughout the years became identified as the "Southern Emigrant Trail."

In the year 1852 various detachments of the Mexican American
Boundary Commission traveled the old Desert Trail between Vallecito
and Fort Yuma, but they all failed to note the palm trees and the springs
at the halfway mark.

While the oasis seemingly languished unnoticed in the desert sun,
events were taking place in the nation's Capital which were to change
all that.

Congress and President Franklin Pierce realized that a southern railway route to the Pacific was imperative, and in 1853 federal funds were
allocated for the government survey. Lieutenant Williamson and geolo-
gist William P. Blake set out to "Explore the almost unknown country
lying between the Mississippi River and the Pacific Ocean, to look for
and determine a practicable route for a railway." It was Blake who
erroneously had christened the region the Colorado Desert and Williamson who wrote lyrically of the friendly Indians and their magnificent
hot mineral spring.

This desert had been known to the early Indians and Mexicans as
"Palma de la mano de Dios," the palm or hollow of God's hand.

Thus it remained for young Lieutenant R. S. Williamson, of the U. S.
Topographical Engineers, to give the classic description of Palm Springs.

Bath house for the original
Agua Caliente hot springs
was built by the Indians
about 1871. Courtesy
Palm Springs Desert Museum.

When his party, exploring the Pacific Railway route across the desert from Yuma to San Diego, arrived at the oasis, he wrote:

"December 15, 1853.
The greater part of the Valley is entirely dry and sandy and almost as forbidding as the Desert. The monotony is broken by a clump of palm trees on the north of the trail and a green bank from which springs issue known as 'Palm Springs!'

"These are situated under a bank of argillaceous sedimentary beds. The water rises at various places, and seems to saturate the ground so thoroughly for a space of two or three hundred feet in diameter, that a hole dug in any part of it soon becomes filled. The water was sulphurous and gave off a slight quantity of sulphurated hydrogen gas. A slight efflorescence quantity of nitro was seen on the surface of the ground around the pools.

"The water, however, was not so strangely charged with these ingredients as to be unpleasant to drink, especially after having used the stagnant and muddy water of the Desert. I found its temperature, under the shade of a palm tree, to be 80; air 70. Three or four palm trees, each about thirty feet high, are standing on the bank from which the springs issue. They are much injured by fire and the persevering attacks of emigrants, who have cut down many of the finest of the group, as if determined that only the trees that grace the sandy avenue to the desert, and afford a cool shade for the springs, should be destroyed."

63

Blake gave the first geological description of the Colorado Desert and wrote enthusiastically of the oasis they encountered:

"This place was evidently a favorite camping ground for the Indians. When we arrived, many Indian boys and girls were bathing in the warm spring, and a group of squaws were engaged in cooking meat for a party returning from a great feast held near Weaver's Ranch, and now just terminated. Willows and mesquite bushes grow there, and I found a young palm tree spreading its broad fan-like leaves among them. The surrounding desert, and this palm tree, gave the scene an Oriental aspect, and the similarity was made still more striking by the groups of Arab-like Indians."

Despite the glowing account, the area continued to bask unnoticed until California attained statehood in 1850. Californianos then began pressing for a transcontinental railroad to link them with other parts of the nation. When the realization of a railroad appeared to be years away, stagecoaches and freight lines sprang into being. The little desert oasis was a natural stopping place for four of these lines.

The largest and best known was the Butterfield Lines with a southern route from Tucson to Yuma, crossing over the desert and going on to San Diego. This line connected with one from San Francisco to Los Angeles. John White, age 32 and a native of England, served as the desert station master. In addition there were three smaller lines in operation.

Stage station at Palm Springs, Carl Eytel. Courtesy Southwest Museum.

The San Antonio and San Diego Mail Line operated from 1857 to 1861. Nicknamed the "Jackass Mail" it had an adobe desert station built by Warren F. Hall, famous pioneer California stage man. Another of the small lines was the Grant Stage running from Prescott, Arizona to San Bernardino in 1872.

Undoubtedly, the most colorful of all the stage operators was "Big Bill Bradshaw" who, tracing out a short way to haul freight across the desert from the gold camps, chose the little desert oasis as a stopping place. It was Bradshaw who christened it "Agua Caliente." His line ran from La Paz, New Mexico Territory, to Los Angeles through Prescott, Arizona, Ehrenburg and then on to Chuckawalla, Indio, Palm Springs and Banning during 1863 to 1877.

With the coming of the railroad in 1877 the days of the overland stage routes came to an end. Among others the Bradshaw oasis station was abandoned to the Indians.

To encourage the building of the railroad, the Federal Government awarded alternating sections of land on each side of the tracks to the Southern Pacific Railway. The government retained the even-numbered sections until years later when these mile-square pieces were converted by the President to reservation lands for the Cahuilla Indians.

This was a bewildering concept for the Cahuillas who could not comprehend how the Federal Government could "give" them land which had always been theirs. In the words of Old Indian Patencio, who lived to be over a hundred, "What is *reservation?* That's not our language. That's white man language." He would later say, "The way of the Indian is hard. First they learned the way of the Spanish Fathers. Then they learned the way of the Mexicans. Then they had to learn again, very

John Butterfield, whose stages ran through the desert lands, making the trip from St. Louis to San Francisco in 23 days, 23½ hours. Courtesy Pasadena Public Library.

different, the way of the white man. So they could not please everyone.''

The confused Cahuillas had no way of foreseeing that in the distant future these lands set aside for them would one day bring them tremendous wealth. Nor could they comprehend that in several years after the completion of the railroad, two white men would venture down into the desert area, look around and with knowledgeable eyes realize that the land was of commercial value.

The land they favored belonged to an Indian named Pedro Chino.

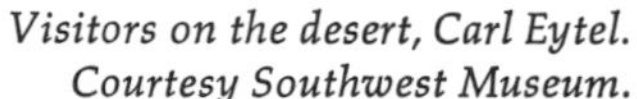

Visitors on the desert, Carl Eytel.
Courtesy Southwest Museum.

IO.

The First Land Purchases

Palm Springs Indians beside a typical Agua Caliente home in the late 1800's. Pedro Chino, from whom the first land purchase was made by whites, is standing in the center. Courtesy Title Insurance and Trust Company, Los Angeles.

PEDRO CHINO had a small ranch located between the hot springs and the mountains. On this land he planted some fruit trees which he irrigated with the flood waters coursing down the canyon. He lived in a small one-room adobe house. But, if rumor is correct, Pedro Chino was an unhappy man.

He yearned for greater things, especially political power. To obtain such prestige it would be necessary for him to live closer to tribal head-quarters near Banning. According to the late Heber Winder, attorney and historian, "Pedro was not very ambitious physically, but he was ambitious politically." He wanted to be elected chief of the Cahuilla tribe. Then, too, according to Winder again, "Chino knew that someday the Indians would have to get off the railroad land which they occupied as squatters."

When, in 1880, two white men appeared, W. E. Van Slyke and M.

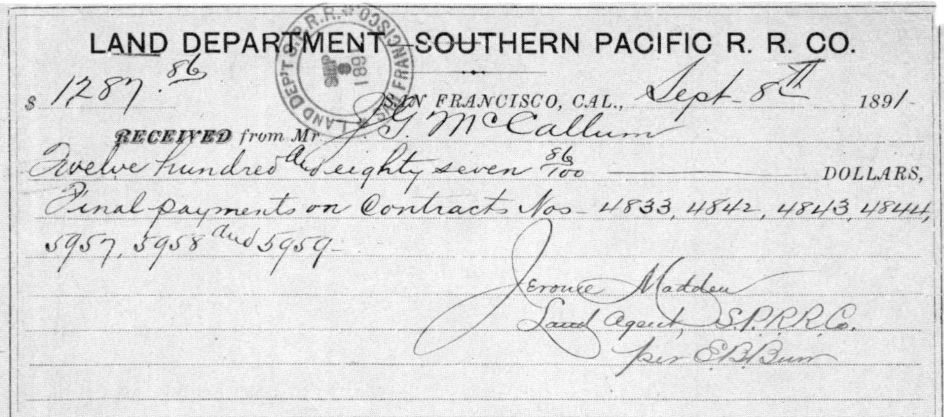

Receipt for the final payment to the Southern Pacific Railroad Company for the acreage purchased at $2.50 per acre by John G. McCallum.

Byrne, and offered him $150 for his little place, Chino took the money with alacrity and rode off on his horse towards Banning and the Potrero Indian village.

Van Slyke and Byrne had no intention of settling down in the desert and when McCallum sought a place, they sold him a fifth interest in the 320 acres they had bought from the railroad. This deed dated March 24, 1885, read as follows:

"We, W. E. Van Slyke and M. Byrne, grant to J. G. McCallum all that real property situated in San Diego County, State of California, described as follows: The undivided one-fifth of Sections 13 and 23 and the undivided one-fifth of all the surveyed part to wit: The North half of the North East Quarter and the East half of Section 25, and the undivided one-fifth of the East half of Section 15, including one-fifth interest in all water rights, connected with said Sections and parts of Sections but excepting from said Section 15, all lots and tracts heretofore conveyed or contracted to be conveyed by the 'Palm City Land and Water Company.' All said Sections and parts of Sections being in Township 4, South Range 4 East S.B.M.

"We also hereby grant and transfer one undivided fifth of all property of every kind whatsoever belonging to said Palm City Land and Water Company including all credits due or to become due to said company.

"The above described lands being the same which were purchased from the S.P.R.R. Co. by W. R. Porter and W. E. Van Slyke by S.P.R.R. land contracts numbered from 3749 to 3761 both inclusive on which two dollars per acre remains unpaid.

"Witness our hands this 24th day of March, 1885.

W. E. Van Slyke

M. Byrne"

The following November 5th in a transaction with Byrne alone McCallum paid eighteen hundred dollars for about 150 acres of land. This bought up all of Byrne's interest in the above-listed properties. McCallum's hunger for more land increased and it is a matter of record that on December 12, 1887, he paid an additional $800 to the Southern Pacific Railroad for 320 acres, the land which today covers the area from Ramon Road to Alejo, and from Indian Avenue to the mountain.

The names Van Slyke and Byrne were to appear on many future land deals with McCallum.

All of the land purchases made by McCallum were recorded in San Diego since Palm Springs at the time was situated in San Diego County, Riverside County not being formed until 1893. One deed was for 320 acres, another covered 640 acres of Section 13 — a mile east of Palm Springs, while another was for 480 acres of Section 13. In addition he bought 480 acres of Section 23, which is immediately southeast of the village, and 167.07 acres in Section 19 — two miles east. His final purchase was 160 acres in Section 3, which was the land situated on what is now known as Palm Canyon Drive, north of Palm Springs where the road turns west toward Banning.

Pedro Chino and Will Pablo,
Indian friends
of the McCallum family.

Evolution of Indian dwellings,
Carl Eytel.

"Where the desert meets the mountains,"
J. Smeaton Chase photographer. Courtesy Palm Springs Historical Society.

I I.

The Earth Home

Old fig tree at Palm Springs,
Carl Eytel.
Courtesy Southwest Museum.

JOHN MCCALLUM began moving his family to their desert oasis. The train took them as far as Seven Palms — now known as Garnet — some seven miles away. Their belongings piled in a buckboard wagon and Johnnie lying upon a stretcher, the family then rode across the desert sands. Judge McCallum led the way on horseback as his little daughter, Pearl, proudly sitting on the saddle, nestled in his arms.

They came to the desert where their neighbors were to be seventy-six Cahuilla Indians. At first their only shelter was the protection of one of the huge grey-trunked old fig trees which bent its leafy branches above them as they camped beneath.

Adobe brick workers at work.
Courtesy Title Insurance
and Trust Company, Los Angeles.

Johnny, still too sick to join in the activities, lay upon a cot under the fig trees. The other children romped and played and watched the Indians, under the guidance of Will Pablo, make the bricks for the walls and pour the cement floor of the new house.

Small as she was, Pearl understood her father's enthusiasm for the home being made of such primitive material. It was altogether fitting that the walls were being made in the ancient manner first taught to the Indians by the early Mission priests.

To John McCallum such simplicity had particular meaning.

Earth — water — sun. "Pais, agua, sol," the Spanish colonizers had said. This mixture tamped down by the feet of man, and then placed in the forms and set out in the sunshine to dry, was basic to his philosophy. From this honest toil would emerge a home the walls of which would surround his family with the elements of nature. The adobe would become the witness of their lives. Like a mother's arms these walls would enclose them comfortingly and shelter them from cold, heat and wind.

This McCallum adobe was built on the site where many years later Pearl was to erect the Oasis Hotel. Eventually she had it moved to its present location in McCallum Green on the main street of Palm Springs.

The family settled down in this charming "L" shaped home. Back of the house ran the stream of water coming from Tahquitz Canyon. This was the source of water for domestic purposes. The water running in the stone-lined culvert, made years earlier by the Indians, was cool and sweet and pure. This water belonged to the Indians. By law the first 18 inches as well as the last 18 inches of water was theirs. It was not until Judge McCallum bored into the mountain tapping the source of the spring that the flow was increased to 75 inches. Even so, some years the water would last but four months and the supply diminished, and then the family and Indians had to return to the waters of the hot springs which were the steady main source of supply. This water had a strong

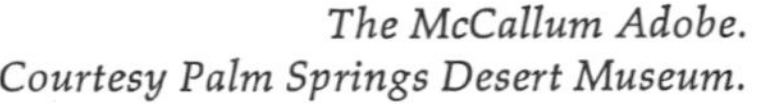

The McCallum Adobe.
Courtesy Palm Springs Desert Museum.

THE TAHQUITZ DITCH

Tahquitz Ditch, as it flowed through Desert Inn grounds.
Courtesy Palm Springs Desert Museum.

THE McCALLUM RANCH

Courtesy Palm Springs Desert Museum.

mineral taste and had to be put into large clay ollas and then hung from
the tree branches during the night. By morning the clay had sweated
and the jars cooled until the water was sweet enough to drink.

The little stream behind the adobe was the life-saver for the family.
It not only provided crystal clear drinking water but it also provided the
only refrigeration. Two large hogsheads were set into the ground and
the waters flowed around them. One was for cooling melons and fruit
and the other for keeping cans of butter cool. A small milk house built
over the ditch kept milk and other foodstuff palatable. Food came by
train from San Bernardino, a butcher in Banning supplying their meat.
All of this was hauled from Seven Palms by wagons, usually at night to
avoid the heat of day.

While the walls of the house went up, the Judge turned to putting the
80 acres of land into condition for planting. With the aid of some Indians
he leveled the land and ploughed it into shape. He then planted 20 acres
of apricots, 30 acres into early grapes, a grove of orange trees, and, as
an experiment, seeded in alfalfa fields.

*The McCallum Ranch House,
Palm Springs, Carl Eytel.
Courtesy Southwest Museum.*

12.

The Taming of Wild Waters

Flume bringing Whitewater to Palm Springs, Carl Eytel. Courtesy Southwest Museum.

IT WAS obvious to Judge McCallum almost from the very first moment he looked out over the seemingly barren wastes of the land around Agua Caliente that the soil was good. When he saw the luxurious growth of the grapes and figs grown by the Indians from cuttings from the old Missions, his convictions strengthened.

If his own plantings were to continue to thrive, he realized that he could not rely upon the uncertain flow of water coursing through the Tahquitz culvert the Indians had used for some time. Despite his having increased the water in this ditch from a mere eighteen inches to a flow of seventy-five inches, this source was too undependable.

Then, too, if his dream of converting the additional land he was steadily acquiring into productive farms raising the earliest crops of fruits, as well as small plots for home owners, was ever to become a reality, the Judge knew that he must find a new source of water supply.

His daughter, Pearl, in an interview in the Palm Springs *Villager* of Feb. 16, 1959, gave a dramatic word picture of her father's efforts to obtain water:

"Father knew that if the desert was to bloom and grow that water, water and more water was the only answer. After much investigation he commissioned J. P. Lippincott, the noted engineer, to study the various

76

canyons and survey the supply that could be brought to Palm Springs and irrigate the thousands of acres of desert land.

"Andreas Canyon, with year round water from the melting snows, was not available. As was right, for it belonged to the Indians. Cool, clear, clean delightful water tumbles down Tahquitz Canyon, but only for a few months. Snow Creek contributes its share but not enough for a thirsty desert.

"But Whitewater. Here was the breast that was never dry. My father tapped this seventy-mile watershed, but it was not easy. It took time and patience, hard work and money to tame these mountain streams. The Whitewater River, like a young colt would kick over its traces. After storms it would break barriers, and cause washouts and floods. The area had a succession of floods and droughts, but through it all men stayed here. The climate, the beauty, the silence and solitude of the desert were worth it.

"At last the water was harnessed and brought across the desert from Whitewater Canyon. Here the wild mountain waters were tamed for the use of those who chose to live in this incomparable desert.

"Yes, in the desert, water is everything. The big redwood flume, on the high trestle that protected it from floods, skirted the base of the mountain at Whitewater until it arrived at a point where the present highway cuts through. Here a tunnel was drilled and the water carried through to the east side of the mountain, from whence it emptied into

Whitewater River before diversion into the stone-lined ditch.

77

The big canal constructed by J. G. McCallum to bring water to Palm Valley.

Stone ditch bringing Whitewater to Palm Springs, Carl Eytel. Courtesy Southwest Museum.

the beautifully constructed eight-mile-long stone canal that could carry a thousand miner's inches of water. This water came from the snows of Mt. San Gorgonio to the Village of Palm Springs.

"People came, planted grapes, alfalfa, apricots, oranges, and various experimental fruits and small experimentation of dates. Can you blame me for having a just pride in my father, whose pioneering spirit not only sensed and felt the needs of the desert, but strode side by side and step by step with other outstanding Californians in securing the natural resources for the people who choose and love the desert?"

This irrigation project was the first in the nation to bring water to the arid lands of the Western parts. With the aid of unskilled Indian workers and battling the scorching heat of the desert sun, the raging, blinding winds and sandstorms, Judge McCallum struggled to bring precious water over 19 miles of rugged desert terrain. He spent over $60,000 out of his personal funds and untold sums to maintain the ditch so the water could continue to flow.

The story of Judge McCallum's struggle to bring water across a desert seemingly possessed with devils which persisted in obstructing every inch of the construction of the rock-lined ditch is an epic of courage, faith and stubborn optimism. Involved also were certain legal aspects.

Judge McCallum incorporated his Palm Valley Land and Water Company on February 1, 1887, for the purpose of bringing irrigating water to the West half of Section 14 and Sections 13, 23 and 25, T4S, R4E, and Section 19, T4S, R5E, S.B.B. & M. This water was brought through his stone-lined ditch but was not distributed to all the land above mentioned. The company was originally incorporated with 5000 shares of stock at $100 each.

On the 17th day of the same month of incorporation, February, 1887, J. G. McCallum as president of the Palm Valley Land and Water Company, signed a contractual agreement with W. H. Hurley. Hurley agreed to excavate one mile of the ditch earlier surveyed by T. M. Topp "near the Whitewater station of the S. P. R. R. from the westerly end of said proposed surveyed ditch." This ditch was to be "forty (40) inches wide on the bottom and sixty (60) inches deep with equally sloping sides and the bottom to the full size thereof for the agreed price of seventy-five (75) cents per rod linial measurement." Hurley further agreed to pay and feed the men and animals required to complete the job which had to be finished within the stipulated time "on or before March 20th, 1887."

Hurley must have faithfully lived up to his agreement for on May 10, 1887, another agreement between him and The Palm Valley Land and Water Company was signed.This time it was for six miles of water line starting at the easterly end of the mile just completed. This section was to be 60 inches wide on the top, 40 inches on the bottom and 30 inches deep, and was to be constructed for the agreed price of "eighty-five (85) cents per rod, lineal measure."

Whatever rejoicing McCallum might have felt when he first saw the waters rushing through his painfully constructed irrigation system and flowing out upon the thirsty desert land, was crushed when there appeared upon the scene one day a special investigator from Washington. By special instructions from the Secretary of the Interior in response to several complaints lodged against the newly organized Palm Valley Land and Water Company, U. S. Indian Agent, Joseph W. Preston, arrived to investigate charges of "fraud, trespass or other interference with the lands and rights of the Mission Indians on what is known as the Agua Caliente and Rincon Reservations, and technically designated as Township Four South, Range Four and Five East, in San Diego County, California, and so reserved and set apart for the use of said Indians."

Fortunately, Agent Preston proved to be a man of perspicacity and after carefully inspecting the land and thoroughly reviewing all aspects of the situation, gave his approval, subject to that of his superiors at the

Aqueduct rounding one of the spurs of the San Jacinto Range, Carl Eytel.
Courtesy Southwest Museum.

Washington level, to the water project. In his lengthy report dated May 10th, 1888, he explained the benefit to the Indians who were to be guaranteed free water for the development of 160 acres of land of Section 14 and water for a subsequent 160 acres should they develop the area. He pointed out the necessity of following the route across Indian lands as it was the only feasible course which could be followed. Furthermore, he agreed that the "Palm Valley Land and Water Company shall have the full, free, exclusive right of way through said reservation for the construction of a water ditch now located and designed through sections aforesaid owned by the said Government . . . . for a distance of twenty-five feet on either side, together with all the rights necessary for the full and successful construction, occupation, use, enjoyment and operation of the same."

In consideration for the rights of use and of easement the water company had to agree to deliver without charge, "One inch of water under a four inch pressure to six acres of land, and to be securely preserved and conducted and delivered on the North-West corner of said section . . . that said Indians shall have the first right to water . . ."

The authorities accepted this proposal and there was no further difficulty from that source. Maintaining an adequate water supply for his hoped for subdivision and for his ranch would prove to be a constant and costly struggle for Judge McCallum. The water flowing through his irrigation ditches, he thought, would be ample to service his own orchards and vineyards and to nourish the small farms he hoped others would come and plant.

Irrigation water gushing from the redwood flume Judge McCallum constructed to bring water across the desert.

13.

A Troubled Benefactor

THE NEXT five years were to be crowded with activity for Judge McCallum. "During those years," wrote Heber Winder, lawyer and early historian of the region, "Judge McCallum was acquiring title to land from the Southern Pacific Railroad. In the meanwhile other white men bought up fractional interests in Palm Springs and vicinity. These in turn sold their interests to Judge McCallum. It was not uncommon for a deed to go on record conveying 'an undivided one-eleventh interest in and to an undivided 167.17 acres in Section 15, T4S, R4E.' "

McCallum dreamed of starting a colony of people sharing his enthusiasm for the desert. To accomplish this he obtained the services of T. M. Topp to survey for a township. He called this Palm City and saw to it that the area was divided into 56 lots or blocks, 48 of them lots and 7 of them sites of 1 36/100 acres, with the remainder of the town consisting of 4 lots of 2 acres each; 4 lots of 4 20/100 acres each; 1 lot of 7 36/100 acres; 8 lots of 8 36/100 acres each; 1 lot of 11 40/100 acres; and 2 lots of 13 36/100 acres. He kept the family 80 acres separate from the survey.

The parcels totaled 76 lots of approximately 199 acres. He called this original subdivision the Colony Tract. Before 1886 McCallum had sold 11 so called "acre lots" and deeded them, and in addition about a total of 35 acres of the outside tracts, thus leaving undivided of the 2000-acre Colony lands about 1,954 acres, of which 153 acres were in the town site.

Taking one of the rooms of a small building, Judge McCallum stocked it with supplies and set up a general store which was described by James' *Wonders of the Colorado Desert* as, "Palm Valley store, a typical desert place, where the prospector and traveler, the tent dweller and the hunter, may alike replenish his stock of canned and other eatables and procure feed for his animals."

It was not long before the Judge realized that if he were to accomplish all of his dreams, more funds would be absolutely necessary. The time

JUDGE JOHN GUTHRIE McCALLUM
Courtesy Palm Springs Desert Museum.

Dr. Welwood Murray at the
entrance to his Palm Springs
Hotel. Courtesy Title Insurance
and Trust Company,
Los Angeles.

was approaching, he was convinced, when it would be propitious to refinance and broaden the scope of his activities.

"Exploitation of the land, or of the people, was not part of his plan," wrote Elwood Lloyd of J. G. McCallum in his book *Enchanted Sands*. "Instead, he envisioned the place as an admirable site for a colony of happy homes, on little ranches and orchards which would produce the earliest fruits in all America."

But first, he decided, there had to be accommodations available for prospective buyers. A hotel, even the most modest, was a priority. He knew exactly the man for this task. In a two-storied house in a canyon near Banning, and which bore his name, lived a lanky Scotsman and his wife. "Dr." Welwood Murray (the title was an honorary one bestowed upon him, it was claimed, for the outstanding medical service he rendered to the wounded upon a battleship during the Civil War, and not one earned in a medical college) was a man of importance in Banning. He was also noted for his irascible nature.

A native of Edinburgh, Scotland, he came to the United States when he was 26 and was employed as a copyreader by Harper and Appleton publishing firms. The gaunt Scot, speaking in a dignified manner with a thick burr, first appeared in Banning about 1876 or '77. Immediately upon arriving in the little settlement which consisted then of four small houses, a few tents, a boarding house, a general store, and three saloons, Murray assumed management of the San Gorgonio Fluming Company. This was a corporation formed to cut and transport lumber, fuel and ties for the Southern Pacific Railway, which by then had been completed as far as Cabazon in the pass. He frequently boasted, "I finished the flume in what is known as Banning and brought the first water down June 3, 1877 at the cost of $20,000." The timber rushed down this flume in Water Canyon, but as one old timer put it, "Every stick was in debt by the time it reached the track."

Murray bought eighty acres in Banning and began his ranching. He became manager of the local orchards for a San Jose company which operated a cannery at Colton, planting Washington plums, ten acres of blackberries, prunes, peas, peaches and apricots for this firm. He also purchased ten inches of water to irrigate these plantings and thus started the flourishing Banning fruit-raising industry.

It was this man whom Judge McCallum and his little daughter called upon. He evidently spoke so enthusiastically of the potentialities of the desert oasis that the usually cautious Scot was swept into acquiring a five-acre plot across the way from the McCallum adobe. The Judge urged him to start immediate construction of a hotel.

Murray actually took very little interest in the proposed hostelry, but became engrossed with planting orange trees and ornamental and exotic

Palm Springs store, Carl Eytel.
Courtesy Southwest Museum.

trees and shrubs. While her husband was in constant communication
with the Bureau of Plant Industry in Washington, eagerly seeking information about some new tree, vine, shrub or flower to experiment with on
the desert, Mrs. Murray taught at the Indian School at the Potrero Reservation. Murray became recognized as one of the leading horticulturists
in the state.

THE garrulous Doctor was the only person nearby with the same excellent education and cultured literary tastes as Judge McCallum. While
differing in personality and frequently disagreeing, the two men enjoyed
an intellectual companionship.

McCallum loved the Bible as did Murray, and they both quoted from
it at length. The Scot recited the native bards of his homeland, while
McCallum resorted to quoting Shakespeare and often Milton and Tennyson, during those rare moments when he could relax, enjoy good conver-
sation, and take time from his many duties as rancher, builder, and
government Indian Agent.

So it was that one summer afternoon Judge McCallum invited Murray
to accompany him and Johnny on a pleasant buggy ride up one of the
canyons into the primitive area where grew some scraggly trees. This
outing was in response to a request from one of the Indians who suddenly appeared one day and requested permission from the Judge for the
Indians to cut some of this timber.

The Judge, realizing that the Indians lacked employment and were
badly in need of money, agreed to inspect the stand of timber. After a
leisurely ride up the mountainside they reined the horses and the men
got out of the buggy to walk up the slope to the trees. Judge McCallum
looked over the situation and after checking the trees, granted permission for the cutting of one hundred cords of wood.

The sum agreed upon was from $2.50 to $3.00 per cord with the
Indian receiving 50 cents per cord for supervising the cutting and hauling of the wood to Banning for sale. Recalling how experienced his friend
was in such matters, Judge McCallum then told the Indian to work with
Dr. Murray who would assume responsibility for the deal. Murray
agreed to undertake this task.

They drove down the mountain and the Judge, preoccupied with
other responsibilities and believing this matter was in the capable hands
of Dr. Murray, immediately dismissed the day's events from his mind.

AGENT John G. McCallum submitted his first annual report dated August 22, 1884, from San Bernardino, California, to the Commissioner of Indian Affairs in Washington, D.C.

The report began with an historical and statistical account of the Mission Indians and described their locations, their civilization and then led into an analysis of their character as McCallum saw it:

> "They are peaceable and honest with but few exceptions. The young are generally ambitious and quick to learn, but not to provide for the future. They are superior in appearance and intelligence to other California tribes."

He went on to express concern over the ejection proceedings against Indians living upon what had been the original Mexican land grants. This legal action had been instigated by whites holding those grants. McCallum stated, "Similar complaints will likely be filed against other Indians living in villages upon such grants this year . . ." He pointed out that in addition to the Mexican grants, a large portion of the reservation lay within the limits of the land granted by the federal government to the railroad in excess of 200,000 acres.

> "Nine tenths of this is practically worthless, rough mountain and desert land; half of the remainder is good land, having sufficient water and timber, and the remainder would be valuable if water should be brought upon it . . ."

He explained that under his tutelage the Indians were showing increased interest in wider cultivation of their lands. "The two wagons, making seven in all, and the eight large plows, with proper harness, were furnished by the Government which have had a good effect."

The Judge then returned to a discussion of possible means of protecting the interests of the Indians in safeguarding their lands so that they could not be deprived of their heritage:

> "It may be suggested that their village sites on Government land should be patented to the Indian bands who possess them, the same as town sites are patented for the whites who possess them, but as to the Indians, with the usual restrictions against alienation. And the Indians who desire to engage in agriculture outside of their villages should be allowed a reasonable time to select their homesteads on the reservations, as well as outside, under the act of the last session of Congress on that subject. It seems clear that it is only a question of time when the reservation system in Southern California will give place to

Indian homesteads, and the sooner such homesteads can be secured the better it will be for the Indians as well as the whites. In this view I shall try to have them take homesteads under the act referred to, and on their reservations, unless instructed to the contrary, as there is very little land left outside these reservations that would be suitable for the Indian homesteads . . ."

The Judge discussed the unscrupulous white persons who sold illicit liquor to some of the Indians. However, the Judge pointed out, "A large proportion of them (Indians) do not indulge, and this proportion is evidently increasing." He found that this increase in sobriety was owing in part to "better public sentiment, and in part to the successful prosecution, mainly in the local courts under the State law of those furnishing such liquors to the Indians in the past year." In this the agent had the cooperation of the "local officers and juries and the aid of public sentiment, which were not formerly given, as it seems from the official reports that no conviction could be obtained (formerly) in the courts. There were about fifteen convictions in this county alone in the last half of the year . . ."

Under the heading on Education, he pointed out that there were "six day schools under this agency in the latter part of the year, a new school having been started April 1 at Rincon, where it was very much needed, as will be noticed by the large attendance there." Schools had been repaired and plans were under way for the construction of three new ones and when these were completed, two additional teachers were to be employed.

He brought the report to a close with a discussion of the citizenship rights of the Indians. This was a matter of keen concern to him, for the Judge wrote not merely out of his regard for his Indian charges, but as a staunch respecter of the Constitutional rights of all people living within the confines of the United States.

"Many of these Indians are of right citizens, although not yet recognized as such, for the laws of Mexico made no distinction among races as to citizenship. The Indians who were in a condition of civilization when the treaty of 1848 was made were citizens of Mexico, and are by the terms of that treaty, now citizens of the United States. The progress made in the last few years indicates that the Mission Indians generally will before long become a part of the people of this State having and exercising the rights of citizenship."

The report was forwarded to the Commissioner of Indian Affairs in

Washington, D. C. and subsequently published in the official *Indian Office Report*, 1884, pages 12 to 15.

McCallum could very well look back upon his first year as Indian Agent and derive some satisfaction for the work accomplished. There was still, he knew, much more to be done and he set about to accomplish this.

Banning, with Mount San Jacinto on the right and Mount San Gorgonio on the left.
Carl Eytel. Courtesy Southwest Museum.

14.
The Attack Begins

Difficulties developed between factions in the reservation. Interfering whites began taking sides in a situation which was entirely an inter-tribal affair. The difficulty was further augmented by the influence coming from the former Indian Agent S. S. Lawson, whom McCallum had replaced. Lawson, unknown to the Judge, made certain written allegations against the Agency Doctor, Dr. Albert Thompson, accusing him of pilfering government medicines and using them for his private benefit, and all (so he claimed) with the tacit approval of Agent McCallum.

The Commissioner of Indian Affairs, taking note of these allegations, instructed Special Indian Agent Robert S. Gardner of San Francisco, to investigate the matter when he made his annual inspection tour of the reservation the following spring of 1885. Gardner arrived and was taken on a personally conducted tour of the entire Mission Indian reservation by Agent McCallum.

Gardner turned in a favorable report dated March 14, 1885. He was greatly impressed with the increased numbers of productive little ranches and stated that the Indians, under McCallum, had more acres cultivated than at any time during his knowledge. "The same," he noted, "having received proper care and attention, present an inviting appearance and adds very much to their home comforts and from which they derive considerable revenue."

He then advised that the Agency headquarters should be removed from San Bernardino to the Potrero Reservation. Such a move, he be-

lieved, would help the Indians escape from the temptations of the big
city life where unscrupulous whites lay in wait to ply them with liquor.
The Special Agent commented upon the increasing sobriety he observed
among these Indians and gave credit for this to McCallum and the
change which had taken place in public sentiment towards prosecution
of persons found guilty of selling liquor to the Indians. Jail sentences
were being given where formerly no such convictions could be obtained.

After investigating the charges against Dr. Thompson, and holding a
full scale hearing, Gardner found that there was no foundation for the
allegations. He found Dr. Thompson to be "a good physician . . . both
honest and capable," and that he was giving "satisfaction to the Agent
and to the Indians." The report continued by Gardner writing, "I have
made particular inquiry touching the character of both Dr. Albert
Thompson and S. S. Lawson for Truth and Veracity. The character of
Dr. Thompson . . . is above suspicion and beyond reproach, and has not
been the subject of criticism. The character of S. S. Lawson . . . has to
some extent been the subject of criticism by some of the leading citizens
of this place."

The Special Agent then gave his summation of the character of J. G.
McCallum and his work as Indian Agent for the Mission Indians:

> "The agency is being ably, successfully and honestly managed under the super-
> vision of John G. McCallum as Agent. He is a man of good moral character,
> energy and executive ability, and has the reputation of being possessed of good
> legal attainments. He contemplates severing his connection with the Service
> on or about the 30th day of June, 1885 to engage in the practice of his pro-
> fession at Los Angeles, Cal."

This report was received in Washington and possibly the information
about McCallum's intention of leaving the service leaked out. Two
months later the Commissioner of Indian Affairs received another letter.

The attack upon McCallum was under way.

The letter was dated May 29th, 1885, and was written by James Faris,
deputy marshal in San Bernardino. He told of hearing about a new allo-
cation of government funds for the "promotion of the detection of liquor
selling to the Indians." Faris requested that some of this money be sent
to him to reimburse his fellow officers who, "without encouragement or
assistance of Agent McCallum, ferreted out cases of drunkenness among
the Indians." He claimed there were from ten to thirty bottles of liquor
sold a day, and that often the officers went out in all kinds of weather

at great danger and frequently at their own expense. McCallum, he
stated, just preferred to ignore the situation. Faris added that they "were
tired of doing this work without pay."

This allegation, coming as it did, immediately following the unequiv-
ocal recommendation by the Special Investigating Agent Gardner of
Judge McCallum's character and capable management of the Mission
Indian Agency, must have failed to impress the Commissioner. There is
no record of the charge ever having been called to McCallum's attention.

The dissentious clique of whites, however, had no intention of relax-
ing the attack. Letters with vague innuendos derogatory to Judge Mc-
Callum continued arriving at the Washington headquarters. After brief
flurries of inquiry these defamatory allegations were dismissed as for the
most part being groundless attacks.

There was, however, one letter which contained assertions of a more
serious nature. This was written by S. K. Lankston July 25, 1885. The
letter to the Commissioner began by Lankston stating, "You ought to
know how things are going at the Indian Agency here and I will take it
on myself to tell you but I don't care to have my name mentioned."

The accusations Lankston made, which he intended to be defamatory
against McCallum, interestingly enough were actually allegations
against Dr. Murray, with McCallum being accused of playing a secon-
dary permissive role. Lankston alleged that: Dr. Murray went into a
wood cutting contract with the Indians with McCallum's knowledge
and deprived them of their wood; to protect Mrs. Murray's job as school
teacher on the Potrero Reservation McCallum falsified the pupil atten-

The Van Deventer Ranch,
Carl Eytel. Courtesy
Southwest Museum.

dance records; Dr. Murray stole some of the Indians' water and Mc-
Callum did nothing to stop him; the Agent and "his Doctor" got up a
scheme whereby they paid some of the Agua Caliente Indians a trifle
and then got hold of their lands; there were other "rascalities."

Lankston concluded with a postscript in which he reiterated, "I give
these facts but I don't care to have my name known!"

Judge McCallum was told nothing of these accusations at the time
they were received in Washington.

Dr. Murray's hotel as it first
appeared, Carl Eytel. Courtesy
Southwest Museum.

15.

The Final Coup

FOLLOWING his plans made months before, and as announced to the Special Investigator, John G. McCallum sent his letter of resignation on Aug. 22, 1885, to J. D. C. Atkins, Commissioner of Indian Affairs:

> "Sir; I have the honor to hereby tender my resignation to take effect on the appointment and qualification of my successor; and respectfully request that the same be presented to his excellency, the President.
>
> > Very respy your Obtd. Servt.
> > J. G. McCallum,
> > Indian Agent."

The resignation was sent to the President and a letter of acceptance dated Sept. 8, 1885, was received by McCallum. He began formulating his plans to return to Los Angeles and renewing his law career.

Despite the heavy demands of opening a law office, Judge McCallum had one more duty he wished to perform for the Bureau of Indian affairs. He asked for and received a time extension on his annual report for the year of 1885 until he had completed an accurate census taking of the Mission Indians.

McCallum's second annual report was dated September 30, 1885, and in it he quoted the results of the census of the Mission Indians:

> "With the limited number of employees . . . an actual enumeration, including names, ages and relationships was made of the larger villages, including the eight villages where the agency day schools are established, the remainder being necessarily estimated. The result is as follows: Whole number, 3,070; males over 18 years of age, 876; females over 14 years of age, 1,056; school children between 6 and 16 years of age, 770.
>
> "Of all the Mission Indians (he went on to report) about 250 can read English, of which 100 learned in the last year . . . Two additional day schools were commenced at the beginning of the calendar year. Eight day schools have since then been in operation, at which there was good average attendance . . . The school statistics show that average attendance at the eight schools to be very

good, ranging from 15 to 48 for the year and an average attendance for all of 23½."

In the light of certain charges which were to be made against Mc-Callum, casting aspersions upon his integrity as a man and his efficiency as Indian Agent, it is important to note his remarks in this report concerning the Indian lands:

> ". . . Several of their larger villages are on Mexican grants now patented to whites, and containing no exceptions in favor of the Indians. The Government employed special counsel to defend the Indians in such cases . . .
>
> "A few of these Indians occupy land outside of the reserves. Every opportunity has been taken to inform them generally of their rights under the Act of 1884 . . ."

This report brought McCallum's responsibility as Indian Agent to a close. His replacement arrived at the reservation on Oct. 1, 1885. John S. Ward assumed charge of the Mission Indians.

Ward was immediately swept into the opposition camp. Evidently believing the charges against McCallum could become a cause célèbre, or perhaps out of overzealous eagerness to please, Ward began making reports to Washington. The frequency of these and the intemperate language in which they were phrased made them suspect to being more than just routine accounts. In one such report he stated, "This affair is very much in accord with the general policy of Republican officials in the past." In another he wrote, "The whole Augean stable needs cleaning." In still another, "McCallum demands a trial. And this he shall have."

The opposing faction, with the full cooperation of Agent Ward, moved relentlessly ahead on the almost forgotten charges concerning the wood cutting episode. The Commissioner of Indian Affairs deemed Lankston's charges of sufficient importance to order that another Special Investigator Agent Heath be sent from Washington to investigate. Immediately upon his arrival at the Potrero Reservation Heath went into consultation with Ward, "to whom," he reported, "I am indebted for much valuable information."

After questioning several persons, particularly J. B. Hanna, the white man who bought the wood, the Special Agent then presented McCallum with excerpts of the charges being made against him, but withheld the name of the accuser.

United States Indian Service,

_________________________ _Mission_ Agency,

San Bernardino Cal Aug 22, 1885.

Hon J. D. C. Atkins
Commissioner of Indian Affairs
Sir:
I have the honor to hereby tender
my resignation, to take Effect on
the appointment and qualification
of my successor; and respectfully
request that the same be presented
to his Excellency the President.
Very respy Your Obdt Servt
J G McCallum
U. S. Indian Agent.

J. G. McCallum letter of resignation from Indian Agent position. Records of the Office of the Secretary of the Interior, Appointment Division.

"Sir:

"I have just received the "Extract" from your official correspondence, which you had the courtesy to hand me, at my request, to answer or not, at my option.

"I prefer, as a matter of simple justice to answer, even though the name of the writer is withheld, as you inform me, at his request.

"First. As to the wood cut on the Potrero Reserve, — over a year ago, the Indian men of that reserve, then not of employment, desired to cut some wood — nearly all of it saplings — which were growing on a few acres of the unsurveyed part of that reserve for the purpose, as they stated, of clearing the

LETTER FROM
JOHN GUTHRIE
McCALLUM
TO GEN. H. HEATH

ground for cultivation, and wished to sell such wood, as they had the right to clear the land for cultivation and wished to sell such wood so cut, I consented to it. The Indians did cut a cord or two more or less than one hundred cords, hauled it to Banning, and sold it there, as I am informed, mostly to Dr. Murray, at from $4.00 to $3.00 per cord, which was about its value, and which was the actual cost of the cutting and handling.

"I had nothing to do with the sale or purchase of the wood, the Indians did as all Indians in the Mission Agency have done, sold their own products, without any interference by the Agent. As they are civilized Indians, they are not now, and never have been, controlled or directed in any such matters.

"Banning is over thirty miles from the Mission Agency office, and my knowledge of the matter is mainly what I heard about it.

"When the amount of wood, above stated was cut, there was, I thought, good reason, to doubt whether the Indians were cutting the wood to clear the land for cultivation, or whether that was a mere pretense to get remunerative wages when — as was then the case — they had no other work to do. I, therefore, directed the Indians to stop chopping the wood, and they then stopped. That was the only wood cut and sold by the Indians during the time I was Agent, so far as I have any knowledge or information.

"The land at Agua Caliente was certain odd numbered sections which were granted by act of Congress to aid the construction of the Southern Pacific Railroad and surveyed long prior to the date of the Executive order making the Indian reserve there, which order specified only the even numbered sections and the unsurveyed lands in the three townships, viz: Townships 4 S R. 4E R. S. R. E. E. and 5 S. R. 4 E. Those odd numbered sections were purchased by two citizens of this place.

"I had no interest whatever in the purchase and was not consulted about it.

"After the purchase was made, I learned about two acres of those of the railroad sections so purchased, had been fenced with brush and poles, the whole improvement not being worth as I believed over $100. Two or three Indians claimed these improvements, and wanted the purchasers to pay them a total of $300 for them, which I was informed by these Indians, was paid to them, and with which, the Indians were then and I believe ever since were satisfied.

"The improvements and the land itself together, were not worth what was given to the Indians. Therefore the money simply was a gift, with which I had nothing whatever to do except to request the purchasers to give liberally, which they did and for which they deserved and received thanks from every intelligent, unprejudiced friend of the Indians, who chose to consider it.

"As to reference to Dr. Murray, the complaint made is also notoriously false. Dr. Murray did not try to take the Indians' water, nor did any one ever represent to me that he had tried to do so.

"As I do not know who is the author of such notoriously absurd, and stupid libel, I can only guess . . .

"You will please understand that I am making no defense for I am not called on for any, but have stated so much, simply for the sake of truth and mainly as a matter of justice to others.

Very respy,

J. G. McCallum."

There was nothing more he could say when he was fighting against an anonymous accuser. John McCallum went to Los Angeles and opened his law offices. In due time, the Federal government of the United States took action.

Dr. Murray and Judge McCallum were officially indicted for "felonious removal of wood" from Indian reserves. The case dragged on for nearly four years in the U. S. District Court in Los Angeles. Finally the case was adjudicated and reported in the Banning *Herald* of Feb. 1, 1889, with the headline reading:

"RAILROAD LANDS ON THE RESERVATION"

"On Monday, last, Judge Ross, U. S. District Judge at Los Angeles, decided the long pending case against McCallum and Murray, wherein they had been indicted for taking wood from Government Land. The Court found that the wood had been taken, but decided in favor of the defendents on the ground that the land from which the wood was taken was railroad land, and did not belong to the government. The land in question was one of the unsurveyed sections within the Indian Reservation and located north of Banning. If correctly reported, the decision is an important one and affects this community very materially."

The ordeal of this unwarranted trial undoubtedly left a wound which never entirely healed for Judge McCallum. Many years later Pearl was to say in an interview:

"Historically one cannot separate the desert from the Indians and the Indians from the desert, and my father, a friendly man, loved both. The Indians trusted him for he knew them intimately, their traits and their problems. My father always said that if there was a point of justice for the Indians, the Indians should be given the benefit of the doubt.

"Many say that our Indians were never more happy and healthy than under my father's administration. Even today as I look out from my terrace, I see the same warm sun, the same mountains, and only wish that old Pedro Chino,

97

Capt. Joe and the great old Marcus, Miguel, and Francisco would come riding
by as they used to. . . .

"The Indians were very happy in their desert brush houses through all those
pioneer days. I personally never saw an intoxicated one. They were honest and
latchstrings, not locks, held the doors closed from the dust and the weather . . . .

"As Lincoln felt toward the colored people my father felt toward the Indians.
He was both their benefactor and their champion."

*Marcus family, Palm Springs,
1904. Courtesy Title Insurance
and Trust Company, Los Angeles.*

16.

The Return to the City

THE TIME had come for John McCallum to put his dream of subdividing his desert land into small ranches and home sites into action. To accomplish this as announced to the Special Indian Agent investigator, he left the Indian Service and moved to Los Angeles.

Letters written by him indicate that he first had his office or headquarters at 50-51 Temple Block, Los Angeles. Old copies of the Los Angeles City Directories reveal much about the McCallums during the 1880's. The issue for 1886 contained but a single entry:

"McCallum, J. G., attorney at law. 24 W. First
res. 18 S. Griffin Ave., East L.A."

The City Directory for 1887 contained two entries. Wallace had joined his father and was listed as "Student" residing at 18 W. Pico. The Judge had moved his office to 132 N. Main, and was residing at the "NE cor. South Grand Ave. and Adams." The following year, 1888, Johnny

Spring Street north from First Street about the time Judge McCallum went to Los Angeles to open his law business. Courtesy Title Insurance and Trust Company, Los Angeles.

Exclusive West Adams Boulevard as it appeared when the Judge purchased his home on the corner of West Adams and Grand Avenue in Los Angeles. Courtesy Title Insurance and Trust Company, Los Angeles.

joined them and was listed in the Directory as "Horticulturist" while Wallace was designated as "Law Student." The Judge's office was then at 36 S. Main, Room 76. As was the custom in those days, there was no mention of the female occupants of these residences. Emily and Pearl were not included. The son, Harry, probably assumed charge of the desert projects.

Los Angeles in the '80's was a place teeming with excitement and was fast becoming a rival in importance commercially and financially to San Francisco. It was a place of haphazard streets deep in dust which became quagmires of deeper mud during the rainy season. Wagons had to be abandoned on Main Street and signs posted warning of bogs deep enough to drown a man.

The tinkle of horse-car bells accompanied the clunking of the spindly iron wheels striking dried adobe on the tracks over Main Street, while pedestrians stood aside to permit Martin Aguirre, the sheriff, to ride by on his black charger.

There were two well recognized so-called "best" residence districts in Los Angeles — one the Westlake district extending from about 6th Street to Pico and from Union Avenue to Westlake Park, then the western limits of the city. The other was known as the "Adams Street Section" which included Figueroa Street south of Washington, over Adams Street, and south to 27th, 28th, 29th Streets up to Vermont.

*Tennis party at McCallum
West Adams home
in Los Angeles.*

The McCallum's favored the West Adams section. On January 5, 1888, John G. McCallum purchased a residence for the sum of eleven thousand seven hundred dollars from James O. Seymour. This large home, with stables and various outbuildings, remained the legal residence of Judge McCallum for the next ten years.

The McCallum family to frail little Emily's great pleasure was immediately accepted into the exclusive social circles of Los Angeles and Pasadena. Debonair, handsome young Johnny, when he came up on the train from the desert, was in great demand as an escort for the lovely Pasadena debutantes. Many an elderly lady living today can recall her mother's telling of the gentle-mannered young Johnny McCallum's escorting her to cotillions.

Emily and the young McCallums, who kept their regard for the desert home steadfastly in mind, nevertheless found life in the teeming city of Los Angeles, alleged to be the first city in the world to have its streets entirely lighted by electricity — almost a heady experience. Figueroa, the widest and most fashionable street in the city was unpaved and made an excellent driving course and speedway for horse lovers.

Well chaperoned parties attended the concerts conducted by Theodore Thomas at Turner Hall, and most surely the gala opening of Child's Grand Opera House. Packing picnic baskets they boarded the Southern Pacific train and rode to the junction just behind Wilmington where they

The new pier at Long Beach was an irresistible attraction to young Angelenos who took the train and then transferred on the rickety tram for this outing, but few were brave enough to dare the ocean waves. Courtesy Title Insurance and Trust Company, Los Angeles.

Packing picnic baskets, young excursionists boarded the Southern Pacific train and rode to the junction just behind Wilmington where they transferred to a steam dummy line with open, cross-seated cars and rode to Long Beach. Wilmington and Long Beach Rapid Transit, 1887. Courtesy Title Insurance and Trust Company, Los Angeles.

transferred to a steam dummy line with open, cross-seated cars like horsecars and rode to a frame hotel on the bluff of Long Beach where the more daring bathed in the surf. Upon rare occasions, they took the Banning steamer, ''The Falcon,'' and crossed the rough channel waters to Santa Catalina where they put up at ''Old Timm's Camp.''

The area of Ft. Moore Hill, overlooking the plaza and with little white houses clinging to the steep hillsides, their ladder-like stairways the only means of access, so appealed to Judge McCallum that he purchased nine lots up there from Harry R. Stevens for the sum of two thousand dollars.

While his family socialized, Judge McCallum made many trips to San Francisco to tell his legal and literary friends of the wonders of the Palm Valley he loved so much. His law practice also occupied much of his time and among his influential clients were such important personages as William Monroe, founder and developer of Monrovia, California.

All the while McCallum kept adding to his desert land holdings, much of which he acquired from the railroad for $2.50 per acre. His trips to San Francisco paid off when he found two investors in that city who were willing to participate in promotion of the Palm Valley lands.

17.

The Great Real Estate Boom

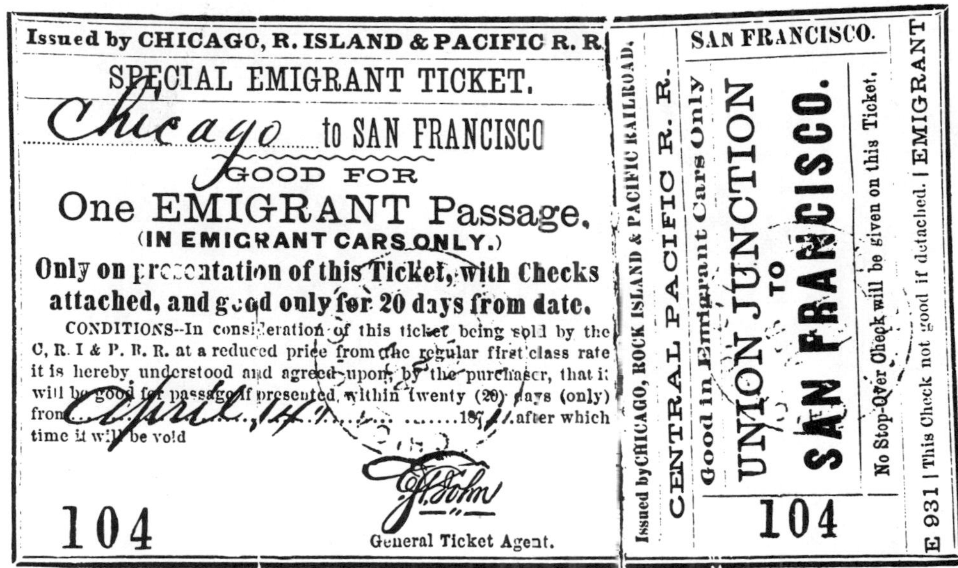

Example of the reduced railroad tickets offered to induce passengers to travel westward to "Golden California." Southern Pacific photograph.

WHEN THE Santa Fe Railroad reached Los Angeles in 1885 the Southern Pacific determined not to relinquish its control and started a rate war. A ticket could be purchased for one dollar in Kansas City, destination Los Angeles and all the golden promises extended towards health, happiness, and instant riches in real estate. The lavish promotional advertising done by these railroads turned California into a major tourist attraction.

Newspapers all over the country carried advertisements of the most extravagant nature, and gullible health-seeking investors raced to California. One piece of the real estate "boom" promotion proclaimed, "In this soft and balmy atmosphere existence even for the afflicted becomes a joy unspeakable." Another promoter is claimed to have said, "We sold them the climate and threw in the land."

Suddenly in the mid-80's real estate developments proliferated, small towns appeared almost over night with glamorous sounding names, and many just as quickly disappeared from the scene never to be heard of again. The real estate boom reached its zenith in 1887. The time was almost too late for McCallum and his dream subdivision.

As the rivalry for passengers to the "Golden West" grew in intensity, the railroads rented halls and staged glamorous exhibits in London as well as in eastern parts of the United States. Southern Pacific photograph.

His sense of urgency was evident in the alacrity with which he moved ahead as soon as he had obtained the interest of O. C. Miller and H. C. Campbell from the San Francisco area and Dr. James Adams, an investor from Los Angeles. McCallum owned 2,748 acres and would ultimately acquire between 5,000 and 6,000 acres, mostly bought from the railroad for $2.50 per acre.

Major Miller must have requested additional information. A copy of a letter written to him by Judge McCallum reveals that "I have deeded to you and Scott 600 acres, to Hill 100 acres, M. Adams 100 acres, to Thomas 70½ undivided acres. So I have still left about 582 acres, all of which appears in the papers which I showed you."

McCallum went on to explain that these previous sales of the original Colony Land Tracts had not, at that time of sale, been duly registered and patented, and few of the papers were recorded, and the final payments had not been paid to the railroad. He urged immediate incorporation so that the syndicate could issue clear titles to whatever land was sold, the railroad be paid, and whatever money was left could then be put to good use "to clear off the town lots and street, improve roads, and plant shade trees."

"If we incorporate promptly," he wrote, "perhaps it would be well to

Enrapt listeners thronged into these halls and were enticed by the thousands to buy cheap excursion tickets on trains rushing them to California and the extravagant promises of sudden wealth and immediate health. Southern Pacific photograph.

put up a Company house . . . The same house could be rented for a hotel. It is evident that Dr. Murray's house of eleven rooms only will not accommodate one fourth of the people who want rooms. So too the company should move the bath house and fix it up on the west line of the springs.

"The whole five enterprises of Town, Mineral Springs, hotel and tillable land promises like a bonanza yet is so much safer than mining commercially. Yet the hotel promises quicker returns give or take a few years for trees and vines to become profitable in production.

"If I had $10,000 to use now, I would wish to take all the stock in the hotel. Hotels at health resorts, where there are mineral springs, is the most profitable business now, even in Southern California, on the money invested."

The prospective partners, caught up in McCallum's enthusiasm, agreed to incorporation, and syndicated under the name of "Palm Valley Land and Water Company" at first, and later reorganized with a capitalization of $100,000.

The first business of the syndicate was to hire H. J. Stevenson to make a survey of the east half Section 15, T4S, R4E, totalling 320 acres, which was the site they had chosen for the proposed township. This townsite extended from North Street (now Alejo Road) on the north, to South Street (now Ramon Road) on the south and from East Avenue (now Indian Avenue) on the east to the slope of the San Jacinto Mountains. Stevenson completed his survey in October, 1887.

The syndicate completed the stone-walled canal, or Whitewater Ditch. All claims to water in Whitewater except one was purchased and owned by the company. Over 1500 inches of constant water flow was available. Besides this, 500 inches of water was taken from Snow Creek, making a total of 2,000 inches. Water was to be deeded with the land as it was sold.

The map prepared by Stevenson in 1887 divided the townsite into thirty blocks, some of which were divided into as many as 36 lots, while Block 30 was but one block. With but slight variations, the legal descriptions of downtown Palm Springs today is by reference to this map.

The syndicate partners held undivided interests in the land which was distributed among them as follows: Judge McCallum 2748/10,000; O. C. Miller 3341/10,000; H. C. Campbell 3355/10,000; Dr. Adams 556/10,000.

The partners signed a written agreement with McCallum assigning him the sole responsibility for all the promotional activities and plans for the contemplated day of auction.

A typical group of tourists who took advantage of the reduced rail rates to come to California to enjoy all the promises held out to them during the boom times of the 1880's for quick riches and immediate health cures. Courtesy Title Insurance and Trust Company, Los Angeles.

AGREEMENT

"It is hereby agreed that J. G. McCallum shall expend such money as he may deem necessary and proper in putting the undivided lands in the Palm Colony in San Diego County, California in proper condition for the auction sale and other expenditures proportioned to our respective interests in said undivided Colony Lands. Also to pay said McCallum pro rata as aforesaid a reasonable compensation for General Agency and superintendence preparing advertising and selling said lands making Abstract Contracts, and to reimburse him for all sums properly expended in connection with such services. And in case it shall be deemed best for a majority of the undersigned to save expenses of conveyancy papers to deed our respective interests to said McCallum (on receiving a declaral of trust from him showing the amount of our respective interests, so to be held in trust by him, the proceeds of which to be accounted for at any sales of said lands or portion thereof of said Colony, which it is now contemplated will be made in the next eight months). Also to incur such expense as he may deem necessary in hiring teams to carry passengers who shall attend such auction sales, from Seven Palms to said Palm City such total expenditures not to exceed $500.00 — each of us hereby agreeing to pay our pro-rata of said.

Dated and signed this August 30, 1887.

O. C. Miller
Thomas W. Scott
(Attorney in fact for
J. G. Hill)
J. G. McCallum"

John McCallum was ready to plunge into the midstream of activities which were to bring his longtime dreams of development of his beloved desert into fruition. Many and grand were the plans he had made. His zeal was boundless.

Then, as always seemed to be his fate, certain unexpected problems arose which demanded his immediate attention. Once again, he was plagued by distractions.

He ran into a set-back when State Engineer Hall, in reviewing the application for real estate subdivision permit, stated that he considered the water supply, the capacity of which was claimed sufficient to supply 6,000 acres, was inadequate. McCallum was able to convince him that the developers contemplated adding other sources to the water supply and that he personally, as president of the Palm Valley Water Company, had posted a notice which announced:

"Is hereby given that I, the undersigned, claim all the waters flowing to the extent of 300 inches measured under a four inch pressure flowing in, and also including the underflow of Cañon with the tributaries and cienegas therewith, connected at the point where this notice is posted, which is about 5 miles northwesterly of Section 15 Tp 4 South Range 4 East S. B. M. in San Diego County, California and within about 15 feet of the junction of two cañons which unite in said Chino Cañon.

"That said water is claimed for the purpose of irrigation on said Section 15 and sections adjoining thereto, in Township 4 South Range East San Bernardino base and meridian.

"That I intend to divert said water by means of ditches, flumes and pipe of sufficient size to carry all the waters of said Chino Cañon to the extent of these three hundred (300) inches.

"Dated and posted this 13 day of February, 1886.

Jno. McCallum"

Visionary dreamer that he was, Judge McCallum also had a hard practical streak in his nature. He knew that to entice prospective land buyers to travel as far as Palm Valley, the railroad fares had to be made appealing. He wrote Manager-General Towne of the S. P. Railroad:

"I would respectfully request that round trip rates may be given for passengers from Los Angeles to Seven Palms and return . . . . The present rate each is $5.40 whereas the round trip rate to Banning from here (only 20 miles east) is $6.00. One hotel for invalids mainly and a boarding house are just started at the new colony Seven Palms and we have started making a canal — with about thirty men now engaged — to be increased hereafter — our company having to pay the fare of laborers and no prospect of income for a year or more makes the present rates come hard for our company and to persons like myself, who have to make the round trip every week or two.

"The interest of your R.R. Company in the success of such colony enterprise is no doubt too obvious to you to need mention here.

"I trust there is no rule made by the directors of the S. P. Company to prevent giving round trip rates between here and Seven Palms proportionate to those given to other colonies. This letter is written at the special request of all persons interested in the settlement in Palm Valley near Seven Palms.

Very Respectfully,

J. G. McCallum"

Who could resist the lure of such advertisements as this which the Southern Pacific had printed in newspapers all over the country? Southern Pacific photograph.

Somehow, despite being involved in these time consuming interruptions, McCallum found time to make frequent trips to San Francisco to promote interest in the desert land project and to prepare dramatic promotional material which was mailed to prospective buyers.

He knew that it was imperative for this advertising information to be as appealing as possible if it was to attract the type of people he wanted in his valley. One of the most lavish pieces of promotional material was a brochure of sixteen handsomely mounted photos of the most beautiful scenes in the Palm Valley region. A copy of this costly brochure is presently to be found in the California Room of the State Library in Sacramento.

Another beautiful piece of advertising was a single folded page illustrated by steel engraving of these same views. The written script proclaimed "Perfect climate, wonderful scenery, pure mountain water: The earliest fruit region in the state: Absolute cure for all pulmonary and kindred diseases."

Advertisements ran in San Francisco, Los Angeles and Riverside newspapers. These ads repeated the promises of the brochures but added "The home of the Banana, Date and Orange. No Fog! No Frost! No wind storms!"

The date for the auction was set for November 1, 1887.

The Great Land Auction

This ad, reproduced from the San Bernardino Weekly Times of October 29, 1887, promoting a railroad excursion to Palm Springs for a land auction, was undoubtedly composed by Judge McCallum.

EXCURSION
—TO—
PALM SPRINGS,

Leaves Los Angeles on S. P. R. R.,

October 31st, at 8 A. M.

Rate of Fare for Round Trip.

San Francisco to Seven Palms, and return............$25 00
Los Angeles, San Gabriel, Monte and Pomona, and return 3 50
Ontario and Cucamonga, and return:............... 3 40
Colton, and return 2 70

Take train leaving S. P. R. R. depot at Los Angeles at 8, a. m. Monday, October 31s , reaching Seven Palms at 12:20, p.m. Leaves Colton at 10:20 a. m. Returning on any regular train in two or three days.

Invest at Palm Springs, where there is

NO FROST!
NO HEAVY WINDS!
NO FOG!

THE HOME
OF THE
BANANA, DATE AND ORANGE.

Only Spot in California where Frost, Fog and Windstorms are Absolutely Unknown.

The Earliest Season in the State. Best Opportunity for Men of Moderate Means. Every Fruit and Vegetable Matures a Month to Six Weeks Earlier than Anywhere Else on the Coast.

In a sheltered spot at the base of the San Jacinto mountains lies Palm Valley, famous all over the southern part of the State as being the location of the Agua Caliente Springs, whose waters are an absolute specific for rheumatism and a host of other diseases. The soil of this Valley is remarkably fertile and it has been demonstrated that every deciduous and citrus fruit and every vegetable will mature a month or more in advance of the most favored localities elsewhere.

There is a

MAGNIFICENT WATER SUPPLY

Derived from the Whitewater river and other sources, and a fine canal has just been completed, some eight miles in length and stone lined, which conveys at all times an abundance of water. Ten acres of this land in fruit and vegetables will furnish an ample income.

These lands have been subdivided into town lots, and 5, 10 and 20 acre tracts, and will be sold to the highest bidder on easy terms.

AT AUCTION, TUESDAY, NOVEMBER 1st.

For further information apply to CONDEE & STORY, San Bernardino; J. B. FISKE, Redlands; C. B. WEEKS & CO., Colton; HARVEZ POTTER, Riverside; B. L. MUIR, San Diego; J. L. MOOTE, Ontario, or WATSON, STOLL & CO., 245 N. Main street, Los Angeles.

The sale will be conducted by Mr. S. W. Fergusson, Manager of the Southern California Land and Immigration Co (Incorporated).

Principal Office, 10 California Street, San Francisco,

Note—All the unsold portion of this property will be on sale by above mentioned agents, and by S. W. Fergusson, at 10 California St., San Francisco, and at 245 St , Los Angeles.

AT LAST the great day arrived!

The special train of eager prospective land purchasers arrived at the Seven Palms station at 12:30 P.M. The train left San Francisco at 9:30 in the morning of October 30 arriving in Los Angeles and leaving that city at 8 A.M. October 31. Stops were made at San Gabriel, Puente, Pomona, Ontario and Banning. The round trip fare was $25.00 from San Francisco and $3.50 from Los Angeles.

As the curious passengers stepped off the train at the desolate little weatherbeaten station of Seven Palms they were met by Dr. Murray's "Indian-Arab" Willie Marcus dressed in colorful flowing robes and his camel, and by musicians, and greeters. They were then pushed into carriages and driven across what probably appeared to their unaccustomed eyes, bleak wasteland. Once they rounded the protective point of the mountain, the harsh winds stopped and they soon came to Murray's hotel. As one writer put it, . . . "Before long we entered a sort of real fairyland, green fresh, alive with birds and filled with the murmur of running water — a lovely oasis where the desert and mountains meet."

The excursionists were treated to more music, refreshments, speeches and all the trimmings. Murray's little hotel, filled to the rafters, could have taken care of many more had the facilities been available.

Southern Pacific Station at Palmdale, McCallum wagon waiting to pick up visitors and supplies. Courtesy Title Insurance and Trust Company, Los Angeles.

The auction began the next morning with the sonorous voice of the auctioneer, S. W. Ferguson, extolling the virtues of the parcels of land as they were presented. By pre-arrangement it had been announced that lots were to be sold to the highest bidder at "One-third cash, balance in 6 to 12 months at 8% interest."

Caught up in the enthusiasm of the occasion, W. J. McIntyre, an attorney from Riverside, was the first bidder and bid on Lot 1, Block 22 for $50.00. Other bidders leapt into the action and the next two sales of $45.00 each were for Lots 2 and 3 of the same block. These lots today are the very heart of Palm Springs and were ultimately regained by McCallum's daughter, Pearl, and have increased in value a thousandfold.

McIntyre continued to bid as the day wore on and finally ended up buying eight lots, all in the same vicinity as his original purchase and averaging $2.80 per front foot. Most of the excursionists preferred the land along Palm Canyon, or Main Street as it was then called, but several "venturesome souls" went as far out into the desertland as what is now Deep Well Ranch. One person bid in and was successful in obtaining a 20-acre site out there for $1,000.

The weary visitors returned to the excursion train leaving an exhausted but satisfied real estate promoter in the tiny far off spot on the desert. McCallum must have breathed a sigh of satisfaction. A total of $50,000 worth of land and 137 parcels were sold on that one day.

The back and front of the brochure widely circulated extolling the virtues of Judge McCallum's Palm Valley real estate venture. Courtesy History Division, Los Angeles County Museum of Natural History.

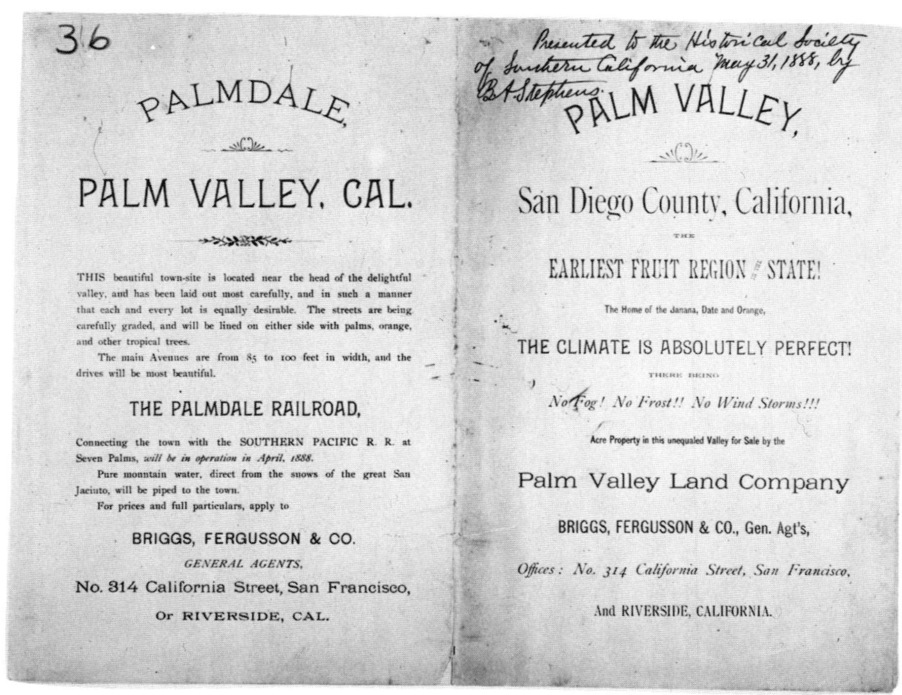

19.
"Pearlie"

Pearl McCallum at about twelve years.

PROUDLY the tiny girl nestled safely in her father's arms as she sat upon the front of his saddle that day they rode across the sands and she first came to Palm Valley, as her father had named the place. From the first moment Pearl shared in her father's enthusiasm for the "strange, sun-blanched land, the pale, mysterious desert."

As they rode over the sandy boulder-strewn wastes, the father told his five-year-old daughter about the poem of Tennyson's which had so inspired him on that first visit to the Agua Caliente springs. The story of *The Lotos-Eaters* and the Land of the Afternoon in which they found peace and contentment would ever after linger in Pearl's memory, and she loved the long afternoons coming with the sudden disappearance of the sun behind towering Mt. San Jacinto.

Whatever discomfort and loneliness her gentle little mother, Emily, might have felt in the simple adobe hut the Judge had the Indians make out of adobe bricks, to Pearl it was always a place of charm and comfort. Camping out under the brilliant stars in the protection of the grey-trunked, sprawling old fig tree until the house was completed was an adventure for Pearl and the other McCallum children.

Her first impressions of this strange new land of such haunting beauty were gained from horseback. The McCallum children roamed the sandy

"Pearlie" and her burro.

stretches nearby and out into the open desert and at other times rode into the canyons. There in the shade of the towering palm trees they played and fished in the icy pool of the canyon stream.

When she was not riding her little burro, Pearl romped and played with her Indian friends. With hair streaming back from her sun-tanned face, her bare feet streaked with silt and mud from wading in the irrigation ditch, the little girl, the only white child at the time, found life a constant source of wonder.

Sometimes she would go with these children into the canyons. Shuddering with delicious fright, they would keep their distance lest the evil spirit dwelling, so legend had it, in Tahquitz Canyon would snatch them into angry threatening arms and take them away. Sometimes, when the shadows crept over the steep granite walls of lofty Mt. San Jacinto, if one was fortunate and the time of day was exactly right, an imaginative child could see the outline of an Angel, or in another place, the face of her father's hero, Abraham Lincoln, would loom up.

The Indian children called her "Pearlie."

But most of all her greatest joy came from riding, and astride her burro Pearlie loved racing over the sands to the railroad station to watch the trains rush along the tracks. As she rode she learned the names of the desert plants and their characteristics. The lacy mesquite trees, indicators

Harry McCallum, left,
and Wallace McCallum.
Courtesy Palm Springs Desert Museum.

of water hidden below the surface of the sand, were an important source of food supply for the Indians who gathered the twisty beans and stored them in baskets. The golden-green of the Palo Verde tree with the shower of pale yellow blooms in the spring contrasted delightfully with the blue flowering of the lacy grey smoke trees — both lovers of the hot desert sun and frequenters of the dry desert washes. She puzzled over the mysteries of the ironwood tree which sank in water and the pumice rock which floated when tossed upon the same pool with the sinking wood. The strong, pungent fragrance of the creosote bush wafted up and around her as some of the leaves were crushed as she rode through a patch.

The desert wildflowers — the lavender verbena, the desert primroses, the host of others, scarlet, yellow, and crimson — delighted her. She would always remember the beauty of the spring flowers in the meadow behind the spot where the Desert Inn would stand one day.

The little wild desert creatures became her friends.

She loved to lie awake at night and listen to the shrill, haunting yapping of the coyote packs. The sound of their barking seemed ominously near as the stillness of the night was interrupted. Frequently, along with the coyotes would come the pounding hooves of the shaggy wild horses which lived in the canyons and came down to forage off the tender young orange leaves and to devastate the grape vines.

Pearlie claimed the small birds as her very own. She adored the small mauve-colored doves even more than the quail. Their faithfulness and gentleness endeared them to her.

On rare occasions, when her brothers could take the time, she rode with them, and they took lunches and climbed high along the canyon walls. Sometimes when she was very still, a wonderful sight came into view. The graceful, surefooted Big Horn sheep, infrequently during the heat of the summer days, came down from their mountain heights to drink. They grazed off the mesquite trees and rested in the shade. Perhaps, if luck held, a venerable ram, his huge horns curled and twisted with age and his barrel-shaped torso heaving with caution, stood guard as the dams and lambs frolicked in the coolness.

There were other times when her mother was feeling well and not suffering from one of her incapacitating migraine headaches that she took Pearlie to bathe in the hot springs.

School house at Palm Springs,
Carl Eytel.
Courtesy Southwest Museum.

Mountain sheep in their haunts
on Mt. San Jacinto, Carl Eytel.

"We used to bathe," Pearl later reminisced, "Ladies first, wrapped in Mother Hubbards for bathing suits. You would put your feet in first, and as the sand moved all of a sudden a pool of hot, soft water about a yard wide would burst forth."

At first the spring from which bubbled sand and warm water had merely a timber across it to help the bathers steady themselves. Later the spring was enclosed by a small ramshackled building built out of rough timbers. Bathers hung their clothes upon nails driven into the walls. Few of the settlers took advantage of the healing waters, although anyone was welcome to do so. After awhile, the Indians charged a few cents for bathing privileges.

The shy, soft-spoken Indian woman always smiled a welcome to them when they came to the oasis. Pearlie loved to sit and chat with these gentle women as they gathered reeds growing near the springs. Made of epicampes grass and of a juncas weed and using a deer-bone awl for piercing and threading, these Cahuilla Indian women made some of the finest baskets in America.

In the early days Johnny was too ill to roam the desert with her, but to everyone's delight the warm air soothed his sickness until he could breathe normally and was strong enough to help his father with the

117

chores. Pearl followed her big brother as he helped with the irrigating.

Bands of spirited wild horses coming to drink sometimes broke down the walls and the water ran wildly as though eager to escape the confinement of the stone-lined ditch. Pearl rode as close to these wild creatures as she possibly could and watched in fascination as the Indians showed her how they trapped the best of the lot, hobbled, and then tamed them. She greatly enjoyed watching these same Indians, about seventeen of them, pick apricots, peaches and figs and haul them off in huge wagonloads for the two or three hour ride to the railway (seven miles across the sand) for shipment to the early market in Los Angeles. The excitement caused by a fifty-pound watermelon, which took first prize at the Riverside Fair, never left her and she loved telling about it years later.

Pearlie was a sombre, serious child and often was left alone. With her horse to ride and her playmates she wasn't lonely, however. There were two Indians whom she regarded with special affection and she considered them "twinky" people — Rosie and Marcus Pete were very good friends of the McCallum family. After settlers came and purchased land, there was one family she always remembered. In an interview with Jane Ardmore which appeared in West Magazine, Pearl recalled, "At one time there was a rancher named Bradshaw with an orchard of apricots where El Mirador now stands. He had two children, a girl about my age and a boy. We played family. That was the only time when we had enough children to play Mama and Papa and Child. When snow came — and we did have snow, this land had everything — we made a sled, using heavy pieces of lumber for runners, cracker boxes for seats, and with harnesses of leather and baling wire, we hitched up burros and had ourselves a sleigh ride."

Pearl's early schooling was in the one-room board and batten shack which was heated by a wood stove. Her sister, May, who was seventeen at the time, was the teacher for Pearlie and the twenty-six Indian children.

If the solitary, self-sufficient little girl sometimes looked wistfully at the father whom she silently adored and yearned for him to share some of the attention he lavished upon Johnny and May, his favorites, she said not a word. The home place was called "Johnny's Ranch" and it was the gay, talented sister May the father took with him on outings. May had inherited her mother's sweet singing voice and was a fine musician, playing the piano with great skill. Judge McCallum delighted in

*On the trail up Palm Canyon, Carl Eytel.
Courtesy Southwest Museum.*

showing off this lovely daughter's progress. The other children of the family simply accepted this favoritism as a way of life.

And so the halcyon days of Pearlie's solitary, but strangely happy childhood blended one into the other. The crops flourished. The real estate development prospered. Johnny was strong and well. Life was good except for the fierce migraine headaches which had plagued her mother all of her life and which also had come upon Pearl when she was about nine. These headaches were to increase in severity until she would average at least two migraine attacks every month.

Pearl always, even as a very old woman, looked back upon these first nine years of her life with nostalgia.

The McCallum sisters, May and Pearl.

20.

The Rejoicing Desert

FOLLOWING the "great day" of the successful auction came a time of happiness and promise. Judge McCallum continued his promotion of the area by continuous writing to his friends and associates throughout the State and at the same time supervising Johnny's Ranch.

On the eighty-acre ranch the twenty acres of apricot trees became laden with luscious fruit; the thirty acres of early grapes responded equally bountifully, and the oranges were particularly delicious. Wrote Ed Ainsworth in his book *Beckoning Desert*, "Pearl McCallum, the youngest child of Judge McCallum, later Mrs. Austin G. McManus, described to me the plantings of her father in rhapsodic terms. She said that the Indian River sweet oranges, originally from Florida, the most beautiful oranges she ever saw, had a purplish luminescent cast which won for them the first prize at the Riverside Exposition. The grapes bore the beautiful names: Rose of Peru, Flaming Tokay, Early Sweetwater and Black Hamburg. The giant fig trees bore fruit as sweet as honey."

The original McCallum groves. Mountainside house which was built in the late 1880's shown to the left of the picture. Courtesy Palm Springs Desert Museum.

Ernest Braunton, resident of the little community, wrote in his diary in 1889 and described the ranch, "On the McCallum ranch, known as Section 29, was some of the most fertile land in the valley. In 1889 it contained alfalfa fields, figs and apricots . . . Also covered in some spots by well-developed native plants. It had the largest and most northerly Palo Verde (Parkinsonia) known in the section."

Braunton continued his entries: "May 16, first crop of black figs and watermelons ripe. I shipped some figs to L. A. and received $1.25 a pound for them. All fruits grown on the desert are superior in flavor on account of the fact that the extreme heat generates less sugar. June 1 — Ripe apricots from McCallum's ranch. June 15 — Second crop of water-mellons ripe, second crop of figs ripe, also Muscat grapes from Murray's ranch." Because it was the first to reach the markets his fruit always brought high premium to the growers.

At holiday times, there was much jollity in which both whites and Indians shared. Some of the Indians had worked with McCallum in building his adobe home. Among these were such people as Magill Saternino, who also had worked on the water ditch, Pedro Chino, Marcus Belardo, Baristo Sol, Allejo Patencio, and others. Most of these men were one day to be honored by having streets named for them in Palm Springs.

JULY 4, 1888, came and Judge McCallum seized upon this to stage the first patriotic civic celebration witnessed by the people in the valley.

A CIVIC CELEBRATION

Pearl McCallum in the original orange grove just before the long, devastating drought. These oranges were the famous Indian River sweets from Florida which won many awards at agricultural fairs.
Courtesy Palm Springs Desert Museum.

In spite of the warm weather they made of the day a round program of sports, flag displays, firecrackers, and speech making. There were few celebrants, but they entered into the spirit of the occasion with a zest.

The *Riverside Press and Horticulturist* reported the gala celebration in its column called Palmdale Letter dated July 14, 1888:

> "Did Palmdale celebrate the Fourth! Celebrate! Yes, in the early morn with bang of gun and bray of burros. Later by excursion to the 'realms of shade at Palm Springs' and latest with fireworks (no firewater) and a big bonfire as a finale. Our habitations were gayly decked with flags, games were played, patriotic airs sung and Palmdale enthused."

Although the Palmdale correspondent failed to make mention of the fact, Judge McCallum most assuredly must have delivered a patriotic speech similar to those he gave during the halcyon days of his former political career.

THE PROMISE OF GOOD TIMES TO COME

FOR A time it appeared that Palm Springs was going to become almost overnight one of the great agricultural centers of Southern California. Other settlers came and joined in the agriculture dream.

The McCallum wagon, pulled by mules "Judy and Maud" on the old Bradshaw road. Courtesy Title Insurance and Trust Company, Los Angeles.

A Mr. Twogood planted his ten-acre tract on Section 19 in grape vines and Miss Chilson seeded her ten acres in the same section into alfalfa. Both plantings did very well. Cutter and Dinsmore contemplated cultivating their thirty acres. McCallum wrote F. A. Koetitz in San Francisco setting forth the progress in the Valley and concluded his letter by saying, "I returned from Palm Valley two days since. Two hundred acres planted there all look very well. The water system has been working regularly since I resumed charge of the company nearly two years ago. I will return to Palm Springs in a week or so. I suggest that you or your brothers visit the valley as soon as possible. The hotel is now open there; or you can board with Mrs. Bradshaw if you prefer."

Dr. Murray's little hotel flourished. His motherly wife watched over the needs of the guests while the irascible Scot tended his trees and plants and read poetry to the visitors. He had little patience with the sickly ones who came. Many famous literary figures were to register at the hotel and remain enraptured with its surroundings and then go off to extol the virtues of this enchanting spot.

But this terrestrial paradise was not to last.

A plow used on the McCallum ranch during those first years of cultivation. Now owned by Moorten's Desertland Botanic Gardens.

The wagon Judge McCallum used to haul fruit to the railroad and to bring visitors to Palm Springs. This wagon is now in the Desertland Botanic Gardens. Courtesy Mr. and Mrs. Chester (Slim) Moorten.

21.

The Absentee Rancher

EARLY in the summer of 1890 Judge McCallum began to feel the strain of his efforts. The struggle to build the 19-mile stonelined water ditch, and to organize, promote the sales, and then supervise the development and oversee the progress of the little settlement had exhausted his reserve energies. His daughter May was not well and so the family urged him to take a respite and go to Chicago for a visit.

Mrs. McCallum and Pearl were living in the West Adams home. Harry, as secretary of the company, assumed the responsibilities of supervising the Palm Valley Water Offices at 209 S. Broadway. He wrote daily reports to his father and busied himself putting files of correspondence in order. He also was in frequent communication with J. D. Greenwade, the foreman in charge of the desert ranch.

Conscientious Harry, despite his youth, tried to be the father figure. He arranged excursions to Long Beach for Pearl and his mother. Johnny's illness had returned and Harry wrote long letters to him and to the wandering Wallace, both brothers evidently failing to write as frequent-

Agua Caliente, 1889. Picture taken by W. B. Forsythe of Orange and presented to the Palm Springs Historical Society by his famous son, the artist Clyde Forsythe. Courtesy Palm Springs Historical Society.

ly as he hoped they would. He rejoiced when he could write his father about the health of his two brothers which seemed to be improving.

The warm bond of affection existing between all members of the family and their love for the father are repeatedly revealed in Harry's letters. In his frequent notes to his father are to be found such phrases as: "Hoping to see you soon and that complete health and happiness confronts you." "Pearl well and mother in good health and spirits." "There is nothing further to write except to repeat my former wishes for your health, etc. and to state that we are prospering." Harry continually sent comforting and reassuring news items to the obviously concerned father in Chicago. "May and Pearl," he wrote, "Both diligently studying and both happy." (May had dashed out for a brief visit.) Another message stated, "Mother has lately been improving. She is having the garden fixed up to surprise and please you, no doubt."

Wishing to comfort his father, Harry once wrote, "Looking at everything at this time it seems that the sun which so long a time has been behind the clouds for us, is now coming out and all will be prosperous and peaceful again."

Sentinel Palm, Carl Eytel. Courtesy Southwest Museum.

Money was a problem and he constantly sent requests for funds to his father. Most of the amount received in return went to Johnny to pay the bills at whatever hotel he was frequenting. Harry struggled to collect payment due the McCallums and often failed. He listed the West Adams house for sale with a realtor and in one letter when funds were lacking, wrote the ranch foreman "A distressing state of impecuniosity forbids my going to Palm Valley at present."

The welfare of Palm Valley and its products were of constant concern to the young man. He arranged with the State Chamber of Commerce to send one of the watermelons raised on Johnny's place on the "California on Wheels" exhibit. All of the newspapers carried extravagant notices of this alleged 100-pound giant melon (which, in fact, probably weighed around fifty pounds) and gave Palm Valley splendid publicity.

In a letter to A. R. Briggs on June 6, 1890, Harry wrote, "At present I am using my influence to have this office moved to Palm Springs which will do away with about $20 per month rent expenses and will be more convenient there, and also give the Valley more renown and will increase the Post Office service very materially. And by the way, I might inform you that after July 1, 1890, "Palm Springs" is the P. O. address and not Palmdale, which it has been."

He kept his father informed on the daily happenings both in Los Angeles and at Palm Springs. Three items must have been of great interest to the Judge:

"I wrote to Greenwade last Friday to send me the first few bunches of ripe grapes," wrote Harry, "I want them for exhibition and to have it in the papers that Palm Valley has the *first*. Prof. Wheaton has a bunch of grapes (a fine variety but not the Mission — I forgot the name) about a foot long, large and fine; and he intends to send them to the State Board of Trade where they will receive the most notice and be officially reported."

The second news item was concerned with a project afoot at the time on the desert, "Wheaton, Hanscom, Murray and other Palm Springites are raising a subscription to send Murray, "Jimmy" and others up Palm Cañon from the Van Deventers to the north to prospect for a way through that Cañon from Palm Springs to San Diego. Their report will be sent to the proper authorities, and they feel pretty sure the county road will be opened in accordance with their report."

Mother McCallum, deeply distressed over the ill health of her two older sons, evidently expressed concern over Harry's working and living conditions. He wrote his father about this and also about continuing his education as his mother wished. "When mother writes you about the office injuring me, you naturally want to discontinue it. But it is all a mistake about me dissipating. I have too great a regard for my future, and also, the happiness of others, to ever do myself such an injury. Even if I decide to go to City College, I think the office should still be open and that you hire an assistant to aid you . . . Now about the College: You are aware of my defective education in science studies, and it would be impossible to consider the higher ones without passing an examination on the former, which I could not do. However, if they are not involved, the embarrassment of having to enter a very low class might be saved me. Circumstances have been such during the past that my studies have from time to time been interrupted just long enough to make me forget what I had learned each time . . . . Another objection to attending college is the expense in going there, of an outfit, and getting started which would be felt heavily just at this time."

Harry continued sending his father newsy items. At the same time he was busily endeavoring to carry on with the family enterprises without much financial success. He kept an increasingly growing list of names of those who had participated in the land venture and who were fast becoming delinquent in their payments, both for the land and for the assessments charged to keep the ditch in repair and the water supply constantly flowing.

Carl Eytel's concept of the life-giving waters of Tahquitz Ditch. Courtesy McCallum Estate.

22.

The Return to Palm Valley

JUDGE MCCALLUM returned from this trip east on Oct. 8, 1890, and immediately again began assuming a leading role in the activities of his Palm Springs. His crops were flourishing, and as he stood looking out over the panorama dotted with his neighbors' orchards, his faith in the future of the Valley was undaunted. He could brush aside the annoyances of the costly maintenance of the water ditch and of a few persons who were delinquent in their assessment payments, and the weak-of-heart who, after a brief time, were giving up and returning to the city life they once had tried to escape. Others would come, he was confident, and it was to these he addressed his efforts by writing letters and mailing them the attractive brochures he had prepared describing Palm Valley.

His typical promotional efforts are illustrated by the letter he wrote to Dr. J. W. Dennis, dated Oct. 31, 1890:

"Dear Sir:

"In answer to yours of the 23 inst. — The land I offer for sale is on Sections 11 and 19 in ten or five acres and upwards. The enclosed diagram will show you the tracts and relative prices. You will see by the map heretofore sent you, their relative positions to stations, railroads, Palm Springs, etc. and the exact distances, you can measure by the section lines of your map.

"The regular terms are, ⅓ cash, ⅓ in one year and ⅓ in two years, interest 8 percent per annum. A liberal discount will be made for cash payment in full; and a liberal extension as to time payment of those who improve this season. Parties who pay all cash will have a still more liberal discount, say 15 percent, at least on those prices.

"Some of the adjoining lands, no better than these offered, were sold at $150 to $175 per acre in the last two years. But as I am the original purchaser and holder I can afford to sell at a much less rate. In all cases one share of stock in the Palm Valley Water Co. of which I am president, and owner of the majority of the stock, goes with the land. This is deemed sufficient and is about ⅓ more water per acre than the average in Southern California.

"As to cost of trees and vines: deciduous trees cost about $20 per 100 which is the usual number per acre. Orange and lemon trees cost about three times as much per acre. *Rooted* grape vines $3 per acre, but grape *cuttings* cost about one dollar per acre and grow about as well as the rooted vines.

"Most of the planting in Palm Valley so far, is in grape vines of many choice varieties, as they do very well, ripen very early, are excellent fruit to ship; the whole country being a market, they bring high prices: cost of production being less.

"Reliable parties will cultivate, irrigate, and take care of trees and vines at from $12 to $15 per acre per annum. But the cost is less to the person who does his own work. As to fencing: our state law provides that no fences are required where Palm Valley is situated. In other words, those who keep live stock must fence it in. However, I have so far preferred to fence rather than take any chances. Wire fencing is not expensive.

"As to selecting your land it is much preferred that you select it in person or by your agent. I would prefer not to select for anyone. If you should wish personal references in your city, I refer you to James P. Kilbreth, of 490 W. Sixth Street, and to Col. J. V. Guthrie of Mt. Auburn.

"In Palm Valley tree and vine planting commences in January and may continue to the first of May for the season.

"Whether you do or do not purchase in Palm Valley this seems to be the best time to come to Southern California. The demand for good land is evidently greatly increasing as well as the population. And lands are bought now for profits or production rather than for speculation. Ten acres intelligently culti- vated in this country will give larger net returns than 160 acres of average land in Ohio, or in the other older states.

Very Respectfully,
J. G. McCallum"

It was about this time the U. S. Government announced its interest and intention of importing date trees from Arabia.

Never ceasing in his efforts to bring new crops into the Valley, Judge McCallum hastily wrote H. E. Vandeman, Pomologist, Department of Agriculture, Washington, D. C., the following letter:

"Dear Sir:

"Your letter of the 27th ult. to the Los Angeles Chamber of Commerce relative to the date palms received by our government was shown to me today; because, as I suppose, that Chamber had selected Palm Springs in San Diego County as the point of distribution for some of these trees under the erroneous impression that the government had not already distributed them.

"On careful reading of your letter, I notice that you state that the 'valley of

THE FIRST
DATE TREES

the Colorado is perhaps the best place' for such trees, and that you state that five points of distribution as already selected by the government. As this leaves one of the male trees not distributed to any one point, I would respectfully request that Palm Valley, which borders on what we call here the Colorado Valley, or rather Colorado Desert, be selected for one of those date trees. By reference to the San Francisco Weekly Chronicle of the second instant, of other leading newspapers in this state, the well-known fact is referred to, that in all the United States there is no place where the conditions seem so favorable to the date palm as Palm Valley where there is now abundant water for all horticultural purposes because of the recent completion of the Palm Valley Water Company's irrigation system. In Palm Cañon which is at the upper end of the Palm Valley and connected with it there are over 1000 Palm Trees growing close together of remarkable size and height which bear fruit prolifically. It has the flavor of the dates of commerce. These are supposed by many to be wild dates, but the trees look like what are commonly called the fan palms. The temperature there and the sandy soil, and all the surroundings are said to be similar to those where the date palm flourished in Africa.

"In case this selection should be made the trees should be consigned to me at Seven Palms, San Diego Co., Cala., which is on the main line of the Southern Pacific Railroad about 109 miles east of Los Angeles and 5 miles north of Palm Springs in Palm Valley where I suggest these trees should be tried. Many date tree palm seeds have been planted at Palm Springs already. In case you should desire reference as to myself, I refer you to the Chamber of Commerce here and to our representatives in Congress.

Very Resp'y Your Ob'dent Serv't
J. G. McCallum

P.S. I should have stated above that the date palm seeds before mentioned have grown remarkably well.

Very Resp'y
J. G. M."

Thus it was that Judge McCallum was among the very first to introduce date growing in the Coachella Valley and the above letter disproves the statement of his daughter Pearl, who was frequently quoted as saying, many years later, "My father was never a rancher at all, but somehow he used great intelligence in deciding what to plant, which of course was anybody's guess then." On the contrary, he was in constant communication with the national Department of Agriculture and the Bureau of Plant Industry in Washington. As a small child, Pearl was unaware of his correspondence throughout the years.

Palm Springs Railroad Station,
Carl Eytel.
Courtesy Southwest Museum.

Finally, as the length of the list of named delinquent property owners grew to such proportions he could no longer shrug them aside, Judge McCallum's sanguine faith became weakened.

Two rival subdivisions in the desert region had failed ignominiously. A group of Boston investors had started a settlement they named "Palm-dale" and despite vainglorious efforts of promising "Wide tree lined streets" and even going to the extreme of building a narrow-gauge rail-road from the mainline, the enterprise never got really underway. The developers' dreams of prosperity and their $100,000 faded.

The other development was that called "Garden of Eden," a small tract at the mouth of Andreas Canyon. Lack of water supply doomed this tract sponsored by Riverside capital and subdivided by B. B. Barney.

The Judge began the heartbreaking task of trying to revive interest in Palm Springs. Many of the original purchasers proved to be sources of great disappointment to him. Instead of settling down upon their little ranches and helping to establish a real community of people sharing the love of the region and reaping the benefits both physically and financially from the warmth and equable climate, for the most part, they came to the desert only during the cooler months. Frequently these

131

owners put their places in the charge of some member of the family
suffering from bronchial trouble who had neither the strength nor the
inclination to take proper care of the plantings.

The water ditch and irrigation system constantly silted up and the
cost of keeping the sand which choked off the water shoveled out, was
becoming prohibitive. The settlers rebelled at paying the assessments
and McCallum found himself paying these repairs largely out of his
own pocket.

At a meeting of the stockholders held in Los Angeles on February 12,
1889, an assessment of $1 per share had been voted upon and notices of
this duly published in the *Evening Express* in every issue for four weeks.
An affidavit to this effect was filed in the Superior Court of Los Angeles
County.

Some of those assessed paid immediately, but eleven of the original
purchasers failed to do so. A second directors meeting was held on Jan.
5, 1891, and another $1 assessment voted. This was duly advertised for
the required period of time in the San Diego *Weekly Union*. Commencing March 5, 1891, a list of delinquent names was published in four issues
of the newspaper and among the names was that of O. C. Miller, one of
the original organizers of the syndicate. This was notification that all
such delinquent lands were to be sold by public auction on March 12th
of that year.

Eventually, a large portion of the land was to revert back to the State
for non-payment of taxes. The syndicate partners differed heatedly and
as Pearl commented in an interview later, "They had split up," she
recalled. "They had a very heated argument — they thought my father
was selling the land too cheap. They broke up without any reconcilia-
tion — they were old friends, they should have reconciled — and they
abandoned everything. Later I spent great sums of money to buy back
the land and clear the titles."

Distressed and harassed as Judge McCallum was during this financial
struggle, his anguish was compounded by the realization that Johnny's
health had worsened to an alarming degree. The family had been lulled
by word that their son was greatly improved. But then he came home to
them a mortally stricken young man.

23.
Johnny McCallum

FROM the moment of his birth in the primitive, small Gold Rush town of Placerville in 1864, the boy was a cherished pivotal point in the lives of John and Emily McCallum. Their anguish over the death of their first son was somewhat assuaged with the coming of this child two days before Christmas. It was the recurrence of the miraculous Nativity scene for the two young parents. They named him John Guthrie McCallum, Jr. Other children were born to them, but it was always John who came first.

It was without a qualm that they uprooted their lives when he was stricken almost mortally the year of the fierce typhoid epidemic in San Francisco, and eventually went to the desert warmth. The land purchased and cultivated there was always called Johnny's Ranch.

One writer after visiting the desert described Johnny by saying "In this place dwells a young man who was brought into the Valley two years ago in a cot, in the last stages of consumption. Then he was a mere skeleton. Now he is a stalwart man — robust and hearty — a living example of the curative effects of this dry, wholesome air. He spends his days in caring for a small orange grove and vineyard, both of which delight the eye with their vivid green in this land of ashen-hued sand and rock."

As he rode horseback to inspect the condition of the water ditch, little Pearl followed behind on her pony. She later recalled, "Father acquired this property where I live, for my brother, Johnny. It was his ranch and a good choice it was. The warm sunshine, pure water and outdoor living restored his health. Johnny took his place alongside father and traveled with him working with and for the Indians. He was able to assist in the management of the canal and supervise construction." Another time Pearl said, "Johnny was a good brother and a fine son." His genial nature and handsome looks put him in great demand socially when he made trips on the train to visit the family home on West Adams in Los Angeles.

For a brief period of time, it seemed that the anxiety over Johnny's health could cease and the parents were able to relax their vigil. Suddenly, all this changed.

An inexplicable accident occurred. Johnny told them that on one hot summer day he went into the fields to irrigate the alfalfa. After opening the sluice gates, he said he lay down in the shade of a cottonwood tree and fell asleep. He slept so soundly he was unaware the water had broken through the ditches completely saturating him. The sun had set and he caught a severe cold. During his illness the lesions of the tuberculosis scars broke open and Johnny was caught again in the dread illness.

This was a story which taxed the credulity of the few villagers who remained in the desert during the heat of the summer. Rumors were rampant as to what actually did happen that day in the alfalfa field. The distraught McCallum family ignored the idle chatter and started once again the painful ordeal of restoring their beloved Johnny to health.

Then began frantic two-year efforts on Johnny's part to find a place where he could be free from the painful congestion destroying his lungs. He went up to Ventura and for a while found relief. It was finally the famous Hotel del Coronado near San Diego which attracted him. The brochures and advertisements in the newspapers proclaimed that this hotel was "America's grandest seaside resort . . . A veritable earthly paradise."

Johnny McCallum registered and remained there two weeks. On Friday, Jan. 17, 1891, Dr. Bowditch Morton was called but Johnny could not rally. He died of "Phthisis" at the age of 26 years, 8 months.

The following Sunday there was a small item in the "Arrivals" column of the San Diego newspaper that said, "H. C. McCallum down from Los Angeles is at the Brewster."

Faithful Harry had come to bring Johnny back to his family. They buried him in the large family plot of twelve graves his mother Emily had purchased in Rosedale Cemetery just outside the then city limits of Los Angeles.

More than a little of Judge McCallum's heart was also buried that day.

"JOHNNY"

John Guthrie McCallum, Jr.

24.
The Waters of Affliction

AFTER YEARS of struggle to obtain sufficient water to irrigate his orchards and vineyards and those of his neighbors, it was inconceivable to Judge McCallum that too much water could bring disaster. Such became the case when in 1893 devastating, torrential rains beat down upon Southern California with a fury which has never been equalled.

The "Big Flood" raged continuously for twenty-one days. Up in Los Angeles the usually dry docile little Los Angeles River became a relentless, raging fury, washing out bridges and tearing out houses. Everything within its flow was uprooted and hurled along to destruction by the onrushing flood-waters.

In Palm Springs the rains hurtled against the side of the mountains and plummeted down the canyons. The White Water River became engorged and broke through its usual course tearing out portions of the painstakingly constructed stone-lined ditch, cutting off the life line of water to the small settlement of Palm Springs. Silt and sand covered everything.

Such a rain was unheard of in the desert regions. Judge McCallum tried to protect his plantings against the impact of the damaging water.

Fortunately, there was no danger from the water racing down Tahquitz stream, but the rain caused seven waterfalls at the back of his ranch. All of these, with one exception, ran into the Tahquitz ditch and were carried safely away. The streams from the largest waterfall at the southwest corner of the property tore across the badly damaged twenty-acre field. Thousands of inches of water flowed down this canyon. When the rains stopped McCallum began the hard task of "digging out." He built a dam near the southeast corner of the ranch and filled in the sections washed away by the floods and replanted his washed-out orchards.

Suddenly, without any warning the rains stopped and eleven long years of drought began. McCallum's Ranch began dying. "The Whitewater ditch flow trickled off to nothingness," recalled Pearl, "until we didn't have drinking water except from the springs."

Judge McCallum struggled to save his planting, even to hauling water by wagon three and a half miles in the vain attempt to save his apricot trees. There was nothing he could do but stand by and watch the delicate tendrils of the new grape shoots and the budding trees wither and turn brown. The drought continued unrelieved through long endless and hopeless days.

Settler after settler gave up and left the desert. During the summer of 1894, the white population of Palm Springs was reduced to but a handful of residents. M. French Gilman, who carried the mail at the time, recalled that these few were Dr. Welwood Murray, Professor Wheaton, former distinguished organist of Trinity Church of New York, Judge McCallum family, George Hayman, the zanjero, and the Broesemle family.

AMAZINGLY, Judge McCallum rallied enough to participate in a large patriotic celebration which was recalled by Gilman and reported in several interviews. Gilman reminisced that either in 1894 or 1895 a most enthusiastic celebration, the largest of its kind ever seen in Palm Springs, was given. Gilman resided at the time in Banning.

THE BIG CELEBRATION

He recalled, "Nathan Hargrave and I rode down to the desert on horseback . . . Celebration activities started about 10 o'clock. Ceremonies were held south of the hot springs on Indian Avenue which in those days was the principal street through town. Fireworks were few that year, but there were plenty of foot races and horse races and games. For altogether too many folks, some kegs of beer were the main attraction. Speech making came late in the afternoon. They all gathered around an improvised bunting-trimmed stand placed under the big cottonwood trees which in those days lined both sides of the street for a short distance. Chief man in the athletic contests was a youthful Cahuilla Indian named Lee Arenas — a lithe, beautifully built specimen of young manhood and an exceptionally good runner. He won all the foot races where speed counted. Present that day were Judge McCallum and his son, Harry, Eugene Van Deventer, who grazed cattle through upper Palm Canyon and Pinyon Flats."

Participants came from surrounding communities of Banning, Indio, Garnet and Mission Creek. Some 350 people participated that memorable day and enjoyed free ice cream, lemonade, beer and in quantities to "satisfy the most thirsty."

Horsemen played the game of "Saca el Gallo" in which a $20 bill was tied to the feet of a rooster. The hapless creature was then buried in the sand up to his neck. The horsemen rode by at breakneck speed and bent down to try and pull the rooster out by the head. Whichever rider succeeded in snatching the rooster out of the sand, and then flailing the other riders with it until he managed to unfasten the $20 bill and put it into his pocket, all the while riding at full speed, was declared the winner.

As reported in the newspapers, the big patriotic celebration ended with Judge McCallum reading the Declaration of Independence. Harry McCallum had served as master of ceremonies during the day.

THE CONTINUING DROUGHT

McCALLUM managed to salvage a few citrus and apricot trees from the withering blasts of heat and the drought, which persisted with dreary monotony day after day. The few white settlers were not the only ones to suffer this lack of water. The Indians grew increasingly bitter and complained to their official U. S. Indian Agent.

In 1893 Agent Frances Estudillo wrote in his annual report to Washington: "Their (the Indian) lands are good and fertile, but their water supply is in bad condition. They have suffered seriously this summer losing a large portion of their crops, for want of water to irrigate with . . ."

Again in the report of 1894 Estudillo wrote: "This reservation situated on the desert requires an abundant supply of water during the summer months. All products are from two to six weeks in advance in maturing in this section than elsewhere in Southern California. This has caused venturesome whites to interfere with the Indian's water privileges in what is known as the Toquitch Canyon and the Andreas Canyon. Either of these water sources would furnish sufficient water for the number of Indians using or requiring the use of these waters tributary to the lands they inhabit. I have now under process of settlement an arrangement by which this difficulty will be overcome and the Indians have their just dues . . ."

By July of the following year, the water question of the reservation remained unsettled. Agent Estudillo received a letter from Washington and went to call upon McCallum. The letter instructed Estudillo to give ten days notice to McCallum and others to remove their property from the reservation. Failing in their doing such, the Agent was instructed to take possession of the property at "as little loss as possible to the parties concerned."

The constant harassment of both nature and the government was beginning to take its toll upon Judge McCallum. His health began to fail, but he summoned enough energy and persuasive powers to negotiate the matter with the Agent.

In the midst of these delicate negotiations tragedy which seemed to haunt McCallum, struck again. This time it was his son Wallace.

THE THIRD McCallum son, Wallace, remains almost unknown. He was away studying and traveling most of the time the family was developing the desert property. Only fragmentary mention in family letters and diaries is made concerning his activities and whereabouts.

One of Harry's letters written to Wallace on June 27, 1890, remonstrates with him for not writing:

"Dear Wallace,
"Patience becomes exhausted when one waits months for the letter that never comes and so I write first trusting that it be so dry as not to deserve an answer, i.e. one of those interesting letters descriptive of scenery and mankind, or nature and human nature — which you so clearly bring out. In fact the contents of your answer, whatever they be will no doubt be very acceptable and interesting, especially to myself ..."

By Sept. 24, 1890, Judge McCallum wrote to the Tax Collector of Shasta County:

"Dear Sir:
"Will you please inform me at your earliest convenience whether any tax arrears from the record of your county was assessed for the year 1889-90 against Wallace McCallum. He was interested that year in Sec. 18 in T 41 N or R 2 E, MDM. I will pay for your trouble if you state the amount in your reply.
    "In case the property was sold for delinquent taxes please inform me to whom the redemption money must be paid and the amount.
                    Yours truly,
                    J. G. McCallum"

On this same date the Judge also sent an inquiry to the Register and Receiver U.S. Land Office, Shasta, California, regarding this same property purchased by Wallace, but for which McCallum then held the receipts. Wallace had appeared before a notary in Jefferson County, Kentucky, the previous year and on January 4, 1889, made out a quit-claim deed placing these lots in his father's name.

Wallace's lengthy absences from home and neglect in notifying the family of his whereabouts was a continual worry to the harassed mother. She was distressed over his failing health and drinking problem which had grown worse at the time of Johnny's death. Again Harry wrote to his father: "Wallace's health improving . . . I wrote to him yesterday a letter of five pages and invited him to answer . . . Mother thinks it might be well to start Wallace in some business pursuit, if he and you are willing."

His aversion to steady employment was first indicated in November of 1891, when he refused the appointment of Postmaster for the desert village.

Wallace's heart condition grew increasingly worse, and so correspondingly, did his drinking. During September or October of 1895 he went to Chicago. Six months later at 9 p.m. on March 4, 1896, he died of heart disease brought on by alcoholism. His funeral was held the following day at Oakwood Cemetery, Chicago. He was not quite thirty years old.

Wallace McCallum's name was later engraved upon the tall memorial granite obelisk in the Los Angeles Cemetery where lay the body of his brother Johnny.

The ailing father could take no time to grieve over the death of this son, but continued working as always, finding what little solace life could offer in keeping busy. Emily stayed on in the West Adams home. Pearl was in Chicago at her mother's insistence that she get away from the desert and attend school.

The Judge and Agent Estudillo worked many long hours evolving an equitable plan whereby the Indians as well as the whites could be assured a water supply sufficient to the needs of each. Estudillo was then able to report to Washington, "Many visits to McCallum have been made in order to secure such rights as would benefit the Indians and do justice to all concerned." An agreement was finally arrived at, which was submitted to the Department for action.

There was nothing more to be done. The long wait for officialdom in Washington to read and act upon this agreement began. The drought dragged on. Financial distress for McCallum increased.

WALLACE McCALLUM
Courtesy Palm Springs Desert Museum.

Just how critical the situation was becoming was revealed in a letter McCallum wrote November 19, 1896, from Palm Springs to I. S. Clark, one of the property owners:

"I have yours of recent date. In reply, I would say 'yes, I have a majority of the stock: viz, 3300 of the total of 6000 shares. If offered $3,000 cash for a majority of 6000 shares I might feel tempted to accept it, but I am not prepared to say more on that point. The stock has never sold even in large blocks at less than $20 per share. The last large sale was for $25 per share and since then about $8 or $9,000.00 has been expended on the system, which was much improved.'

"Referring to my proposition to you, it is important that I should have a prompt answer as the time has come for me to act."

Clark must have been one of the property owners who had simply walked out and abandoned his land for the Judge continued his letter by stating:

"I visited your land last week after writing to you. Your alfalfa looks well and all of it can be saved . . . About 15 head of cattle were pasturing on it. I was told they belonged to somebody who stops above the White-Water ranch. Not being herded they go to our main ditch for water and damage it by pushing the stones into it . . . I saw your agricultural implements also. They seemed all right except for being in the sun . . . . If not prepared to accept my offer make me an offer and decide as promptly as possible. It is plain to me that it is our plain mutual interest to cooperate and I have no desire to speculate in the water — as my former letter will show.

Very respy,
J. G. McCallum"

THE FATEFUL DECISION

THE NEW YEAR came and still no word arrived concerning Washington's decision on the agreement. When the report came, the carefully worked out agreement had been ignored. The decision was entirely in favor of the Indians. McCallum and the other whites were entirely cut off from their water supply coming from the Tahquitz and Andreas Canyons.

The blow was too much for his weakened heart. John McCallum succumbed without medical attention on Feb. 5, 1897, in Palm Springs.

The custom down in that little desert settlement when a death occurred was to wrap the deceased in blankets and transport him to the Seven Palms railroad station to await the arrival of a Banning undertaker and casket. The undertaker performed the required routine of preparation for burial and the remains then were returned to Palm Springs for interment. Judge McCallum was denied the privilege of returning to his beloved Palm Springs.

Certain other events had to take place before he could be laid to rest. The coroner's jury listened to Coroner Dr. D. C. Sherman's diagnosis and declared that John G. McCallum, 70, a lawyer from Los Angeles, had died of "natural causes and not contagious."

He was released to friends who escorted his body to his grieving widow in Los Angeles. The daughter Pearl had been sent a telegram which stated that her father had suffered a sun stroke. She arrived from Chicago in time to attend the funeral on Feb. 10, 1897. The fact of her father's failing in health during the last two years had been carefully concealed from her.

Repeatedly throughout her long life, Pearl was to say in grief-stricken bewilderment, "He'd never been sick a day in his life. He lost his boy, John, and then his son, Wallace died, and there was this drought. It couldn't have been anything but a broken heart."

*   *   *   *   *

John Guthrie McCallum died believing himself to be a failure. His work had collapsed into nothingness, so he thought, and his dreams of a desert paradise where people could come and find health and happiness thwarted and destroyed. It remained for his daughter Pearl to carry on and bring those dreams into reality.

As she stood by the graveside in Rosedale Cemetery that wintery day in Los Angeles when her father was buried near Johnny, Pearl recalled his words often said to her, "Pay the taxes. Hold onto the land."

The land became her love, her obsession, her life.

Part Three

The Steadfast Dream

An outing in Tahquitz Canyon.
Courtesy
Marjorie Forline Stephens.

25.

Into a New Era

THE EXCITEMENT of witnessing the ending of one century and the expectation of greater things to come in the new swept across the nation. For the McCallum family the long span of years during the 19th century, from 1826, the year of his birth, to the time of his death in 1897, was the story of the dreams and disappointments of John Guthrie McCallum. During the next years, and long into the 20th century, their saga would tell of the struggle, especially by Pearl, to bring the father's hopes into reality.

One month to the day after John Guthrie McCallum died intestate, a judge of the Superior Court in Los Angeles appointed Harry McCallum administrator of his father's estate.

The property affected by this decree was described as follows:

"To wit: Personally,

"Cash on hand $4.71: Store accounts and stock of goods in General Merchandise Store at Palm Springs, Riverside County, State of California: Furniture and fixtures in "Hillside House" at said Palm Springs, as follows: books, Japanese whatnot, rocker reclining chair, plush lounge, carpet, six rugs, two bedroom sets, four leather chairs, cot, dining room table, six dining room chairs, kitchen stove, utensils, etc. Furniture and fixtures in "Ranch House" at Palm Springs, Riverside County, California as follows: carpet, two fancy tables, one lounge rattan rocker, six dining chairs, dining table, side-board, kitchen stove, utensils, etc. three bedroom sets, three porch chairs, marble top sideboard: tools, materials, livestock etc., on "McCallum Ranch," at Palm Springs, Riverside County, California, as follows: hayrake, tools, phaeton, grind-stone, anvil etc. box shooks, light wagon, lumber, mower, buggy, two carts, two cultivators, old implements worn out, scraper, two plows, two harrows, chickens, wheelbarrow, new wagon, large old wagon, hay harness, hay press, six horses, two mules, two cows, one heifer, one calf, office desk, etc. one watch and chain, diamond stud, one pair cuff buttons.

"Two hundred and fifty (250) shares of preferred stock of Bear Valley Irrigation Company, with coupons numbered 4 to 201; certificate of proof of claims

Judge John G. McCallum's desk. Now owned by Mr. and Mrs. F. Thomas Kieley of Palm Springs.

against the Pacific Bank of San Francisco, California, No. 919, for $3853.63 less 30% of dividends paid thereon, three thousand three hundred and twenty eight and ⅝ (3328⅝) shares of the capital stock of the Palm Valley Water Company, a corporation organized under the laws of the State of California."

This personal property went to the widow along with one half of the real property. According to the Decree of Distribution dated January 25, 1898, the three children, May, Harry, and Pearl, each received one sixth of the land. Harry and Pearl immediately deeded their complete share back to the mother, but May sold a portion of her allotment for approximately $10,000. This was a blow to Pearl. She never became reconciled to what she considered to be a regrettable act committed by her sister when she sold 140 acres and thus ignored her father's admonitions to hold on to the land.

The sisters had never been close, but the breach widened and never healed.

Young Harry took his duties as head of the family seriously. He found there was an outstanding debt of $2,500 against the estate. The Judge had borrowed this money for the restoration of the badly damaged water canal. Next to his concern over his mother and sisters, protecting the flow of water became Harry's greatest anxiety.

On October 2, 1897, as president of the Palm Valley Water Company, he filed upon the waters of Chino Canyon (West Canyon) as shown in Book 1, Page 184 of the Water Claims of Riverside County. The purpose of this filing was to correct any possible errors in the previous filing. Apparently, at this time, a four-inch pipeline was laid from this canyon to a small reservoir in Section 3, T4S, SBB&M. The water when available was to be distributed from that point to the twenty-three consumers then living in the village of Palm Springs.

Water, or lack of it, continued to be an urgent problem for which there appeared to be no solution. The long drought continued. The little village languished as reports reached the McCallums in Los Angeles of many cases of typhoid and other fevers brought on by impure, dreggy waters on the Morongo and Agua Caliente Reservations. The Indian Agent reported to Washington that the death of Judge McCallum had left the water situation but partly solved.

The following year the Los Angeles City Directory carried the entries:

McCALLUM ESTATE—H. F. McCALLUM, trustee, 335 Wilcox Bldg., 206 S. Spring St.

McCallum, Harry—Pres. Palm Valley Water Co. and trustee McCallum Estate, 335 Wilcox Bldg., 206 S. Spring, residence 1049 W. 7th Street.

It was from these offices that young Harry endeavored to carry on with the McCallum problems.

At Emily's insistence Pearl continued with her education. Lacking sufficient funds for her to return to the Stone School in Chicago, Pearl finished the semester at the Marlborough School for young ladies in Los Angeles.

Palm Canyon.

149

26.

Miss Pearl McCallum

Miss Pearl McCallum
in gymnasium suit,
Friday, March 18, 1898.
Marlborough Field.

THERE IS a photograph taken, according to the inscription written upon the back, on Friday, March 18, 1898. It is of Miss Pearl McCallum in gymnasium suit, standing upon the Marlborough athletic field.

This costume consisted of voluminous black bloomers, black blouse with leg-of-mutton sleeves, black cotton stockings and tennis shoes. The dark wavy tresses were firmly held in place by tight braids topped by a large ribbon bow. In the girl's right hand, tucked against her side, was a basketball.

Marlborough, the famous finishing school for young ladies, was very proud of its basketball team newly organized but two years previous. In fact, the school itself was but ten years old, having been first established in Pasadena and then moved to Los Angeles by its founder, Mrs. Mary S. Caswell.

As one studies the picture of the fresh-faced, round cheeked, pretty young woman, it is noticeable that the deep-set eyes have a mature, pensive and contemplative look. The soft lips are firmly set. The girl appears to have withdrawn into some inner recess.

This expression is to be found in marked evidence in many photographs taken of Pearl McCallum McManus during her long lifetime. It is as though, one assumes, she was always with a group, but never actually part of it. She was to become an elderly, greatly honored and respected lady of Palm Springs, but this same expression of deep thoughtfulness, often with a slight shadow of sadness would be evident in most of her pictures.

An energetic game showing the Marlborough team in action! Courtesy Marjorie Forline Stephens.

But, at the time of the above-mentioned picture, Pearl was undoubtedly, along with the more than sixty other young ladies attending Marlborough, basking in the inspiration of the amazing woman directing the school. Mrs. Mary S. Caswell, widowed early, and left with a small daughter to support, brought to her teaching some of the granite qualities of her beloved New England. She was an able teacher with an outstanding ability of presenting academic subjects or questions of manners and morals with an unusual twist which made them unforgettable.

"In the early days," wrote one of the former Marlborough students, "Mrs. Caswell was not interested in making of us college material. Being a lady was of greater importance than the completion of a broad education."

Such an educational philosophy would seemingly have little to offer such a girl as Pearl who had a life of freedom roaming over the desert on horseback, unbound by strict circumspection, and would do nothing to prepare her for the hard times ahead. Yet, undoubtedly, the influence of the stern admonitions and rigorous life rules Mrs. Caswell imparted to her young charges, made a lasting impression upon Pearl.

Life at Marlborough, located at Twenty-third Street in Los Angeles, and with the wide verandas on the frame building, was to be but a brief respite from the rigors and tragedies of Pearl's life. Much as she loved being there, Pearl was destined to be at Marlborough but one year.

Marlborough School, 1897. Courtesy Marlborough School.

Today most of her classmates are gone, but of those remaining few recall the shy, awkward, frightened young woman, still grieving for her lost father, who came to the school at an age when most of the students were graduating. Pearl was nineteen. They remember how threadbare her clothing was and how much they wanted to share their dresses with her.

Unidentified tennis-playing friends and Pearl McCallum. Marlborough classmates?

Memories of the school remained with Pearl always and she would recall as did another Marlborough girl who wrote, "The Marlborough Violets (non-boarding day students) arrived at eight-thirty by bicycle, horse and carriage, pony cart, horse car or cable car. Then there were chapel prayers, roll call, ten minutes of calisthenics in long wool skirts that dusted the floor, swishing petticoats, stiff collars and rigid boned corsets restraining waists to eighteen inches — The most enjoyable time of the day was the hour after dinner when the girls sat by the fireside with their embroidery while Mrs. Caswell read to them." Sometimes, during Mrs. Caswell's hour, she lovingly lectured to her girls, often warning them against being "fuzzy minded."

The remarks Mrs. Caswell made to one of the graduating classes stayed firmly imbedded in Pearl's memory. "Be each of you," admonished the school leader, "day by day, the noblest woman that your present circumstance call you to be; live up to your present needs, your present growth. So, only as you stand strong where you are, will the next step be made clear. So, only shall you come to the true woman's kingdom."

Pearl became strong. There would be no shedding of tears for her.
Those would be reserved for her mother whose failing health required
them to remain in Los Angeles to be near the doctors. Pearl once recalled
that, "Mother never recovered from heart break of Johnny's death,
then Wallace died, and this was followed by the sudden death of her
husband. She was a beautiful woman, with a lovely singing voice, but
she was a little girl woman — not a pioneer. She did the best she could
in this strange and, to her, relentless world, and when it was unbearable
she cried like a little girl."

It would be eight long years before Pearl returned to the adobe home
she loved. Meanwhile she had a living to earn, a sickly mother to care
for, all the while doing everything possible to assist Harry in the salvag-
ing of the meager estate left by her father.

THE Los Angeles City Directory for 1900-1901 contained a revealing TEACHING DAYS
listing for the McCallum Family:

McCallum, Emily—1004 Florida
McCallum, Harry—Pres. Nome Co-operative Gold Mining Co.—1004 Florida
McCallum, Pearl—Teacher L.A. School of Dramatic Art—1004 Florida

All traces of whatever structure that once existed at 1004 Florida
Street have been removed long since, and the lot upon which it stood
is presently a parking lot in the shade of the towering pillars supporting
the roaring traffic hurtling along the Harbor Freeway. From the appearance of the nearby buildings still standing we assume that it was one
of those rangy two-storied rooming house types so prevalent during
the 1880's and 90's in Los Angeles. The McCallums possibly lived
above the classrooms of the School of Dramatic Art.

This school, run by Mr. and Mrs. George Dobson, incorporated in
1899 under the laws of the State of California, was affiliated with the
Emerson College of Oratory at Boston. No record exists which reveals
exactly what subjects Pearl McCallum taught, but a small brochure
tucked in the files of the Los Angeles Public Library lists Mr. and Mrs.
Dobson as conducting the courses in dramatic reading, humorous dialect,
voice culture, public speaking, interpretive delivery of poetry and prose,
with personal reminiscences being given of Dickens and Thackeray.

Other courses listed in the brochure include: hygienic and character
building, right habits of living, dynamic breathing and function of the

lungs, physical culture and gesture. Because of her enthusiasm for the outdoors and her love of horses and horseback riding, it might very well be assumed that Pearl taught some phase of the Physical Culture aspects of the school curriculum.

Then, too, she had been summoned from the Stone School in Chicago at the time of her father's death. The sole existing record of such a school in Chicago at the turn of the century was one by the name of Stone School of Scientific Physical Culture at the 16th Street Masonic Temple. This school did not continue for any great length of time and there is no record listing the names of any students who attended there. It is a marked coincidence that Pearl was in Chicago at the time there was a school by the name of Stone listing in its curriculum the same subjects later found being part of the instruction of the Los Angeles School of Dramatic Art when she was on the faculty. The drama school moved to larger quarters in a new building on South Hope Street between 10th and 11th and the name changed to Dobson School of Expression during 1903-04.

By this time, all the McCallum names were missing from the Los Angeles City Directory.

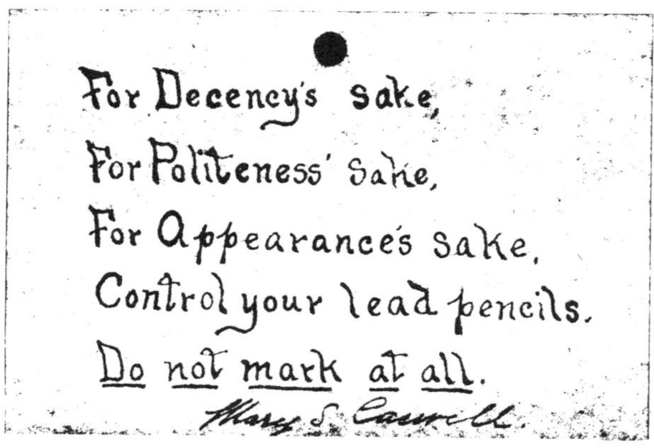

A typical gentle remonstrance
printed by Mrs. Caswell to guide her students.
Courtesy Marlborough School.

27.

Harry McCallum

A VERY lonely young man, burdened with responsibilities too heavy to bear, wrote in his diary, dating the entry February 8, 1899. Harry F. McCallum turned to the pages of his personal record to find release in pouring out his thoughts. The ink is faded and the pages of his diary are water stained, but the plaintive story has been preserved:

"Over two years since the last writing herein! On February 5, 1897 my father died of heart failure leaving my mother, two sisters—May and Pearl—and myself the last of the family. Words of mine cannot describe the changes since. Yes, it was a terrible affliction and now it is a great loss. Many years ago we were all carefree. We were ambitious and life was the usual thing which most people have found it to be. Then our time came commencing in 1891 when Johnnie died. Next my health broke and is delicate to this day. Then May married and left us to live in Chicago, which was not a trouble but it was another of the steps which were breaking up our old home. Then the country had a financial panic and times became hard with us . . .

(Note: Two lines blurred by water stain and are undecipherable)

the expense of maintaining a burdensome water company and an unproductive ranch. Yet mostly matters have been easy since June of last year as my credit appears to be good. Mother and Pearl have had everything they wished for. At present the ranch is paying a little and the store and Post Office well. After a hard fight I was appointed P.M. here in June of 1897. The water company expenses are reduced to a minimum and there is a good prospect of disposing of the White Water River owned by the Company at a good price. The reason of the financial pressure is that Palm Valley has ceased to improve and is going backward. It being proved that after all it is a desert region and not much of a fruit region. The Water Company depends upon the planting in Palm Valley and all the stockholders depend upon the Company. The McCallum interests consist principally of this stock. We were hard pressed for the expenses of maintaining the company's ditches, and protecting its water rights remained nearly the same as when more land was irrigated, and this deficit was raised by stock assessment. I am President of the Company and upon realizing that Palm

Valley could never support the Company, I tried to dispose of one of our water rights to other places — the White Water River Company, the company's other water source for the use of Palm Valley, which would be abundantly supplied therewith. This matter kept me pretty busy and some prospect of success has come our way. In 1897 I negotiated with three different canaigre companies, but they all quit doing business as their experiment in raising canaigre proved a failure. Then one company spring from these and I negotiated with them
(Note: two lines blurred by water stain)
route of the line of conduits. One company paid $1,000 for an option on December 1 to purchase for $15,000 in cash and certain first mortgage bonds, but failed to take it up. I am now trying to force them to and meanwhile I am looking into the question of advertising and selling direct to Redlands City and water power to the S.P. R.R.

"My father had been failing for two or three years before his death but his mind was as strong and vigorous as ever.

"My mother and my sister, Pearl, have been here for three months and my sister, May (Mrs. Dr. Forline), arrived two weeks ago to remain until Dr. Forline can close up his business in Chicago and come to California to settle. The health and prospects of all of us are very good, excepting my slight cough. —

"There has come in an era of things which promise well. For instance, my health is infinitely better while last year I had repeated attacks of congestion of the lungs and began raising blood. Then financial matters are promising. The health of my two sisters and my mother is splendid and they are in fine spirits.

"In addition to all the changes in our fate and fortunes during the recent past, there have also been great changes in larger matters and public affairs. Southern California has been going ahead rapidly and a boom is predicted within two years — a healthy boom. Then the U.S. itself has just had a war with Spain, defeating that country overwhelmingly within three months, and a treaty of peace has just been ratified granting to us the Philippine Islands, and Puerto Rico and also Cuba —"

*　　*　　*　　*　　*

The segment of the journal came to an abrupt end with the mention of the war. Harry evidently was too busy with family business affairs to write at length in his diary again for some time.

No picture of the industrious and serious-minded young man is to be found among family portraits. The Great Register of Riverside County for 1896 listed Harry McCallum as being a resident of Palm City Precinct (consisting of 19 registered voters). He was 25 years old at the time and was described as having gray eyes, dark hair, dark complexion, and being six feet in height.

156

TAHQUITZ FALLS

J. Smeaton Chase photographer. Courtesy Palm Springs Historical Society.

28.

The Bleak Future

THE NEW CENTURY, long awaited by a nation tired of war, finally became a reality. Despite the jubilation of the country, the year 1900 found the remnants of the McCallum family at low ebb. Keeping Los Angeles as their home base, the three managed to make occasional trips to the desert place and visits to Chicago.

The financial stress was slightly relieved when mother Emily sold one lot — the site of the present Palm Springs Community Church. Her failing health required her to be mostly in Los Angeles under doctor's care. Although not regularly dwelling in Palm Springs, it was during this year that Emily performed the one public service of her life. When the little wooden school house was erected in Palm Springs, probably at Dr. Welwood Murray's insistence, he, Mrs. John Guthrie McCallum, and a Mr. Blanchard, with the designated Board of Trade, acted as the first committee to handle all negotiations with the Riverside authorities.

Palm Springs School (before 1906). Courtesy Palm Springs Historical Society.

The summer of 1901 was a sad one for the McCallums as well as for the village of Palm Springs. M. French Gilman wrote in his diary that while the McCallums were in Chicago he served as postmaster and was in charge of the store. He and the mail carrier were the only white residents in Palm Springs that summer.

While they were visiting in Chicago, tragedy again struck the McCallums. On the 19th day of September, at about 1 a.m. while a resident at 3907 Prairie Avenue, Harry F. McCallum, age 30, died of pulmonary tuberculosis. The fourth son of Emily and John Guthrie McCallum to meet an untimely death was cremated in that far off city.

Harry left a brief holographic will written the same year of his father's death, in which he simply stated: "I give and devise all my estate, of every name and nature whatsoever to my mother. I nominate and appoint my mother, Mrs. J. G. McCallum, the executrix of this, my last will and testament, without bond. Dated this 23rd day of Dec. A. D. 1897. Signed, Harry F. McCallum."

The Superior Court of Los Angeles granted a Letter of Administration to G. C. Edwards on February 25, 1904, who claimed that the estate had filed notice to the creditors that Harry McCallum had died showing no property on hand for distribution. His estate, when the will was finally probated by Pearl nineteen years later on October 29, 1923, consisted mainly of real property valued at approximately $23,962.56. While Harry's property had been distributed to Emily by court decree and then subsequently by her to her daughter, it was necessary for Pearl to take this late action to quiet title.

On the way to a picnic in Palm Canyon: Pearl driving Mrs. Jarvis Barlow of Los Angeles, Mrs. McKenzie, and Jack Forline.
Courtesy Palm Springs Desert Museum.

The bereft women, without financial guidance of father or son, faced a bleak future and sought means of obtaining some sources of livelihood. Their sole negotiable asset, apart from their land, was the water system badly in need of repairs which financially they were totally unable to accomplish. Of necessity they were forced to sell their family's controlling shares in the Palm Valley Water Company to liquidate a debt and obtain money for sustenance.

They made the sacrifice not only for themselves, but for the welfare of the village. Had they not done so, the vital irrigation water might have been lost. Because of no repairs having been made on the flume as was required by California law, they were in danger of having to forfeit their claims. Fortunately they were able to sell to Ralph Rogers, a Los Angeles promoter from the Garvanza area. Rogers in turn, by repeating

the superhuman efforts Judge McCallum had undergone years before, with Indian help managed to make the necessary repairs with but three weeks to spare. The water system changed hands several times during the ensuing years until today domestic and irrigation water is supplied to Palm Springs and environs by the Desert Water Agency and the Whitewater Mutual Water Company.

Pearl began the long, often painful, struggle to hold the land for which she believed her father had sacrificed his life.

29.
The Lonely Struggle

SUDDENLY, the long drought ended. The rains started again and water flowed in the streams and through the stone-lined irrigation ditch.

Mother McCallum, despite fearing and mistrusting the desert, returned to Palm Springs. Shortly afterwards Pearl also returned to her beloved adobe home and found complete devastation and chaos.

Along with the ordeal of caring for her widowed and invalided mother, Pearl faced coping with a ranch which had reverted almost to its original state of desert wasteland. During the years the family remained absent, disinterested and untrustworthy employees neglected the place until there were left only the grapes, a few bearing apricots, and a half acre of very choice orange trees. Pearl carried buckets of water and managed to save and harvest the small crop which yielded between $300 and $400. This was their sole income for the year except for the pittance they received when Pearl hired the Indians to cut down the dead apricot trees to be sold as firewood.

Pearl tried to supplement the small sum received from the firewood by picking the remnants of fruit and carrying it on either side of her saddle as she rode around selling to the Indians and neighbors.

Dr. Welwood Murray, brooding all the while over his parched trees and shrubs, in a gesture of desperate defiance against the restrictive mandate from Washington, D.C., opened the sluice gates one night and watered his garden, after vowing that he would keep it alive with his own tears if necessary. When he diverted the last trickle of forbidden water in the flume to the roots of his dying trees, the water gates were again locked. Murray, it is said, went out with an axe and broke open the locked gates. An indignant delegation of the Indians sped on horseback to the Agent in Banning to present their case for water rights. It was then that the fateful decision granting the water solely to the Indians was enforced.

A flash flood intervened to postpone the water crisis, but when the

Pearl McCallum.

rains stopped the struggle for the water was resumed. The whites, under the cover of darkness, again opened the sluice gates, so frantic were they for irrigation water.

Pearl recounted this tragic period in a legal deposition given when the water rights were being adjudicated in 1911:

"From the occupancy of the McCallum Ranch by white men and the development of water with building of the big ditch by white men to the year 1904, the water was justly controlled by them, but as the Indians had lived here in the valley first and although they had little or nothing under cultivation, the first 30 inches was always allowed them. Later on when they, the Indians, had planted from 5 to 18 acres we willingly gave them the first 40 inches.

"In 1904, however, through a misunderstanding the government represented by the attorney for the Indians, Mr. Collier of Riverside, issued an order stating that no white man should touch the ditch or use the water under threat of arrest. This order was the consequence of a report that a certain white man located on other property in the village had used some of the first 30 inches for irrigation purposes. The attorney, Mr. Collier, has personally told me that the order was related to the first 30 inches only and should have stood only until the rains came, as he knew that the Indians had no further right to the water. The order was, however, very naturally interpreted by all as it read and later when there were thousands of inches of water running to waste on the desert, and flooding the streets, etc., by Federal decree the white people were not allowed to touch the water.

"Previous to this, and due to the great drought so well known to Californians that lasted so many years, the ranch had gradually been dying.

"In 1904, due to Mr. Collier's order not to use the water, the trees began to wither and a George Blackburn, passing through the village, noticed the dying

The long drought ended leaving the apricot orchards dry and fit merely to be cut up and sold for firewood. Courtesy Palm Springs Desert Museum.

162

Two years after the devastating drought had ended. Struggling Palm Springs had few settlers and land was cheap. Courtesy Palm Springs Historical Society.

trees and offered to take all chances of being arrested, assisted and offered to irrigate them at his own risk and expense. This he was allowed to do but later Mr. Mendon, a tourist, stated it was an outrage upon the part of the government to cause Mrs. McCallum to lose the trees with quantities of water running through her own ranch, and that he should irrigate the trees in spite of everyone. He was threatened but removed the water gate, hid it, and turned the water into the grove for two days. But the water had come too late and the trees died. Upon my arrival in 1905 I found the leaves yellowed and dry and the trunks with bark mostly peeled off."

Pearl's bitterness towards misguided government officials was very keen when she thought of the twenty years of labor and sacrifice that had gone into the McCallum Ranch (the first to develop and use the waters) and the tremendous loss of income to herself and her widowed mother. She believed it was unjust that the government failed to protect the invalid widow. Her dismay was compounded when the attorney, Mr. Collier, stated in her presence that he was "sorry" such a blunder had been made and then ordered the water turned on again. All too late, the trees were dead and the vineyards too far gone to bear well again for years.

A woman Agent was appointed for the Mission Agency who pursued the water problem "far exceeding her authority and to the detriment of all — the white settlers, the Indians, and the Government," wrote Pearl.

This Agent went so far as to have policemen patrolling the ditch to enforce her orders that no white man should touch the ditch or take water under penalty of arrest and probability of forever losing the use of the water. The ditch was broken in two places, and although repairing these breaks was but a simple matter requiring less than a half day's work, this was not done and the water was permitted to run wildly over the desert for some months.

While her bitterness towards uninformed, interfering government officials never abated, Pearl's affection and high regard for the Indians remained steadfast. They returned her friendship until the end of her life. She sincerely believed there was no problem concerning water, land, or whatever, which could not have been amicably settled between the McCallum family and the Indians had they been left alone and permitted to evolve a fair solution.

So outstanding was this mutual regard between the McCallums and the Cahuillas, John Raymond Gabbert in writing the History of Riverside City and County deemed it worthy of mention. He told of the jolly holiday celebration during the Christmas season of 1927 when Pearl entertained old Indian friends in the Fiesta House in memory of good old days. Many of the old Indians of the days of her father, or their descendants, attended. In appreciation of the events of gone-by days, the Indians entertained with songs and dances.

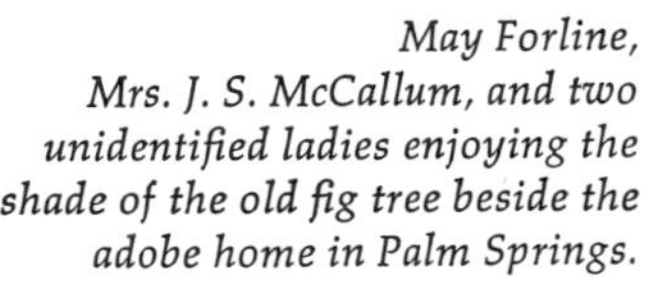

May Forline, Mrs. J. S. McCallum, and two unidentified ladies enjoying the shade of the old fig tree beside the adobe home in Palm Springs.

In the midst of all the anxieties over her mother's health, and the constant difficulties with water problems, Pearl again underwent the tragedy of death in her family. This time it was her sister, May, the last of the McCallum children who had evidently been permanently weakened by the severe typhoid attack so long ago in San Francisco.

The Forline family had moved from Chicago and settled in Redlands. Mother McCallum upon occasion visited her elder daughter but the coolness between the two sisters continued until May's final illness. Pearl rushed to her sister's bedside. When May, realizing that she was dying said to Pearl "Take the baby," three-year-old, sunny little Marjorie Forline became her "Auntie Pearl's" constant companion and helper for the next thirty or more years.

According to Pearl's personal records, the next grievous water situation arose after the heavy rains of September 1, 1910, visited the desert. This storm would not have wrought any havoc had the "intake" gate controlling the flow of water into the ditch been replaced by the government. With no controlling gate "an enormous head of water roared down the line of the ditch, tearing out the dam, sweeping north and east diagonally across the 20 acres where formerly grew the apricot trees, thence down Park Avenue, then back across the 20-acre field following the White Water Canal, breaking through that and tearing a great hole; then northeast through a five-acre field into Park Street again and out on Main Street (Palm Canyon Drive)."

A rare photograph of little Marjorie Forline, age five, and her grandmother Emily McCallum taken under the old pepper tree by the adobe home. Dr. Jaeger later was to tutor Marjorie in the shade of this tree. Photograph taken about 1910. Courtesy Marjorie Forline Stephens.

The missing gate was the cause of the first wash. The second washout, or enlargement of the first, was caused, according to her written report, by "deteriorate action of government men."

"The first week in January, 1911, the Government sent under Mr. Oldberg and Mr. Makosky, boss of field work, a gang of men to construct a new cement pipe and stone ditch to carry Tahquitz water to white people and Indians. Permission was very gladly given for the Government men to camp upon the McCallum Ranch. From the first it was evident that the men in charge were prejudiced against the owners of the property although they had never met them before; this being shown in many little ways and a total disregard for the welfare of the property."

The crew needed water for personal use and for mixing sand and concrete. Pearl continued her account, "A large head was allowed to come down from the Canyon and this was *deliberately* turned out of the old ditch just south of the southwest corner of the ranch where it became an uncontrolled wild stream that ran through the broken dam through the entire length of the wash causing it to be greatly widened in all places, deepened in some and filled with tons and tons of white sand in others. This water ran directly in front of the Government camp and the men therefore saw from day to day the havoc the water was creating."

Pearl remonstrated with the gang boss who ignored her protests. The water was permitted to rampage until it worked its way out to the main street of the town and gutted and tore it up so severely cars could not drive over it. The waters ran crazily over the land for three months, washing out and practically ruining the McCallum Ranch. "The white sand deposited can never be carried away," lamented Pearl, "and good soil can never be substituted for what has been washed away."

"In all fairness to the men doing the work," she wrote, "The work the Government has done with the new ditch and pipe has been very good and both my mother and myself esteem the men in charge for their proficiency and we have done all in our power to facilitate the work. But this is our home and practically all we have left in the world and the income derived from it is our only living. We have held it through years of hardship and care and sorrow looking forward always to the day when the water question could finally be settled with fairness and consideration for all, Indians and whites alike; with the happy possibility of restoring the fields once more to their original cultivation and beauty.

"Instead, we have at our door acres and acres of devastated land that can never be made the same, and the knowledge that this was caused by the carelessness for the need of a water gate and secondly, by the deliberate indifference of those in charge of land that is, indeed our all."

Pearl for years carried on the water struggle alone until other residents, under the leadership of Nellie Coffman, undertook lengthy litigation against the Federal Government which eventuated in a settlement fair to all concerned.

Picnickers enjoying the shade of the cottonwood tree
beside the murmuring waters of Tahquitz ditch.

30.
The Fruit of Sunshine

"It was an experience that comes and goes like a mirage on the desert," Pearl once said when recalling the sorrowful early tragedy-stalked days of family travail and the furious assaults from nature. She continued, "During the drought our ranch began to revert to the desert, leaving only a few vines and some old trees which I was able to care for personally. As I lived on, a new aspect of the desert came to me and the desert gave forth with a new and equally precious substance to sustain interest and life. I choose to call it the fruit of sunshine, for it seemed that the people who came here, and particularly those who came to stay, reflect a rare quality of genuine friendship."

These were the words of an 80-year old woman who had mellowed in her outlook and had either forgotten, or had chosen not to recollect the bitter days of her rejection and suspicion of newcomers to Palm Springs. Friendship did not come easily to Pearl during those early days.

Carl Eytel, first artist to come to Palm Springs. Courtesy Palm Springs Historical Society.

At 26 years of age she returned to Palm Springs to make it her permanent home. There was but a handful of residents and scarcely anyone her age with whom she could have formed a friendship had her shyness and reserve permitted. She found it difficult to converse with even those who had known her father and family for many years. She made the acquaintance of two men who became her sincere friends.

Camping in one of the canyons on her land where the Tahquitz stream musically tossed its way down the mountainside, Pearl came upon an interloper when she returned after her long absence. This was a "Little slouch of a man with a big brush of a mustache, long sideburns, and baggy pants" as George Wharton James described him. Carl Eytel, educated in Stuttgart, Germany, was the first of the many artists who would come to paint the beauties of the desert. He had worked his way West as a cowboy.

Eytel, a poverty-stricken waif, lacked funds to buy paint and canvases for his pictures. He lived precariously in a small 6 x 8 redwood shake cabin with a single cot, a small home-made unpainted wood table, and his painting paraphernalia. Of necessity he slept outdoors for lack of space. All cooking, which was very little, had to be done over an open, outdoor fire ringed around with a few small smoke-blackened rocks. Mostly Eytel relied upon canned milk as his staple diet since he did not like to take time to cook and frequently had not the money to buy food.

This shy, strange little man loved the desert with the same fierce intensity Pearl felt. Always withdrawn and lonely, Pearl felt none of the hesitancy to converse with Eytel that she underwent with other people in the village. He loved the small creatures as she did. He held every plant in reverence and with Eytel Pearl could talk of the wonders of the many-hued glowing desert sunrises and smoldering sunsets.

It was Eytel who said when asked why he remained so long upon the desert, "Just so I may learn to paint some time, one tiny bit of its spirit, in peace—"

Eytel came to the California desert in the fall of 1898. It was, he said, "A spot with which I am very much in love." He could look far upon the peaks of mighty mountains, at the changing glow of venerable hills, and feast his vision upon ironwood, smoke trees and cactus, and forget the meagerness of his habitation.

Eytel became acquainted with everyone in the village despite his shyness because there were so few to know. He was always pressed by poverty as was Pearl during those hard days. She did what she could to help and encourage him even to deeding him the property upon which his tiny shack was built.

He sold little sketches and hand-painted Christmas cards to anyone who could buy them. Gradually his work attracted the attention of important men visiting Palm Springs and he did book illustrations in 1906 for George Wharton James, author of *The Wonders of the Desert* and other books.

The friendship between the little recluse artist, hiding the scars life had inflicted upon him and who found life cruel almost beyond endurance, and the lonely, overly burdened young woman deepened into a close friendship. It was not until Eytel proposed marriage that Pearl realized such a relationship would be wrong for both of them. Eytel left Palm Springs and went to New Mexico, returning some years later to die and be buried in the Indian cemetery in Palm Springs. He had penciled a note upon the deed to the property Pearl gave him years before

George Wharton James and Carl Eytel gathering material for James's books on the desert. Courtesy Palm Springs Desert Museum.

Dr. Edmund Jaeger, botanist and world-renowned desert authority and Pearl's good friend. Courtesy Palm Springs Historical Society.

which stated that upon his death he wished the property to revert back to Mrs. Pearl McCallum McManus.

The second man whose friendship was to become so meaningful to Pearl came to Palm Springs some years later. One day this small, learned man appeared and asked her permission to set up his camp in the cottonwood trees at the back of the adobe. Edmund Jaeger, a young botanist, eventually became the village school teacher for the handful of white and Indian children. Pearl shared his enthusiasm for desert plants and when Jaeger organized the Nature Club, she opened her home for the meetings. Their friendship continued until the day of her death.

Dr. Jaeger recalls that Pearl was generous to those she liked and, when not stricken with migraine, enjoyed inviting neighbors to come for chip-beef gravy dinner. Fresh meat was hard to come by and was to be had only when an infrequent supply arrived by train from Banning.

One of his favorite recollections of those days was the time he did something which aroused Pearl's ire after she had invited him to a chicken dinner.

"Now, a chicken dinner was something to look forward to in those days," recalled 83-year old Dr. Jaeger in his home in Riverside, "I went believing that Pearl would have forgotten the incident which had upset her, but as soon as I stepped inside the adobe she gave me a dressing

170

*Entrance gates to
Nellie Coffman's
boardinghouse, 1910.*

down I never forgot. I began to think she was going to order me from
her house. When she finally ran out of words, she served dinner, but I
knew I was still in disgrace when she gave me just the neck of the
chicken!"

The world-renowned botanist and desert authority chuckled fondly
as he spoke of his friendship with Pearl during those days. "She really
could be very kind and generous, but I have to laugh every time I think
of that chicken dinner. How like Pearl that was."

Pearl always found she could converse with greater ease with men
than women. As she gained in wealth and prestige during the years,
many famous men, especially those in financial circles, sought her advice
and shared their business acumen with her. Among these were the men
of the Du Pont family. Perhaps she thought women posed a threat to
her in some way.

The first woman to upset Pearl was an ebullient, energetic, strong-
willed person named Nellie Coffman. Mrs. Coffman arrived with her
two small sons during a fierce desert wind storm in December of 1908.
Despite the ravages of nature, Mrs. Coffman became enchanted with
the desert and soon returned determined to open a hotel.

The story goes that the Coffman family stayed at Murray's Hotel
and the wily old Scot, disappointed at her refusal to buy his hostelry,

*Nellie Coffman, developer of the
famed Desert Inn and "patron
saint" of Palm Springs. Picture
taken when she was seventy years
old. Courtesy
Palm Springs Historical Society.*

Tahquitz irrigation ditch running through the grounds of the Desert Inn and beside one of Nellie Coffman's tent house accommodations, about 1913 or 1914. Courtesy Palm Springs Desert Museum.

fed her upon tea and prunes and then insisted upon her washing the dishes. Mrs. Coffman refused to be distracted from her purpose and went ahead and bought the piece of property directly across the dirt lane from Murray. Using the structure already upon the ground as rooms for her guests, she brought tent houses from Los Angeles and thus began in 1909 what has since become known as the "Sanitarium Era" in Palm Springs history. Word soon spread of the good care and superb food at "Nellie's Boarding House" as she laughingly called it, and it became the mecca for "lungers."

More and more people came to the Desert Inn and these understood that outside the fence they might have "tuberculosis," but as soon as they stepped inside Nellie's fence, it was "bronchitis." So wide had her fame grown, Mrs. Coffman no longer wanted her inn to be known merely as a sanitarium. She built spacious permanent guest accommodations and made her place one of the great hotels of America.

Compassionate and generous, she saw to it that the Indians had hot food and medicine. Soon she was being called by everyone "Mother Coffman" and grew so high in the regard of her neighbors, she was practically given the role of "Patron Saint" of Palm Springs. Pearl's unhappiness increased. She believed these honors bestowed upon Nellie Coffman rightfully should have been reserved for her father, Judge McCallum, as the founder of the desert community.

Tenter hauling water at Palm Springs, Carl Eytel. Courtesy Southwest Museum.

172

Mountain home of Judge McCallum, built on the mountainside to catch the stray breezes and the magnificent view of the desert below. Artist Jimmy Swinnerton standing upon the roof. Is that little Marjorie Forline astride the burro? Courtesy Palm Springs Historical Society.

Friction between the two women developed and many heated words were exchanged. Other strong women settled in Palm Springs until it became almost a matriarchy during those early formative years. These were gifted women who played important roles until it is now impossible to review the city's history without noting how names of women loom up in its record of events. Again and again these names appear: Pearl McCallum McManus, Nellie Coffman, Zaddie Bunker (owner of the first garage and later on famed as the "flying grandmother"); Dottie Stein, Julia Cornell, The White Sisters (Dr. Franilla, Cornelia, and Isabel), Rose McKinney, the beloved school teacher Katherine Finchy, and at a later date, Melba Bennett and Patricia Moorten.

All were women of great vitality, keen intellect, and were highly imaginative, with definite ideas on how the town should develop. Each made a great contribution in her own positive way. It was inevitable that some of these strong-minded women occasionally engaged in a clash of wills. The heated disagreements between the ladies often resulted in bitter animosities. Publicly they maintained frigid politeness towards each other, but privately the feuding raged. The uninvolved citizenry sat back and chuckled over these contests of wills, but no one ever denied that the ladies were making outstanding contributions benefiting the entire community.

As with most difficulties, time healed many hurt feelings. New people

Festive scene at Murray's Hotel.
Courtesy Palm Springs Desert Museum.

came to the desert, tent houses dotted the area, and with them came new problems and challenges, until there would come the day when Pearl truly could count her friends by the score and enjoy what she liked to call, "The Fruit of Sunshine," or the joys of genuine friendship.

Tent life at Palm Springs,
Carl Eytel. Courtesy
Southwest Museum.

31.
Mrs. Austin McManus

Austin and Pearl McManus.

THE YEAR 1914 was filled with events having important implications for Pearl, for the village of Palm Springs, and for the entire world.

Mother Emily McCallum's health worsened. Pearl found she could no longer care for her mother's needs and of necessity placed her in a hospital at Loma Linda. There Emily died, after first having signed over to Pearl whatever shares of the family property were in her name. Her

Aerial view of Palm Springs in the early days before the McManus mansion and Tennis Club were constructed. Courtesy Palm Springs Desert Museum.

hands were so crippled with arthritis she could barely scratch an X upon the document.

With her mother's passing Pearl assumed control of the McCallum holdings. At the time of his death, Judge McCallum owned between 5,000 and 6,000 acres, most of which he bought from the railroad at the price of $2.50 per acre, but by the time Pearl inherited it, what remained of the original holdings allegedly was not worth more than $6,500. "I had all this land," she once said, "but the taxes went with it. When my father passed away, his fortune had been absorbed in improvements. We just had the land."

When one old-timer gave an interview to a reporter and stated that like most of the early settlers, Pearl had to let her lands go for non-payment of taxes, she hastened to correct his observation by saying there was absolutely no foundation of fact in what he recalled. Then she added, "I've such devotion to the land, I would never have dreamed of letting it go for taxes."

At the same time, she did ruefully admit that at first she knew nothing

176

*Indian Avenue, south, 1920.
Courtesy Palm Springs
Historical Society.*

of business or property values and that one of her first transactions was to sell a valuable parcel of her father's original 80 acres, plus water rights, for $500.

This was a mistake she did not repeat. She learned rapidly from experience.

The year 1914 also saw the world embroiled in the holocaust of war. Americans who traveled each year across the Atlantic found themselves cut off from Europe and began coming to the little desert spa. Property began to sell and for the first time Pearl began to experience relief from dire poverty.

It was a year which brought a great change in Pearl's personal life. At a social event in the fashionable Netherlands Hotel in Los Angeles she met Austin G. McManus. The genial and impeccably groomed former owner of a men's haberdashery had just returned from an extended sea cruise. Originally from South Orange, New Jersey, Austin was engaged in real estate in Pasadena at the time of the meeting.

177

Indian Avenue, 1920, looking north from Baristo to Andreas. Courtesy Palm Springs Historical Society.

During the short courtship, Austin went down on the night train to visit Pearl. Arriving in the middle of the night he trudged across the seven miles of horrifying desert terrain in his highly polished expensive shoes. Deathly afraid of sidewinders and other crawling creatures he expected to crush down upon one with each step. He laughed later when recounting these terrifying hikes and said, "I realized how much I loved Pearl when I made the trip the second time!"

Laguna Beach had always seemed an ideal spot for a honeymoon to Pearl. The craggy rocks with the foaming waves crashing upon them and the steep cliffs dotted with wildflowers were of special delight to her. She and Austin started off in the used car she had purchased by exchanging 10 acres, some of her precious land, immediately after their marriage in Riverside. Pearl was happy that they had Laguna Beach as their destination.

No paved roads led to the isolated artists' paradise in those days and the rutted unimproved dirt tracks wound through ravines and over stream beds. Sometimes the route was particularly dangerous and frightening to Pearl. She later recalled that despite her screams of fright, Austin seemed entirely engrossed in protecting the shiny car from scratches threatened by the overhanging branches of untrimmed bushes.

By the time they finally reached the beach settlement, Pearl was nearly distraught with fear and fatigue. A soft, steady drizzling rain began and continued for all the time they planned to remain at the beach. Pearl bundled herself up and strolled along the beach enjoying the motion of the sea and the little shore birds darting in and out of the waves, despite the rain. Austin continued his preoccupation with keeping the car shiny-bright and bustled around finding an old blanket with which to cover it. "It was the car which took all his time," Pearl laughingly recalled to a friend, "Austin just didn't have any time left for me."

They returned to the desert and began housekeeping in the charming old McCallum adobe.

Pearl and Austin went into the real estate business setting up Pioneer Properties. She reserved the office of president for herself, but listed Austin as secretary. Austin's genial, affable Irish charm won many a buyer, but it was Pearl who had the final say in every transaction. Her zeal to safeguard the future of "her" village led to her dominating every sale. She permitted sales only to persons she believed would prove an asset to Palm Springs.

Eventually Pearl did sell most of the large McCallum acreage, but retained some of the most valuable Palm Canyon Avenue frontage. This property eventually was estimated to be worth millions. As Mike Jack-

Palm Springs, 1907. Courtesy Palm Springs Historical Society.

179

The McCallum Adobe when it was the residence of Pearl and Austin McManus. Courtesy Palm Springs Desert Museum.

son, columnist for the Los Angeles *Herald Express* once wrote, "When the boom began, she started selling small parts of her vast holdings. She kept most of the key locations. Her shrewdness, her determination to protect the beauty of the desert she loved, her insistence upon her own architectural standards, often put her in conflict with big business, speculators and the local law makers. None has claimed to outsmart her."

Pearl was able to make the deeds to the property subject to reversion of title for architectural reasons, so tight was her control over the property she permitted to be sold to the selective few meeting her strict requirements. These restrictions held true even for the land she donated to various community organizations. Pearl had final architectural approval, always.

Her inflexible demands created animosities which exist to the present time, but Pearl's obdurate insistence upon the restrictions being carried out to her satisfaction undeniably created a city of unsurpassed beauty.

The marriage was to last over 42 years. It was a relationship which few of their acquaintances could understand. There were to be rare moments of tenderness and also many moments of vituperation. Always Pearl played the dominant role, which Austin accepted good naturedly.

When the incapacitating migraines struck Pearl, Austin solicitously cared for her, often driving her to the McManus home in Pasadena to escape the broiling heat of the desert. She enjoyed car travel and he sometimes carried her to the car in his arms when the pain became blinding. During these terrible seizures Pearl frequently lashed out at him, but he would shrug off her tirade with a smile and say, "She really doesn't mean that. She simply couldn't live without me."

In truth, they needed and complemented each other. Her strength and courage bolstered him, while she leaned upon his unwavering loyalty and habitual gentleness more than she ever realized. It was not until her family physician taught Pearl to administer subcutaneous injections for the migraine and she was freed of the almost constant pain, that her entire nature changed. She became more sociable and outgoing, seeking the world she previously avoided. It was then that she began having the parties she loved so much and swept into the social life of the village.

Gradually, as Austin's health failed the headaches occasionally returned to plague Pearl. As late as July 5, 1951, she wrote to a friend, "I have been upset recently with headaches for four or five days and this has slowed me up, but know it will be much better as soon as I get to a cooler climate. It has been 112° here the last two weeks. Austin is feeling much better, so of course, that helps me too."

Pearl and Austin celebrated their 31st wedding anniversary in 1945. Using Tennis Club stationery, Austin penned a letter to Pearl which was found in a small metal box among her effects after she was gone. The envelope was addressed, "For Pearl from Austin, May 6, 1945, Our 31st Wedding Anniversary."

It was to the McManus family residence, still standing at 745 East California, Pasadena, that Pearl and Austin went to escape the severe summer heat of the desert.

"On this our 31st Wedding Anniversary — although at times we do not think alike — the one fact remains that you are my wife, sweetheart and companion thru the years. Having been blessed with more than the average man with good health and with much worldly goods — the latter attributable to your able support in courage, steadfastness of purpose and ability to see that purpose thru — in all that encompasses the real things of life worthwhile, I bow to your fine sense of values and strength of character that has made so much of our life and union one to be envied. Love like this lasts forever thru the years. This is the gift of thought I wish to leave with you today with a devout and sincere wish for your health and happiness.
The Old Fus Box,
Lovingly, Your husband, Austin."

181

Four years later Austin made his will and dated it September 10, 1949. In this document he gave everything to Pearl and stated that she owned all the real property and that he had accrued nothing. His failing health had led him to prepare and give Pearl power of attorney on June 25, 1954. Austin McManus died two years later. The funeral Mass was celebrated in the little Catholic Church he loved so much. Pearl buried him in the Welwood Murray Cemetery among other noted Palm Springs pioneers.

Death had taken another of Pearl's loved ones. Always she referred to her Austin by saying with a warm smile, "Ah, that Irishman!"

32.
"The Oasis"

Architect Lloyd Wright, contractor Quinn Spalding, and Austin watch as Pearl McManus turns over the first spade of dirt starting the construction of the Oasis Hotel.

THE SMALL VILLAGE of Palm Springs grew in fame until health seekers and vacationers from distant places came in increasing numbers. The demand for hotel accommodations could not be met. Pearl and Austin decided the need for another hotel was sufficient to warrant their building one. In 1924 they started construction on "The Oasis."

Pearl conceived the idea for her hostelry and then sought an architect to put her ideas into form. Living in Palm Springs at this time was the son of the world famous architect, Frank Lloyd Wright. Young Lloyd Wright momentarily was estranged from his famous father, but Pearl believed that some of the elder Wright's genius and philosophy towards architecture was to be found in the son.

The father had as his motto "Truth against the World" and she wanted to capture something of his statement, "To know what to leave out and what to put in; just where and how, ah, *that* is to have been educated in knowledge of simplicity toward ultimate freedom of expression."

The Oasis Hotel.

As the building progressed, Pearl became more delighted to see her visions become actualities.

"It took a year to complete and was so beautiful that many people offered to buy it or lease it before it was finished," she once recalled. "The dining room was ninety feet long, glassed in with French doors on three sides, and heated by charcoal braziers. I insisted that the orange and cottonwood trees on the grounds be integrated into the structure even if it cost twice as much, and two huge cottonwoods grew up through the dining room roof."

Unfortunately, by completion time, Pearl found she did not have the capital to furnish or operate "The Oasis." It became necessary for her to find someone to lease and operate the establishment. The brothers Hanner, operators of the Hotel Cecil on Main Street in Los Angeles, took over for her.

"The Oasis" immediately became one of the attractions of the increasingly popular spa. In the brochure issued by the railroad entitled "Riverside County; its hotels and resorts," The Oasis was called "an hotel of home atmosphere and service." This advertisement, illustrated by charming woodcuts, went on to describe "The Oasis" in somewhat florid prose:

"The Oasis" as pictured in promotional material put out by the Southern Pacific Railroad. Historical Division, Los Angeles County Museum of Natural History, the Coronel Collection.

"Down in the land of purple night and golden morning, the land of silver sage and gray-green cactus; where the air is full of the wine of life and you bubble over with vitality there lies Palm Springs.

"The unique Oasis Hotel is of massive cement construction, and is formed around a patio of unusual beauty. Nestled against the walls are heavily ladened orange trees from which guests are invited by the management to help themselves.

"The Oasis is irregular in form with a swimming pool, fountain and an emerald lawn whereon a great brazier holds a cheerful bonfire and a spirit of substantial comfort pervades the entire place.

"The rooms have an outlook over a sunspotted patio. The cuisine is excellent. Then there is the matter of sleeping. The beds at The Oasis are the last word in comfort, and the desert air more than sleep-inducing. Nights when the moon is not shining a million stars are on duty."

This ecstatic pronouncement was signed by W. E. Hanner, as lessee.

The hotel proved so popular that the demand for accommodations increased as did the fame of the village.

Pearl made plans for an additional 26 rooms, but to accomplish this it was necessary to find the space. She faced a heartbreaking decision. What to do with the beloved old adobe which stood in the way of the necessary additions? Pearl could not bring herself to demolish the home of her childhood. As always, she made an impulsive decision which cost untold sums of money, but which was one she never lived to regret.

"It was destroy or move it," Pearl later recalled. "I didn't know how to move anything — but that's pioneering isn't it? Down it came brick by brick and was moved along Palm Canyon Drive to the Village Green, where it was all put together again and still stands.

"Shingle by shingle, even the old Indian fireplace so that it can be used for civic activities and ever serve as a monument to Palm Springs' pioneers, its growth and prosperity."

Not only did she move the adobe, but she spared the old fig tree that had been on the original site and under which they had camped and played during those first months and years. This tree, weighing over 18½ tons, required two days to move.

Great as was her pleasure in watching the old adobe rise upon its new site on Palm Canyon Drive, Pearl felt a twinge of sadness each time she passed the rubble left upon the original location and when she looked upon the gaping hole where once had grown the venerable old fig tree. She made another of her sentimental gestures, which always surprised her neighbors who knew her to be such a practical, hardheaded (so they said) business woman.

John W. Hilton, internationally famed desert painter, recalled the incident when he returned from his island home on Maui for his 25th one-man show at the Palm Desert Art Gallery, "I was just a punk young fellow then, trying to learn how to paint. The desert was new to me, but already I had fallen under its spell and was trying like fury to put down its capricious beauty on canvas. Mrs. McManus saw some of my work and liked it. She called me and said she wanted a picture of her childhood

The McCallum Adobe as painted to order by John W. Hilton. He had to do the painting twice to capture the magic of Pearl's childhood recollections.

Pearl McCallum McManus and
the painting of the old adobe she
commissioned John W. Hilton
to paint.

home. Well, this was big stuff to me and I rushed over. You can imagine
my consternation when she took me to a place where there was just a
gaping hole in the ground and some broken cement and rubble. I looked
at her in amazement and she laughed and handed me a snapshot of the
place as it was formerly, and said, "I want a picture exactly as it was
when I was a child."

Hilton shook his head as he remembered going back to the city and
trying to paint the commissioned scene. "All I could keep thinking of
was that doggone hole in the ground and the vacant place where the
adobe stood. Well, I painted the picture, and if I do say so, it really was
pretty good. I rushed back to the desert and proudly held it up before
Pearl McManus. She took one look and thrust it back at me saying,
"It's all wrong. That isn't the way it was at all."

"I took out the snapshot," continued Hilton, "And said, 'But Mrs.
McManus, I have painted it exactly from this snapshot.'" She looked
at the snap and then insisted, "The fence is all wrong. It isn't high
enough. I do not want this picture until you do it correctly!"

"Well, I lost plenty of sleep over that simple picture. I needed the
money and it was one of my first commissions and I wanted to make
good," continued Hilton. "Already Pearl McManus was becoming a
powerful influence and I knew it would be to my benefit to please her.
Suddenly, it came to me that she was recalling the old home place as she

The McCallum Adobe and the
golden haze of cottonwood trees,
as painted by John W. Hilton.

187

*Pearl doing that which she enjoyed most—riding a spirited horse
across her beloved desert. Accompanied by Frank Bogert, former mayor of Palm Springs.
Courtesy Palm Springs Chamber of Commerce.*

saw it through a child's eyes. To a small girl a fence would appear very tall. I rushed back to the site, and hunkering down on my shanks, I squinted up and tried to envision that confounded fence as it must have appeared to little Pearl McCallum and painted it that way.

"She was very pleased and said that it was exactly right. Pearl was so delighted with the picture, she wanted me to set up a studio in Palm Springs. She even offered me a lot for $300 at $30 down and $30 a month. I didn't have $30 for the down payment and, besides, I reasoned, who wanted a pile of sand way out there in the middle of nothing. Of course," lamented Hilton, "The El Mirador Hotel would have been my neighbor had I bought the lot!"

With the moving of the adobe, Pearl and Austin changed their residence to a small cottage on the opposite side of The Oasis on what today is known as Bellardo Road. Within a few years they built their famous "pink mansion" on the side of the mountain. This was patterned after the Mediterranean villas Pearl had admired greatly on their first trip to Europe. The view from the terrace was expansive and a vantage point from which Pearl could look out over the village and beyond to the expanses of desert sand down across the shimmering waters of the Salton Sea.

Palm Springs, 1924. Courtesy Palm Springs Historical Society.

189

Pearl McCallum McManus; oil portrait by
Gordon Coutts, member Royal Academy of Great Britain.
Courtesy Palm Springs Desert Museum.

33.
"Auntie Pearl"

GAIETY CAME to Palm Springs with the arrival of the famous Hollywood stars seeking "Fun in the Sun." Some of these celebrities settled down and became part of the town. Other large hotels, such as El Mirador, were built for these stars. There was but one paved section of road, near the bridge, and street dances were often held there in the soft warmth of the desert nights. Sometimes during the early evening groups of villagers would stroll down the main street eight or ten abreast. There was not much card playing, and movies were shown once a week at the Frances Stevens School by Earl Strebe. Everyone in town, it seemed, owned a horse and there were horseback rides and picnics.

There was nothing much to do in the way of amusement except to enjoy socializing among themselves. Those still residing in Palm Springs who recall those idyllic days cannot remember Pearl McManus ever participating in these social gatherings. Her duty to her invalid mother, coupled with her shyness and serious nature kept her from joining in the fun. She preferred solitary rides across the desert sands upon her horse.

Pearl's enthusiasm for horses continued all her life. She became a charter member of the Desert Riders and yearly contributed funds for the clearing of the trails when the preparations for the annual ride were underway. She gave the money for the lighted cross which stands today upon the side of the mountain and to which each Easter the riders go for services. She rode horseback until she was well into her 80th year to the amazement of all who watched her handle a fractious stallion.

The little village grew rapidly and with its fame and growth came problems of a civic nature which could only be solved with the community working as an entity. On April 20, 1938, Palm Springs was incorporated as a city of the sixth class. Austin G. McManus served on the first city council.

Marjorie Forline Stephens, Pearl's niece and companion and helper since early childhood.

There was no doubt about Pearl's interest in all civic problems. She regularly attended all meetings of any importance and frequently her mere presence gave the sessions importance. She continued attending until her health would no longer permit and then she always expected and received telephone reports on the happenings of the meetings.

With World War II the entire aspect of Palm Springs changed. Pearl sold the acreage to the government for its landing field. The El Mirador was taken over by the government and made into a recuperative hospital for soldiers on hospital leave. Nearby, General George Patton trained his soldiers for the African campaign, the blistering desert heat being considered a duplication of the torrid sands of the other continent. Tanks roared across the desert and tore into the contours of the hills. Vast sections of desert were marked off and became artillery ranges.

Pearl McManus at the Sweetheart Ball given each year in her honor. Courtesy Marjorie Forline Stephens.

Pearl knew many of these soldiers would one day return to the desert and bring their families to live. She doubled her efforts in trying to influence the city officials, sometimes cajoling them into doing what she thought was best for the city.

Throughout the years, Pearl worried over the land which had been abandoned by some of the original syndicate partners. She began tracing the heirs to this property, and at considerable effort, found them and then spent great sums of money buying back the land and clearing the titles. It was not until the end of World War II when the Federal Government declared certain lands as war surplus that she was able to complete these transactions.

Pearl and the "Henrietta" award she received from the Foreign Correspondents Association.

She purchased "Lots 4-5-12-13-14-18-19-20 and the east half of Lot 21, all in Sect. 13, Township 4, South, Range 4 East, San Bernardino base meridian as per Maps, page 652, Records of San Diego County, State of California, containing approximately 210 acres, more or less."

It was necessary for her to pay $111,510 to obtain a quit claim deed for this acreage, paying approximately $532 per acre for the land which had originally been purchased from the railroad for $2.50.

This gave Pearl great satisfaction. Despite the huge cost, once again McCallum land was in McCallum hands.

As she almost reluctantly sold more and more of her land always placing restrictions upon its future use, her wealth and influence increased. She entertained lavishly many of the world's leading social and financial figures. There were many who feared, and a few who genuinely loved Pearl McManus, but there was none who secretly did not admire and respect the fierce old lady in her pink mansion upon the hillside.

One of those who approached her with trepidation was a returnee from the African campaign. Young Clifford Henderson, without money, but with a dream for a new model city on the desert a few miles from Palm Springs, was cautioned by other real estate brokers to beware the jealous wrath of Pearl McManus who would not, he was told, tolerate the creation of a rival community. Cliff Henderson, as he has become known, recalled his early days in creating the city he named Palm Desert.

"Mrs. McManus was a very powerful figure. She could have easily prevented all my efforts towards creating Palm Desert. Instead, she took great interest in all my plans. She encouraged me in every way." Henderson went on to say, "With one word, she could have wiped me out and prevented my getting any financing. Maybe, she remembered the dream her father once had. I don't know. But I do know she was one of the few people in Palm Springs who appreciated my ambitious under-taking. She was a great lady."

Pearl McManus and Zaddie Bunker, Palm Springs' flying grandmother and pioneer garage owner.

Someone, just who is uncertain, began calling her "Auntie Pearl."
Perhaps this came from her niece, Marjorie, affectionately always referring to her aunt in this term. In any case, this became her title among
the villagers. Inappropriate as it was, Pearl secretly seemed amused by
the name.

"Auntie Pearl," wrote a Los Angeles newspaper columnist, "as she
is called by all, doesn't fit her at all. She's not the 'loveable little old
lady' type. She's a true sophisticate. She has the polish of a Marlborough
School product, which she is. She dresses with the casual smartness of
a woman who has always had the best. Her hair, cut short, suits her
easy elegance. She is not given to small talk. In well modulated tones,
she speaks up firmly and with finality to tycoons, promoters and law-
makers. And what she says, has the ring of a royal edict."

Mrs. Austin McManus and Bob Hope. Courtesy Palm Springs Historical Society.

34.
Building Upon a Dream

THE NEXT THIRTY YEARS were to be the most creative and productive of Pearl's long life. There was an imaginative driving force within her nature which kept her active mind constantly conceiving new ideas. She planned, or better dreamed, always on a grand scale, but she left the humdrum details to be worked out by others. Just as she had no time for small talk and gossip, she abhorred the boring minutiae of life.

She once wrote of herself, "I never thought about what it would cost — that is the way I do business — I just plunge into it and when I get excited and have gone into heavy expenses, but after I achieve what I want to do it always works out and I have created something beautiful like the Oasis Hotel, my own home on the side of the mountain, and the Tennis Club . . . I never have any plans down on paper when I start — I just get crews together and plunge in but I have my own ideas back in my mind — something I have thought about for years. Sometimes it is something interesting or beautiful I have seen in my travels — for instance in Morocco — and when I embodied these ideas in things I did here, they turned out to be beautiful. It is a great source of satisfaction to me to feel that my instinct for the beautiful was true and something that has lived . . . ."

Pearl built the first apartment house in Palm Springs and called it the Hacienda. Her neighbors, not enjoying the lively colors in which she delighted, looked at the bright pink of the paint and called this building "Pearl's tomato cans." She built 16 or 17 residences and lived in some before selling them. Of all her building efforts, Pearl was undoubtedly proudest of the Tennis Club. This won architectural prizes and became proclaimed the "most beautiful club in the world," and was the result of happenstance.

Standing upon the terrace of her pink mansion one day, she looked down upon an undeveloped corner of the old ranch grounds and im-

Pearl McManus on one of her many trips to Italy.

*Pearl's famous "V" for victory palms and the oval pool which she built for her friends
and which ultimately became the start of her Tennis Club.
Courtesy Joan McManus.*

pulsively decided to build tennis courts for some of her English visitors. The project was begun on a modest scale, but as soon as the courts were finished she thought it would be pleasant for her friends to cool off in a swimming pool. She estimated the entire project would not exceed $12,000, but soon found the error in this guess. In her mind she designed an oval pool with two graceful palms overhanging the water. As soon as this was completed it became the model and pattern for resort pools, the dramatic design practically becoming the official insignia for California when the State Chamber of Commerce used a picture of this pool upon its promotional literature.

Just as the pool excelled in beauty of design, Pearl's tennis courts are considered to be among the finest in the world. Despite the variable changes in the desert climate from extreme heat to sudden coolness at night, not a single crack has ever appeared in the cement. However, she was not completely satisfied and began transforming the grounds by creating a magnificent garden. The old irrigation ditch was enlarged into rippling streams of water shaded by the mesquite trees. Each season the streams were stocked with trout and the guests permitted to catch their own dinners in this spot of enchantment.

The Tennis Club officially opened in February of 1937 and received acclaim. Pearl was still not content. She recalled having visited a Capuchin monastery high on the cliffs of Amalfi, Italy, and inspired by this recollection, she ordered a wide terrace built out from the mountain-

The view from the terrace of this Capuchin Monastery, Amalfi, Italy, so inspired Pearl that she had the terrace duplicated for her tennis club.

The Tahquitz Ditch was stocked with trout and guests fished for their dinners while staying at the Tennis Club in the early days. Courtesy Marjorie Forline Stephens.

A typical gay dinner party hosted by Pearl and Austin McManus at the Tennis Club. Courtesy Marjorie Forline Stephens.

Pearl and Austin's sister-in-law, Joan McManus, who assisted in bringing great success to the Tennis Club.

side. She employed the famous designer and architect, Paul Williams, to transform her ideas into blueprints for beauty. The clubhouse grew out of an employee's request for a lean-to headquarters. The dining room, scene of many later banquets and gala affairs, had one entire wall of rugged stone over which splashed a waterfall. Blossoms of trailing bougainvillaea made spots of color on this rock work.

It was in this beautiful club that Pearl became the social arbiter of Palm Springs, entertaining official dignitaries, leading representatives of the world's social, artistic, and financial circles. She was assisted by Austin's sister-in-law, Joan McManus. It was with great dignity that the once lonely, rejected, poverty-stricken woman, now wealthy, ruled over her domain graciously and attractively.

In addition to her social activities at the Tennis Club Pearl began participating in other organizations. Among her affiliations she became a charter member of both the Palm Springs Polo Club and the Desert Riders. She was an active member of the Palm Springs Art Association, the Desert Press Club and the Pathfinders.

The Tennis Club, however, continued to be her main social outlet and she frequently made the facilities of this fine club available free of charge for various charitable functions. It was with some regret when her health began to fail that she sold the club for a rumored sum of over a million dollars to Harry F. Chaddick. Before the sale, she determined in her mind what would be best for the club and for Palm Springs and thus was able publicly to state that she sold, "To give me peace of mind in the security of its future. And I know I'm selling it to someone who will maintain the dignity and who cares about the club . . . ."

*Tennis Club, view of the terrace
Pearl McManus designed.
Courtesy Joan McManus.*

Some of her father's high moral code of ethics was inherent in Pearl
and led her to become interested for a few years in the Moral Re-Armament movement. Many of her friends, prominent in Southern California
social and financial circles, were also members. She supported the movement with generous contributions and went to Europe in its interest. A
group of the MRA ''Seniors'' arrived by chartered bus from Los Angeles
to celebrate her eightieth birthday at the Tennis Club. A special song,
composed in her honor, was sung to her as a token of their gratitude for
her generosity.

Pearl gave of her time and her wealth to all groups she believed were
performing beneficial acts for Palm Springs and for youth of the community. Those who knew her well were always surprised to be reminded
of her age. Her faith in young people and her extremely active enthusiasm for all cultural activities kept her young and vibrant.

Her gifts to educational purposes were large and varied. One of Pearl's
first major gifts to the Graduate School of Claremont was, according to
Dr. Robert J. Bernard, ''To bring here a professor of municipal and state
government to develop young people to take hold of civic responsibilities
and prevent the careless exploitation that so often destroys the beauty
and long-term health of our communities.''

Heedless exploitation of the land was a danger of great concern to
Pearl. In the movement for conservation of all plant life and protection
of the land she was truly a pioneer. Ecology, the word so popular today,

*Pearl McManus beside the
famous Tennis Club pool.*

PEARL

may not have been in her vocabulary, but she foresaw the urgent necessity of protecting the natural resources of the land, particularly of her cherished desert. When Dr. Fritz Wendt, Professor of Plant Physiology of California Institute of Technology, came to the desert and began his studies of the plants, his interest and enthusiasm were infectious.

When Pearl learned from Dr. Lee A. DuBridge, president of the California Institute of Technology, of Dr. Wendt's hope to measure the carbon dioxide intake and the water vapor and oxygen output of desert plants such as the ocotillo, pygmy cedar, creosote and cat's claw, she gave the California Institute of Technology $10,000 to build a mobile vehicle and house trailer which became the roving laboratory of the desert. With the assistance of Dr. Loyd Tevis, California Institute of Technology resident zoologist, Dr. Wendt was thus able to follow the rains from place to place and move to the different plant life zones.

Her funds also were used to purchase the newly developed instruments for the measurement of plants. The work of these men was no casual frittering of scientific curiosity, Pearl well knew. Their studies might very well have tremendous implications for the future of mankind, for, as Randall Henderson wrote in *Desert Magazine* for July, 1958, "Every living plant is a little factory using radiant energy from the sun, taking carbon dioxide and moisture and converting them to sugar and other compounds which have good value for the plant and animal world, and giving off water and vapor and oxygen which help maintain the atmosphere conducive to life on this planet. To women with the vision and understanding of Mrs. Austin McManus, Americans owe a great debt of gratitude for the services they are rendering."

Pearl loved the native desert plants and she enthusiastically enjoyed watching their adaptation into the ever increasing numbers of beautifully landscaped areas in Palm Springs. She delighted in walking alone at sunset through the Desertland Botanical Gardens owned by her friends, Slim (Chester) and Pat Moorten. She took great interest in the work being done in their cactus propagation lath houses.

When she heard Walt Disney had asked the Moortens to plant the cactus garden at Disneyland, Pearl requested them to take her to see the plantings. She thoroughly approved their artistic use of desert plants and then turned her attention to the magical wonders of Disneyland. It was obvious to the Moortens that she had used the cactus as an excuse to go to Disneyland! The dignified, prestigious, elderly lady rode in the pilot's

Wildflower-bordered Tahquitz Ditch flowing through the grounds of the Tennis Club.

The magnificent, ever-changing desert that surrounds Palm Springs is an eye-filling attraction, beautiful to contemplate at any time of the day or year. It is hard to imagine that this section of the desert can be seen along Bob Hope Drive just a short distance from Palm Springs itself. Courtesy Palm Springs Convention and Visitors Bureau.

seat of the monorail and looked down upon the merrymakers and the joyful scene below with the delight of a child.

There had not been too much joy in the life of Pearl McManus and what pleasure she derived came to her through the "little miracles" as she referred to the commonplace pleasures of everyday life — her Scotties, Becky and Sheba, her gardens, her friends and always "her desert." The long years of hardship and deprivation left an indelible scar upon her, until even when her wealth assumed great proportions, she was unable to spend money upon creature comforts of life. She did not love money for itself. In fact, so strongly did she fear the power of wealth, she frequently spoke out against what she considered to be the possible corrosive effect of inherited wealth upon the individual receiving the gift. Money should be earned she genuinely believed and then used wisely for the community which was its source and for the benefit of its citizens.

She endured the furies of summer heat because she could not bring herself to lavish enough money upon her own comfort to install a cooling system in her large mansion. Frank Bogert, former mayor of Palm Springs and Pearl's close friend, recalled one exceedingly humid summer when he was serving as manager of the Tennis Club. Pearl's migraines were particularly severe and the heat was compounding her pain. He strongly urged her to put in a cooling system and when she couldn't bring herself to do this, he arranged accommodations for her at the La Jolla Beach and Tennis Club on a reciprocity reduced rate basis of one resort owner to another. Bogert chuckled in admiration at Pearl's spunk

Becky and Sheba,
Pearl's faithful Scotties.

when he recalled that she phoned him long distance the night of her arrival at the club.

"Frank," she protested in distress, "This room is $20 a day. That's too much. I have had the manager change me into a $12 a day room."

"But, Pearl," admonished Frank Bogert, "That must be an inside room without a view of the ocean, isn't it?"

"Yes," she responded, "But I can go outdoors if I want to look at the sea!"

Her one indulgence was the love of simple but elegant dresses of rich fabrics. These she would have sent to her home by the local shops for her selection. Her jewelry consisted of a fine strand of pearls worn as a choker and ear rings. She favored a bracelet made of imitation pearls and towards the end of her life she developed a slight nervous gesture of twisting this as she talked.

Frugal as she was to herself, Pearl's gifts to charitable and educational institutions throughout the years came to significant sums. She gave in the same rugged, individualistic manner she did everything. A cursory examination of her personal ledger for the years 1961-65 reveals that, without any fanfare or public notice, Pearl McManus contributed thousands of dollars annually to the charities which interested her. These gifts ranged from one dollar to those amounting to thousands of dollars. Her gifts to educational purposes were always in addition to these more personal and private contributions.

Aside from her large gifts to colleges, Pearl established local scholarships for the benefit of Palm Springs students. A $500 scholarship to the outstanding high school student was usually presented on her behalf by someone other than Pearl, who preferred to sit unnoticed in the audience. Once when the Palm Springs Women's Club was working hard to collect funds for their annual scholarship, Pearl said for the members to find a student and she would do likewise and would put the recipient entirely through college.

The welfare of the Palm Springs Women's Club continued to be of great interest to Pearl. Aside from her land donation, she gave funds whereby the quality of the monthly programs were enriched. In appreciation of her benefactions the members had written into the club bylaws, "The first meeting in November, hereinafter, shall be known as the 'Pearl McManus Day.' "

Her donations of land to various organizations were frequent and

Unique feature of Palm Springs is the picturesque effect created by the 1200 palm trees which line both sides of Palm Canyon Drive. At dusk, the trees are individually lighted, creating a pixie-like atmosphere for evening strollers and window shoppers. Courtesy Palm Springs Convention and Visitors Bureau.

generous during the years. Among such gifts were the land for the Palm Springs' Women's Club; the Boy Scouts, and the Chamber of Commerce. Always, with each land donation, Pearl retained architectural rights of approval and placed stipulations as to the future disposition of the land in the deeds.

This architectural control was rigidly kept even in the land she sold for a good price. Her keen sense of design and beauty never failed her and she appreciated this in others as well. She was always quick to offer words of praise to those who shared her dream of a beautiful city. In 1959 she wrote to the president of one of the local banks and commented upon the new building under construction at that time:

"I enjoyed meeting the architect, Mr. Wong, and also Mr. Lehman. Both were so kind to me. They couldn't have been more considerate had I been their own mother, or should I say, grandmother! I think your bank is going to be extremely interesting. The golden tones of rock chosen blend beautifully with the architecture, and the entire setting accomplishes so well the purpose of tying the building with the mountains and desert. Best of all, the rock is from Whitewater. All these years we have been looking at it from this side of the mountain, not realizing its extreme beauty."

She signed her note of praise, "Auntie Pearl."

Aside from her Tennis Club, perhaps the buildings which gave her the greatest esthetic satisfaction were Saks and the Robinson store which won such acclaim throughout the nation. Pearl worked closely with the architect and many of her ideas were incorporated in the design of the Robinson store.

Palm Canyon Drive boasts some of the country's finest department stores and chic shops. Location shown here is a part of the acreage owned by Judge John Guthrie McCallum, Palm Springs' "First Citizen," and constitutes part of the original site of the City of Palm Springs.

35·
Every Grain of Sand

PEARL'S FAITH in the future of Palm Springs remained steadfast despite the proliferation of little shacks and tent houses which sprang up and defaced the area. When the floods of 1916-17 again devastated the little community and washed out many of these squalid, unattractive huts, Pearl did what she could to alleviate the suffering of those undergoing the loss, but at the same time she could not help feeling relieved that such eyesores had disappeared overnight.

From the very first she voiced her belief that if her father's dream of a fine community was ever to become a reality such haphazard, uncontrolled building must be regulated. Her convictions were strengthened in 1938 when the great architectural genius whom she admired so greatly for his innovative and imaginative approach to the entire field of architecture, Frank Lloyd Wright, visited Palm Springs. He took a hurried look and then castigated the entire community for permitting erratic, unplanned subdivisions to mushroom into being with architectural monstrosities. The outspoken and controversial genius seemed to relent somewhat in his critical analysis of Palm Springs when it was pointed out to him that his son had designed the Oasis Hotel.

Pearl was in complete agreement that some architectural control was essential. She gained the reputation for being a "hard and stubborn woman." She became anathema to real estate brokers. Eastern financiers and speculators, who came to Palm Springs for the winter for the first time and looking around decided the land offered great potential, found themselves firmly outmaneuvered by the "old woman" when they tried to buy some of her land. Brokers approaching her with such offers were requested to bring their clients for tea. There seated upon the wide veranda of her pink mansion overlooking the wide vista of the desert she served them tea and toasted pound cake.

As these men visited with the charming, regal lady of the mansion

She loved to mount her horse, ride to some promontory, and look out over "her" desert. Pearl and Austin McManus.

View from the terrace at the Tennis Club.
Courtesy Joan McManus.

and sipped the fragrant brew, they found themselves being questioned and sometimes pilloried as she conversed in her slow, softly modulated voice. George C. Wheeler, financial authority, wrote of her in his *Desert Letter* of September 1966, "Mrs. McManus was probably the most astute business personality that Palm Springs has known. She acquired whenever and wherever she could. She parted with a holding only after a long negotiation. If she ever came out second best, it is not generally known. Many a deal ended just before the papers were to be signed. What was thought settled at a late hour was completely unsettled the following morning. She had a knack of thinking of eventualities and protecting herself from any bad effects."

While protecting her own interests, Pearl's goal was always the betterment of her beloved Palm Springs. She sold, almost with sorrow, piece by piece of her land until in the last years of her life her real estate became less and less and her wealth greater and greater. Each parcel sold never entirely passed out of her thoughts and affection. She watched over the community, fretting and scolding sometimes when she disapproved of certain actions, but always there was love and pride in her heart.

Desert riders picnicking at McManus Point, 1958.

*Airport fountain built through Pearl McManus' financial assistance and dedicated
in her honor by the Palm Springs City Council after her death.
Color photo by Petley Studios.*

Her verve and enthusiasm continued and one time she tried to express this sentiment she felt so keenly in an interview. But, as was so frequently the case, her words were misinterpreted and taken out of context by some. Those who respected Pearl McManus understood that she was attempting to put into words the emotion she felt in her heart when she said for publication, "Even now, on occasion, I can mount my horse, ride to some promontory and look far out over the desert, sometimes in the daytime, and sometimes at night when your houselights twinkle with the stars, and even though you have true titles and deeds to your home, your lands, and your ranches, so long as I am here on the desert in my fancy, in my love, and in my friendship, every palm, every house, every tumbleweed, every grain of sand and branch of mesquite is my own, all my own . . ."

Preservation of the beauty of this desert increasingly became more and more important to Pearl. By personal influence and example she set the standards she hoped others would follow. At the end of World War II, when the city resumed control of the airfield, she took special interest in beautifying the grounds and urged the construction of the fine new airport terminal building.

As she continued to give considerable thought to the beautification of the airport, increasingly she favored the installation of a large fountain to greet the visitors coming to the desert. Despite her interest in such a project, it was not until Frank Bogert brought the Mexican architect Julio de la Pena to her attention that she contributed $25,000 towards the construction of such a fountain. This amount of money was found to be insufficient and the McCallum Desert Foundation created by Pearl, later gave $28,000 to the Palm Springs City Council for the completion of the project. In view of her public-spirited generosity, the city fathers, following her demise, voted to name the fountain in Pearl's honor.

The frolicking waters in this beautiful fountain give a delightful welcome to visitors. Pearl also gave land for the right of way for the spacious boulevard leading from the airport to the center of Palm Springs. Her only request was that this avenue be called McCallum Way in honor of her father. The Indians likewise gave land through reservation territory and when they asked that it be given an Indian name, the hyphenated Tahquitz-McCallum designation was given.

Desert riders visit Indian Canyons.

Inscription upon Palm Springs Airport fountain reads:

This Fountain Honors
PEARL McCALLUM McMANUS
"Auntie Pearl" was the first non-Indian child in Palm Springs
arriving with her Father, "Judge" John Guthrie McCallum in 1884.
This fountain was designed by Architect Julio de la Pena of
Guadalajara, Mexico, as a gesture of friendship. Its
398 pieces were hand cut from contera stone in the State of Jalisco.
Dedicated April 27, 1968

The lovely fountain would have pleased Pearl McManus for she pioneered in community beautification projects. She joined in cleaning up and planting the streets, the first such major effort in the town. The Park Patencio South Project, as this improvement association was called, consisted of some nineteen property owners. Pat and Slim Moorten of the Desertland Botanical Gardens worked with Pearl and supervised the selection and planting of shrubs and trees. Those neighbors who were reluctant to pay their share found their obligations being assumed by Pearl.

When Marian (Mrs. Cliff Henderson) began organizing Desert Beautiful in 1962, Pearl gladly permitted her name to be used in the list of directors. To everyone's pleasure, Pearl also faithfully attended many of the organization meetings and gave generous financial support. When her failing health no longer permitted attendance at the meetings, she enjoyed telephone reports from Mrs. Henderson. Pearl listened to the account of the Desert Beautiful activities and would often say, "I approve. I like what you are doing."

36.
"Dreams for the Children"

Her dreams for the children of
Palm Springs area were exalted.

THERE WAS one ugly area of her land which bothered Pearl for years.
She dreamed and planned methods of beautifying this large space. Her
schemes never came to realization. This was the acreage known as
Section 23.

Originally part of the syndicate property, her father having been one
of the five members of this syndicate, it consisted of an area ¼ mile
wide and one mile long and had never been offered to public sale as it
was always subject to the Tahquitz river floods.

From the time Pearl acquired this acreage, she struggled with the
problems of constant flooding. Each major storm tore new channels
through the once beautiful area until practically the entire mile was
devastated. During the years, Pearl tried to clarify the channel for short

*Pearl McManus on the terrace
of her "Pink Mansion."
Courtesy Marjorie Forline Stephens.*

distances at the more crucial points. She lacked the funds for dredging the entire length of the river, the south line of which flowed all the way to Deep Well property and the adjoining location where the Cahuilla School later was built. She tried to guide the first waters of oncoming storms along a straighter and less devastating line.

It was about this time she leased this land for twenty-five dollars a month, to a builder's supply company, not realizing that they planned to excavate for rock and sand. Soon the entire area from the eastern boundary up to the highway was filled with deep scarring excavations which filled with water whenever a cloudburst or heavy rainfall occurred. The great floods of '36 and '37 were cause for constant anxiety to Pearl when these deep pits sometimes extended over acres and reached a depth of nearly 70 feet.

Young people, particularly very small children, went there to swim both day and night. This water, coming as it did from the snow-capped Mt. San Jacinto, was icy cold and could result in severe cramping for the swimmers. This, together with the great depth of the pits made it very dangerous. Finally Pearl, realizing the great appeal water held for children, especially during the hot summer days, and where there were no other amusements or attractions provided for them, hired guards to protect the children while they enjoyed the cooling waters. This was an expense she could ill afford, especially since she also constantly kept

Havoc created by Tahquitz River fifty feet from Palm Canyon Drive.

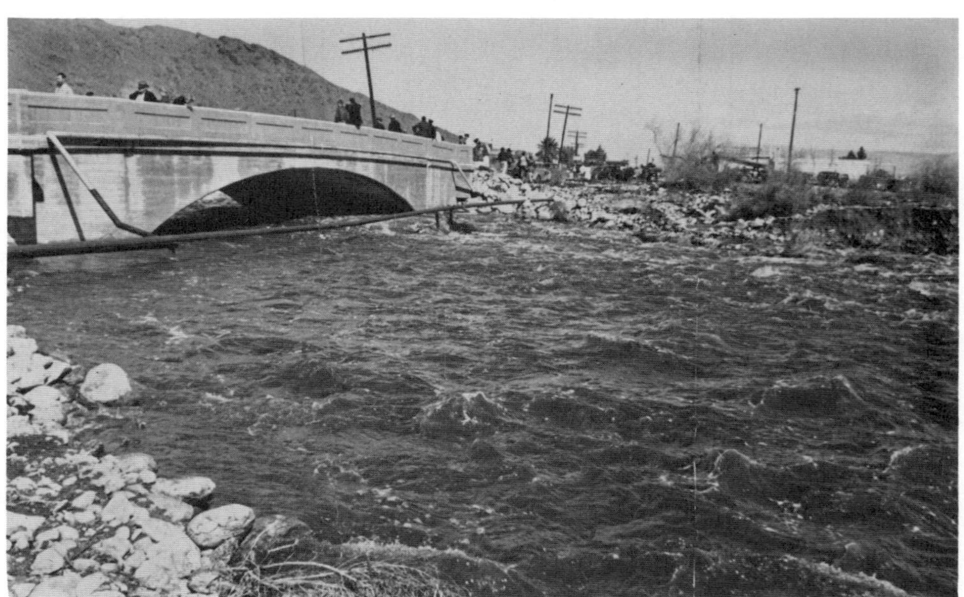

Tahquitz flood waters rampaging east of the bridge over Palm Canyon Drive.

hiring contractors to keep the channels clear so the waters could flow from these pits. No sooner had these channels been dredged out to keep the water from spreading onto the acreage on the south, when the next storm would tear these out and the waters would rampage again.

Sometime after the floods of '36 and '37 which tore away sections of the highway and both ends of the bridge, county apparatus was sent down to repair the damage. Pearl assumed the men had been instructed to continue the opening of the flood control east of the bridge for a mile or two. Such was not the case. The bridge alone was repaired. Once again she was forced to assume full cost of filling in some of the more dangerous pits and in addition she had removed the hazardous piles of sand the builder's supply company had left on her property.

No other property owners in that entire area offered to help financially, although they too were concerned, and Pearl struggled with these problems alone throughout the years.

To a person with less tenacity and narrower vision this section would have become too great a burden to bear and would have seemed but a wasteland. To Pearl, Section 23 was a challange. She loved beauty and could not abide waste. Plans for this land began formulating in her creative mind. To her, nothing was impossible.

She looked upon this ugly stretch of land and envisioned a lovely park for the village of Palm Springs. In this park would be swimming pools and wading pools for tiny children, particularly for use during the hot summer days. On the banks of the controlled stream bed she planned an outdoor theater on one bank with the seats for the audience on the other. There would be an equestrian trail through the entire mile stretch. She saw a driving golf range and possibly a nine-hole golf course. The road, going along the entire north and south banks of the river would become beautifully developed highways and with such an approach over the river, all who passed through Palm Springs would see the lovely and extensive park.

Pearl went so far as to employ Harry Williams, leading architect in Palm Springs, to draw some plans for the project as she envisioned it. There were to be beautiful stone pilasters to break the monotony of long, straight walls. She wanted the stone to be cut similar to the terraces and retaining walls of the Palm Springs Tennis Club which were copied from beautiful stone work Pearl had seen in Morocco.

Enthusiastically, she had surveying crews come to plot out the land. Immediately difficulties were encountered because of the faulty surveying work done by the original crews during the 1880s. Pearl also joined in with other civic-minded citizens and contributed to a fund with which the city hired a city planner for a year.

Perhaps because her plans were too costly, her vision too exalted, or city officials too limited in the availability of public funds, Pearl McManus's dream for such a recreational beauty spot was never realized and remains for dreamers such as she in the future to bring to fruition.

Andreas Canyon.
J. Smeaton Chase photograph.
Courtesy Palm Springs Desert Museum.

One of the more photographed attractions in this bronzed desert resort community is the
Palm Springs Aerial Tramway. Visitors are taken in 14 minutes from the desert floor
through five climatological zones to the Mountain Station of Mt. San Jacinto.
Fifty-four miles of hiking trails at the top lead through pine forests to campsites,
picnic areas and a secluded lake.
Courtesy Palm Springs Convention and Visitors Bureau.

37·
The Other Side of the Mountain

"If you dream," Pearl McManus once said, "you always wonder what is on the other side of the peak."

She was 83 years old at the time and could look out from her sun-drenched living room in the "pink mansion" and gaze down upon the town she had guarded so fiercely all the long years. It was beautiful beyond her greatest dreams and world famous. All was well down in the "village."

Behind her home loomed the gigantic, brooding mountain peak, San Jacinto, rising majestically 10,805 feet in the azure sky. Unconquered, except for the occasional intrepid soul who clambered on foot up the jagged forbidding granite sides. The solitude of the mountain was about to be overcome. Men planned to build a tramway rising from the desert floor to the height of the mountain.

Always the mountain had slumbered above her and at last the trip she had longed for took place. Pearl, curious and excited as a young girl, was bundled into warm clothing hurriedly gathered by friends — ski pants, two pairs of socks and soft leather boots, an orchid turtleneck sweater, a heavy Kelly-green cardigan sweater atop this, a padded parka, and over all a heavy Canadian coat. Friends then pushed, hauled, and tugged her into a helicopter for the ride up the mountain.

The super-charged Bell G-3-B helicopter whisked her gently as a cloud across some of the world's wildest and most rugged terrain to set her down close to 9,000 feet on the other side of the mountain peak.

It was one of the most thrilling experiences of her life. "It was so beautiful up there, with tall pine trees pointing to the sky. The snow was about 18 inches — and, of course, I wouldn't be happy if I hadn't pitched a few snowballs," she exclaimed.

On the return trip she requested the pilot to come back by the southern route. The copter came back by way of the former McCallum ranch land

The view of the other side of the mountain. Pearl McManus visiting the proposed tramway site.

and made a low circle over the Tennis Club. Pearl described the experience vividly, "The city's blue swimming pools look like jewels from the air — like something out of the Arabian Nights." She looked down upon her city, the city she had watched grow from a few Indian grass huts squatting around the mineral pool until it became one of the most famous spas in the world.

The trip was more than a mere outing. It took on symbolic significance for Pearl. Just as her city had grown to great fame, she had grown in compassion, love, and to a magnificent stature as a human being. She had seen "the other side of the mountain." Time was running out, she was realist enough to acknowledge. Trouble with her vision and more recently a developing heart condition made her realize she must set her affairs in order to make sure her fortune would be put to the use she truly wanted.

She believed, as she often said, "Life is growth. The more you 'live' the wider your vision becomes."

Her vision for the young people of the future and for her treasured Palm Springs was wide indeed. She must make plans to realize her broad intentions. For several years she pondered the problem of how her wealth, still largely represented by property, should be distributed.

With the aid of her attorney, Mr. Edward T. Dillon of Palm Springs, she drew up plans for family and charitable trusts.

To charitable and educational institutions, her will provided for major bequests as follows:

California Institute of Technology and Claremont Graduate School and University Center, $500,000 each; College of the Desert and the University of Redlands $250,000 each; the Women's Club of Palm Springs and the Palm Springs Humane Society, $10,000 each.

But before making major bequests to the four educational institutions above mentioned she gave her time and thought to a long and careful evaluation of the character of their work and the quality of their contribution. Her bequests were undesignated as to use, as she had visited many times the institutions that interested her and had come to know well their leaders and some of their trustees, preferring to leave to them the best ultimate use of her benefactions. This searching process of becoming personally informed about the enterprises under study she carried on objectively yet with warm understanding and appreciation.

She knew that major investment must be made in the next generation if it is to fulfill its greatest potentials. And she delighted to be able to have a part in developing those worthy of such investment.

It is interesting to record that at Claremont Graduate School and University Center her bequest of $500,000 was used to accomplish a handsome arcaded two-story building in the central quadrangle of this institution which the college elected to give the name McManus Hall.

"Pearl McManus," said Robert J. Bernard, President Emeritus, at the dedication of this building, "was a true pioneer in spirit and in action. We are deeply grateful for her confidence in this institution and for her generous benefaction."

The California Institute of Technology has been able to keep the Pearl McManus bequest in its discretionary reserves, where it will be available if needed at some future date for building or other purposes. Meanwhile the funds are invested with the Institute's endowment funds for long-term growth of principal and income. The Institute considers itself most fortunate to have unrestricted current income of over $20,000 annually from this bequest for support of general operations.

At the University of Redlands, the bequest of $250,000 was used to cover a portion of the cost of achieving the attractive library named for President George A. Armacost and dedicated in 1970, where the name of Pearl McManus appears with others on a plaque.

Her contact with the College of the Desert well illustrates the personal interest and care with which she familiarized herself with all the institutions involved.

"Early in the life of College of the Desert," said President Roy C. McCall, "she manifested an interest in plans for its future."

"As the College opened in 1962 she asked to see Mrs. McCall and me at the campus residence to discuss a gift of scholarship money, some $4,000, later augmented by $10,000 for "something special." She continued her interest in the College by telephone even during the period of her failing health . . ."

Her bequest of $250,000 the trustees of the College elected to hold toward a major performing arts center. "The Coachella Valley," concluded Dr. McCall, "has been blessed by the vision and clear purpose of a few leaders who have caused it to become what it is, and Mrs. McManus well deserves to be named among them."

Pearl McManus contemplating "the other side of the mountain."

After providing for the family trusts, and the charitable and educational bequests, she provided in her will that the remainder of her estate was to be used to establish a charitable foundation. She stated in her will:

"Since my father founded Palm Springs and pioneered the early development of the surrounding desert area, and I have resided here since childhood and continued its development and the promotion of its welfare, I dedicate the substantial portion of my estate to charitable and educational purposes for Palm Springs and the desert area, and hereby create and establish in memory of my father the McCallum Desert Foundation."

She then named five director-trustees and three co-trustees, all men in whom she had implicit confidence. The control, management, and disposition of the trust thus was placed in the hands of Robert J. Bernard, Harold B. Meloth, Fred G. Ingram, Justice Hilton H. McCabe, and Edward T. Dillon, as director-trustees. The co-trustees named by Pearl were Leon Parma, grandnephew-in-law, Superior Court Judge Joseph T. Ciano of Redlands, and the Bank of America National Trust and Savings Association. After 20 years, the Foundation was to be terminated with any remaining funds to be distributed to charitable and educational institutions. All funds were to be used for the betterment of the people of her beloved Palm Springs and the desert area.

Ancient palms sheltered Indians and travelers from the desert sun. Oil by Nicolai Fechin.

38.
"Tomorrow's My Day"

SHE LIVED on in splendid solitude in her large "pink mansion" on the shoulders of Mt. San Jacinto with her little Scotty dogs as companions. With the passing of the years, Pearl gradually withdrew from active participation in the political and social life of Palm Springs. Her failing vision made driving a car impossible and she relied more and more on friends to transport her on infrequent outings.

For the last two years of her life her heart beats were controlled by a pacemaker. She never complained or spoke of this operation, but rather looked forward to the next which would give her added time. Her curiosity in the wonders of modern science was keen, just as was her enthusiasm and concern over modern-day human problems. She kept her amazing interest in all the events and problems of her village — one-way streets, high-rise regulations, sign ordinances, and whatever else was developing. She often said to visitors calling upon her when she could no longer go down into the center of activity, "This will be a big city and a great community. Of that I'm sure. I only hope it won't be spoiled by unregulated development."

From the windows of her bedroom on the upper level of her home, she could look down upon the cottages of her former Tennis Club and recall where the McCallum orchards and vineyards once spread across the desert.

"I'm so glad I lived to see it all come out in the sunshine," she once said, and then added, "I'm a great person not to let myself worry over what can't be helped. Tomorrow's my day!"

Pearl's "tomorrows" were coming to an end. She became seriously ill.

As Pearl lay in her bed, she kept her proud, stern-featured face turned towards the windows through which she watched the changing glow of the sunlight as it played over "her desert." She was 87 and the valiant, courageous old heart was wearing out despite the pacemaker. She was in her final illness and she was aware of the fact.

Leaning heavily upon the arm of her grandniece Barbara Parma, Pearl took a farewell look at the bougainvillaea blooms. Thought to be the last picture taken of Pearl McManus.

221

Tranquil pool and a view of Palm Springs below.

Twelve years before, when but 75, Pearl jokingly said, "Used to be I didn't like birthdays, but now I'm rather proud of them."

The years between had been active and good, and now she was ready for whatever fate held in store for her. Her affairs were in good order. The men in whom she placed trust knew exactly what her wishes were for the dispensing of her great wealth. She had but recently been converted to the Catholic faith as Austin would have wished. Several weeks before, she had slowly walked down the steps of her home, leaning heavily upon the arm of her grandniece, Barbara Parma, to see the blooming bougainvillaea vines for the last time.

Attended by Cora Snyder, Palm Springs' favorite nurse since 1910, Pearl occasionally received visitors, but for the most part the "fierce old lady" was alone in her mansion. The visitors who did call found her mentally alert, her capacious mind actively aware despite the diminishing physical prowess and failing heart. The seamed and lined face had softened and the years of tan brought on by the hot desert sun faded until the skin was almost translucent. While her eyes still sparkled, and her hearing remained as keen as ever, Pearl's voice faded to a mere whisper.

She enjoyed recalling the history of her father and mother during those early days in California history. She spoke of their coming to the desert and of their brief happiness in the adobe home. Her eyes filled with tears as she related the deaths in her family and those long, painful years of drought.

"It was a time to break your heart," she whispered, sometimes to herself. As she spoke slowly and hesitatingly, she finally came to the period when she had to sell portions of the land to pay the taxes. "But never the adobe," she insisted, her voice becoming stronger. "Don't call it a house. House is another thing entirely. That feeling of adventure which is part of being a pioneer, I've always thought was given to me by that old adobe. I adored it."

Mostly, she confessed, she missed riding horseback, "That's what's wrong with me," she lamented, "I need the desert."

Once when Nurse Snyder tiptoed to the bed, and after watching the shallow regular breathing of her patient, said softly to the visitor, "She is asleep," Pearl opened her eyes to protest, "I'm not, absolutely. There's moonlight and my memories — You can't grow up in a place, have that as your only background, without getting the spirit of the thing. The desert has been my heart. It still is."

Pearl McCallum McManus died on Sunday, July 24, 1966.

News of her death quickly swept over the village and cast a pall. Those who loved her wept and recalled her many gifts to their city; those who either did not know her or feared her in life, began to look around and to see with clearer vision the heritage of beauty she left them.

The funeral services were held in Our Lady of Guadalupe, the little church on the Indian reservation. An overflowing crowd of the great and the small, whose lives she had at one time or another touched, was there in the small church to say "Goodbye."

Of Palm Springs' leading citizen, the priest said, "She was kind and she was charitable." As the Requiem Mass ended, one of the lighted candles around the casket suddenly went out as though its flame had been snuffed by unseen fingers. Many of her friends smiled and thought, "That's Pearl having the last word."

They buried her in the pioneer cemetery by Austin's side.

The brooding desert, near Palm Springs. Courtesy Palm Springs Desert Museum.

39.
L'Envoi

THE MCCALLUM DESERT FOUNDATION, created by the will of Pearl Mc-
Callum McManus, was legally established by the court Decree of Distribution dated March 21, 1968. The Director-Trustee and Co-Trustee
members, personally selected from her friends and business associates,
met informally on numerous occasions immediately following Pearl
McManus' death and formally for the first time on July 18, 1968.

The members faced the problems Pearl knew the handling of her
Foundation would entail: those of management, preservation and disposition of her properties; and the determination of what charitable
organizations would be eligible to receive grants from the Foundation.
By-Laws were adopted as guidelines. The Director-Trustees became
solely responsible for all sales, investments, re-investments and grants
made by the Foundation.

"Light and shadows."

In addition to these responsibilities, each member of The McCallum Desert Foundation Board, knowing full well Pearl's devotion to the memory of her father, took upon himself her charge of perpetuating the memory of the man who founded Palm Springs that far off day in 1884. It was Judge McCallum who purchased the land from the Southern Pacific Railroad Company. It was he who interested other men of means to join with him in the establishment of the village. He brought life-giving water through the Whitewater ditch, and it was he who proved that early fruit and vegetables could be raised on the desert.

It was Pearl McManus' wish that Palm Springs, one of the great resorts of the world, be recognized as a lasting monument to the vision and courage of her father — John Guthrie McCallum.

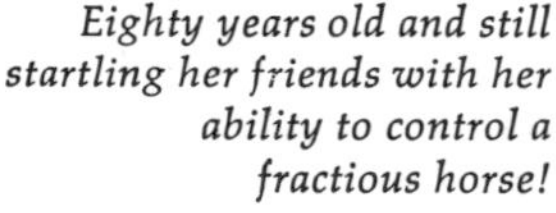

Eighty years old and still startling her friends with her ability to control a fractious horse!

Acknowledgments

THE AUTHOR acknowledges with gratitude the assistance in researching for this book which was enthusiastically provided by: U.S. General Services Administration, National Archives and Records Service, Natural Resources Branch, Civil Archives Division, Washington, D.C. (for Bureau of Indian Affairs historical documents); U.S. Department of the Interior, Bureau of Land Management, State Office, Sacramento, Calif.; Switzerland Circuit Court, Vevay, Indiana; and by the many California governmental agencies which are safeguarding public records.

The Chicago Historical Society, the Indiana Historical Society, and the Palm Springs Historical Society gave inestimable assistance as did the Southwest Museum Library, Los Angeles, the library of the Los Angeles County Museum of Natural History, the Henry E. Huntington Library, San Marino, California, and the Palm Springs Desert Museum.

The librarians of the following public libraries aided greatly: California Section, California State Library, Sacramento, California; Sutro Branch, California State Library, San Francisco; San Francisco Public Library; Oakland; Pasadena; Los Angeles; Redlands; Riverside; San Bernardino; Banning; San Diego; Palm Springs; and Sacramento Public Libraries. An especial word of appreciation must go to the librarians in far-off Chicago; Switzerland County Library, Vevay, Indiana; and the William Henry Smith Memorial Library, Indianapolis, Indiana.

A very warm "thank you" is due the sixty or more persons who generously shared their experiences with and memories of the McCallum family. Patricia Moorten and Betty Kieley were of inestimable assistance, as were Marjorie Forline Stephens, Joan McManus, and Martha Meloth.

Picture Credits

GRATEFUL acknowledgment must also be made to persons and organizations contributing generously the illustrative material which so greatly enhances this book.

Permission to include the original Carl Eytel pen and ink sketches was graciously granted by Dr. Carl S. Dentzel, director of the Southwest Museum. Drawn in 1906 to illustrate George Wharton James's book *Wonders of the Colorado Desert*, these sketches are now cherished items in the Southwest Museum in Los Angeles, as are other Eytel sketches in the collection at The Palm Springs Desert Museum.

Bibliography

Bibliography

BOOKS

Admiral, Don. *Desert of the Palms* (1938)

Ainsworth, Edward Maddin. *Beckoning Desert* (1962)

Anderson, Winslow. *Mineral springs and health resorts of California* (1892)

Atherton, Gertrude. *"Terrible Seventies" in California, an intimate history* (1914)

Bancroft, Hubert Howe. *History of California.* Vol. VI and Vol. VII (1888)

———. *Popular tribunals* (1888)

Baur, John E. *Health seekers of Southern California* (1944)

Bates, Jack W. *The Southern Pacific Railroad in California politics.* M.A. Thesis, University of the Pacific (1942)

Bean, Lowell and Lawton, Harry. *The Cahuilla Indians of Southern California.* Brochure No. 1. Malki Museum, Banning, California (1965)

Bean, Walton. *California, an interpretive history* (1968)

Blake, William P. *Reports of explorations and surveys.* House of Rep., 33rd Congress, 2nd session, Vol. 5 (1856)

Bourne, Arthur Ross. *Some major aspects of the historical development of Palm Springs between 1880 and 1938.* M.A. Thesis. Occidental College (1953)

Bowers, Robert E. *Palm Springs and the Indians* (1965)

Boynton, Margaret. *Stories and legends of the Palm Springs Indians*, as told by Chief Francisco Patencio (1943)

California Blue Book and State Roster (1891)

California State Senate Journals, 1851, 1854-1857

Carlson, Oliver. *A mirror for Californians* (1914)

Carsten, Vernon, ed. *The public lands* (1963)

Caughey, John W. *California*, 2nd ed. (1953)

Chase, J. Smeaton. *Our Araby: Palm Springs* (1923)

———. *California desert trails* (1919)

Crawford, Hildy. *Palm Springs personages*, a directory (1965)

Crofts, Mrs. E. P. R. *Pioneer days in the San Bernardino Valley* (1906)

Cross, Ira B. *History of the labor movement in California* (1935)

Crouch, Winston, ed. *California government and politics*, 3rd ed. (1944)

Daggett, Stuart. *Chapters on the history of the Southern Pacific* (1922)

Davis, Winfield J. *History of political conventions in California, 1849-1892* (1893)

Delamtier, Royce D. *The rumble of California politics, 1848-1970* (1970)

Dixon, Benjamin Franklin. *Palm Springs oasis: old Butterfield station midway between Carrizo and Vallecito* (1958)

Dufour, Perret. *The Swiss settlement of Switzerland County, Indiana* (1925)

Dumke, Glenn S. *The boom of the eighties in Southern California* (1944)

Eaves, Lucille. *History of California labor legislation* (1910)

Elliott, Wallace W. *History of San Bernardino and San Diego counties* (1965)

Ellison, Joseph. *California and the nation, 1850-1869* (1927)

Fox, Maude A. *Both sides of the mountain* (1954)

Gabbert, John Raymond. *History of Riverside City and County* (1900)

Giffen, Helen S. *California mining town newspapers, 1850-1880* (1954)

Goodrich, De Witt C. *Illustrated history of the state of Indiana*

Guinn, J. M. *Southern California: its history and its people; in two volumes, vol. I being historical, and vol. II, biographical* (1902)

Harrington, R. E. *Souvenir of the Palm Springs area* (1962)

Harris, Joseph Pratt. *California politics* (1955)

Heiss, Willard, comp. *Federal census for Indiana, 1820* (1966)

Hicks, Ratcliff. *Southern California or the land of the afternoon* (1898)

Hinkel, Edgar J. and McCann, William E., eds. *Oakland, 1852-1938: some phases of the social, political and economic history of Oakland, Calif.* (1939)

History of Dearborn, Ohio and Switzerland Counties (1885)

Hittel, Theodore H. *History of California*, vol. II (1898)

Holmes, Elmer Wallace. *History of Riverside County* (1912)

Hoyt, Franklin. *A history of the desert region of Riverside County from 1540 to the completion of the railroad to Yuma in 1877*

Hughes, Tom. *History of Banning and San Gorgonio Pass*

Hunt, Rockwell D. *California in the making: essays and papers in California History* (1953)

James, George Wharton. *California, romantic and beautiful* (1914)

———. *Hotel Men's Mutual Benefit Association yearbook* (1898)

———. *Tourists guide book to Southern California for the traveler, invalid, pleasurist, and home seeker* (1904)

———. *Wonders of the Colorado Desert* (1906)

Jensen, Thomas A. *Palm Springs, California: its evolution and functions.* M.A. Thesis, University of California at Los Angeles (1954)

Johnson, J. Neely. *Daily Journal for 1857* (California State Archives)

Kemble, Edward C. *A history of California newspapers* (published as a supplement to the Sacramento *Union* of Dec. 25, 1858, and edited by Helen Harding Bretnor (1962)

Llangsdorf, William B. *The real estate boom of 1887 in Southern California.* M.S. Thesis, Occidental College.

Lewis, Oscar. *The big four* (1938)

Lindley, Walter and Widney, J. P. *California of the south* (1888)

Lloyd, Elwood IV. *Enchanted Sands* (1939)

Melendy, H. Brett and Gilbert, Benjamin F. *The governors of California: Peter H. Burnett to Edmund G. Brown* (1965)

Nelson, Jack. *The history of Palm Springs* (1948)

Nordhoff, Charles. *California for health, pleasure, and residence* (1872)

Owens, John Robert. *California politics and parties* (1970)

Phillips, Herbert. *Big, wayward girl; an informal political history of California* (1968)

Rodman, Paul W. *Mining frontiers of the far West, 1848-1880* (1963)

Richards, Elizabeth W. *A look into Palm Springs past* (1961)

Robinson, W. W. *Land in California* (1948)

———. *The story of Riverside County* (1957)

———. *The story of San Bernardino County* (1962)

Roske, Ralph J. *Everyman's Eden, history of California* (1968)

Sandmeyer, Elmer C. *The anti-Chinese movement in California* (1939)

Scott, John. *The Indiana gazetteer* (1826)

Shinn, Charles H. *Mining camps, a study in American frontier government* (1885)

Shumway, Nina Paul. *Your desert and mine* (1960)

Shuck, Oscar T. *History of the bench and bar in California* (1910)

Shutes, Milton H. *Lincoln and California* (1943)

Swisher, Carl Brent. *Motivation and political technique in the California Constitutional Convention, 1878-1879* (1930)

Truman, Major Benjamin S. *Semi-tropical California* (1874)

U.S. Congress. House Committee on Indian Affairs. *Palm Springs band of Mission Indians*
U.S. Dept. of Interior. Office of Indian Affairs. *Indian Office annual report, 1884, 1885, 1893*

Van Dyke, Theodore S. *Millionaires for a day* (1890)
————. *Southern California* (1886)

Waldron, D. G., ed. *Biographical sketches of the delegates to the Convention to frame a new Constitution for the State of California* (1878)
Whitman, Howard. *Brighter later life* (1961)
Willis, E. B. and P. K. Stockton, eds. *Debates and proceedings of the Constitutional convention, 1879.* 3 vols. (1880)
Willis, William L. *History of Sacramento County* (1913)
Wilson, Neill C. *Southern Pacific, the roaring story of a fighting railroad* (1952)
W. P. A. Writer's Program. *Indiana* (1941)

Young, John P. *Journalism in California* (1915)

PERIODICALS AND NEWSPAPERS

Alta California. Issues of June 3, 4, 5, 1868; Sept. 2, 11, 13, 22, 25, 1868; Oct. 2, 11, 1868.
Ardmore, Jane. "Memories of a desert Pearl," *West,* Sept. 25, 1966
Banning Herald. "Railroad lands on the reservation," Feb. 16, 1889.
Bartlett, Lanier. "When 'Angels' were devils (Los Angeles in the mellow '80s)" *Westways,* v. 26, no. 5, May 1934
Braunton, Ernest. "Diary" (excerpts), *Desert Sun,* May 10, 1930
————. "Palm Springs before the dudes came" *Westways* 26; 20-21, Nov. 1934.
Burke, Tony. "Down memory lane," *Palm Springs Villager,* Oct. 1957, and Jan. 1958.
Crawford, Hildy. "Palm Springs history." *Palm Springs Life.* Annual Pictorial, 1964-65.
Desert Sun. "Tramway," Feb. 23, 1963.

Fitch, George Hamlin. "A trip to Palm Valley in 1892," *Californian,* vol. 8, Oct. 1892.
————. "Where the date palm grows," *Land of Sunshine,* v. 13: 136-142.
Georgetown Weekly News from Oct. 19, 1854, to May 23, 1856.
Gerry, Helen. "In days gone by," *Palm Springs Villager,* vol. 5, Oct. 1950.
Gilman, M. French. "Reminiscences," *Desert Sun,* May 16, 1930.
Henderson, Randall. "Roving laboratory of the desert," *Desert Magazine,* July 1958.
Hicks, Harold J. "You can't live here without water," *Palm Springs Villager,* Dec. 1950.
Jaeger, Edmund. "4th of July in 1889" *Palm Springs Villager,* July 1951.
————. "From cheese to cash, history of the post office," *Palm Springs Villager,* Feb. 1951.
Los Angeles Examiner. Obituaries. Mrs. McManus, July 26, 1966.
Los Angeles Herald-Express. "Moral Re-Armament members' visit to Pearl McManus. I Nov. 13, 1960.
Los Angeles Times. "First lady of Palm Springs dies," July 25, 1966.
McManus, Pearl McCallum. "I remember Palm Springs," as told to Lou Jacobs, Jr. *Westways,* Oct. 1959.
————. "The founding of Palm Springs," as told to Carl Kulberg. *Palm Springs Villager,* Feb. 16, 1959.
Mitchell, Edmund. "Winter at Palm Springs," *Sunset,* 10:352-3, Feb. 1903.
Mountain Democrat. Feb. 15, 1854, March 4, 1857.
Murbarger, Nell. "Palm Springs ghost hotel," *Westways,* Dec. 1949.
Oakland Times. July 1, 1880.
Palm Springs Villager Annual, 1960-1961.
Remondino, P. C. "Climates of Southern California," *Californian,* viii, p. 58.
Riverside Press and Horticulturist. "Palmdale Letter," July 14, 1888.
Riverside Press Telegram. Aug. 13, 1961.
Robinson, W. W. "It all started with Agua Caliente." *Westways,* Feb. 1963.
Sacramento Union. Sept. 4, 1856, March 5, 1866.
San Francisco Chronicle. Sept. 3, 1914.

Shumway, Nina Paul. "Patriarch of Palm Springs," *Desert Magazine*, July 1949.

True, Clara D. "Experiences of a woman Indian agent" (Life at the Morongo Reservation, near Banning.) *Outlook* 92:331-336, June 5, 1909.

"Three health resorts (Beaumont, Banning, and Palm Springs) *Sunset*, Dec. 1899.

"We had a railroad (old Palmdale Land Co.) 1880 boom," *Palm Springs Villager*, April 1950.

Wheeler, George A. "Mrs. McManus watched her desert sand turn into gold," *Wheeler's Digest Letter*, Sept. 1966.

"Wild horses of Palm Canyon," *Palm Springs Villager*, Nov. 1950.

Wilhelm, Jack. "One hundred years in the Coachella Valley," *Palm Springs Villager*, Dec. 1954.

————. "When Palm Springs was a stage stop," *Palm Springs Villager*, Oct. 1947.

Winder, A. Heber. "Early days in Palm Springs" *Palm Springs Limelight.* Jan. 29, 1928; Feb. 5, 1938; Feb. 19; March 5; March 12; March 19; April 2; April 23; May 21; May 28, 1938.

HISTORICAL SOCIETY JOURNALS

Auchampaugh, Phillip G. "James Buchanan and some far Western leaders, 1860-1861." *Pacific Historical Review* (June, 1943), 169-180.

Bacon, Walter R. "Fifty years of California politics," *Historical Society of Southern California Publications*, V (1900), 36.

Dickson, Edward A. "How the Republican Party was organized in California," *Historical Society of Southern California Quarterly*, XXX (Sept. 1848), pp. 200-202.

Florcken, Herbert C. "Correspondence of Gov. J. Neely Johnson," *California Historical Society Quarterly*, XIV (Dec. 1935 and March, June, Sept. 1936).

George, Henry. "The Kearney agitation in California," *Popular Science Monthly*, XVII (August 1880), 433-453.

————. "What the railroad will bring us," *Overland Monthly* (Oct. 1868), 297-304.

Guinn, James M. "The great real estate boom of 1887," *Historical Society of Southern California. Annual*, 1890, v.1, 13-21.

————. "Pioneer railroads in Southern California," *Historical Society of Southern California Publications*, v. VIII, 1911.

Hurt, Peyton. "Rise and fall of the 'Know Nothings' in California." *California Historical Society Quarterly*, IX (March 1930), 16-49.

Kauer, Ralph. "The Workingman's Party in California." *Pacific Historical Review*, XIII (Sept. 1944), 278-291.

Moorhead, Dudley. "Sectionalism and the California Constitution of 1897." *Pacific Historical Review*, XII (Sept. 1943), 287-294.

Parker, Edna Monch. "Southern Pacific Railroad and settlements in Southern California." *Pacific Historical Review*, V, VI (1937), 103-119.

Pomeroy, Earl. "California, 1846-1860: politics of a representative frontier state." *California Historical Society Quarterly*, XXXII (Dec. 1953), 291-302.

Shute, Milton H. "Lincoln's California contacts." *California Historical Society Quarterly*, XXII, p. 183.

Thayer, Mabel R. "California pioneer journalists from 1846-1857." *Historical Society of Southern California Quarterly*, V, XI-2.

Wheat, Carl I. "A sketch of the life of Theodore D. Judah," *California Historical Society Quarterly*, IV (Sept. 1925), 219-271.

Zorrow, William. "California sidelights on the presidential election of 1864," *California Historical Society Quarterly*, XXXIV (March 1955), 29-64.

CORRESPONDENCE AND JOURNALS

McCallum, Harry F. "Diary excerpt," Feb. 8, 1899.

————. Letters to Father. J. G. McCallum, dated June 26, 1890; June 29, 1890; June 30, 1890; July 2, 1890; July 3, 1890; July 4, 1890; July 14, 1890; July 16, 1890; July 19, 1890; July 21, 1890.

————. Letter to brother Wallace McCallum, June 27, 1890.

———. Letters to brother John McCallum, dated June 23, 1890; and July 5, 1890.

———. Letters to Greenwade, manager of desert ranch, dated June 28, 1890; July 1, 1890; July 5, 1890; July 7, 1890; July 11, 1890.

McCallum, John Guthrie. Letter to Major O. C. Miller, Feb. 12, 1887.

———. Letter to Manager-General Towne, S. P. R.R. Co., requesting passenger rate reductions.

———. Letter to Jerome Madden, Esq., Land Agents S.P.R.R. Co., March 11, 1887.

———. Letter to Mrs. W. N. Monroe, Sept. 19, 1890.

———. Letter to Register U.S. Land Office, Shasta, Calif., Sept. 24, 1890.

———. Letter to Tax Collector, Shasta County, Sept. 24, 1890.

———. Letter to F. A. Koetitz, Esq., Oct. 10, 1890.

———. Letter to H. E. Vandeman, Pomologist, Dept. of Agriculture, Washington, D.C., Aug. 10, 1890.

———.Letters notifying of delinquency payments sent to Mathews, Croches, Gilman, McIntyre, McKonkey, Walker, Johnson, Collins, Reeves, Hunt, Mathews, Scott, dated Oct. 28, 1890.

———. Letter to Dr. J. W. Dennis, offering land for sale, dated Oct. 31, 1890.

———. Letter to Maj. O. C. Miller, regarding names on delinquency list, dated Feb. 12, 1891.

———. Letter to Prof. H. F. Wheaton regarding receipt of payment of delinquent assessments.

———. Letter to J. C. Woodward, County Tax Collector, Riverside County, Nov. 28, 1896.

———. Letter to I. S. Clark, offering for sale shares in land company, Nov. 19, 1896.

McManus, Austin. Letter to wife Pearl on their wedding anniversary, April 6, 1945.

McKee, Ruth Eleanor (novelist and author of *Christopher Strange*). Letters to Katherine Ainsworth, dated Oct. 21, and Nov. 28, 1971.

McManus, Pearl McCallum. Letter to Philip C. Boyd, Sept. 1, 1959.

———. Letter dated July 26, 1951.

Miller, C. Letter to J. G. McCallum, discussing high cost of removing silt choking water supply in ditch, Feb. 11, 1889.

Richardson, C. E., assistant registrar Indiana University. Letter to Katherine Ainsworth discuss-ing J. G. McCallum's attendance at that University, Sept. 8, 1971.

DIRECTORIES AND CENSUS RECORDS

Chicago City Directory, 1889 to 1903.

Georgetown, California. Directory, 1862.

Indiana Census, 1820 and 1850.

Indiana Land Entries, Cincinnati District, comp. by Margaret R. Waters.

Los Angeles City Directory, 1887, 1889, 1883-84, to 1901.

Oakland, Calif. City Directory, 1887 to 1900.

Pasadena City Directory, 1914.

Riverside County. The great register, 1894-1896.

Sacramento, Calif. City directory, 1868, 1869, 1870-71, 1872, 1874.

AFFIDAVITS

County Clerk, San Diego, Calif. Death certificate for John McCallum, July 17, 1891.

County Clerk, Cook County, Illinois. Death certificate for Wallace McCallum, March 4, 1896.

Coroner, Riverside County, Calif. Report of Coroner's Jury and Coroner's certificate concerning natural death of John G. McCallum, Feb. 5, 1897.

Los Angeles, County Recorder's Office. Death certificate for John G. McCallum, Feb. 9, 1897.

County Clerk, Cook County, Illinois. Death certificate for Harry F. McCallum, Sept. 19, 1901.

U.S. Dept. of the Interior. Bureau of Land Management. State Office, Sacramento, Calif. Copies of two township plots filed in 1871 and 1872, signed by John McCallum.

U. S. Dept. of the Interior. Office of Indian Affairs. No. 549. Telegram dated July 17, 1883, from John F. Miller, U. S. Senator from California, to Hon. H. M. Teller, Secretary of the Interior, recommending John G. McCallum as Indian Agent.

Letter dated July 17, 1883, following up above recommendation.

Doc. 16879. Sept. 12, 1883. Telegram from J. F. Miller, U. S. Senator, to Hon. H. Price, Commissioner of Indian Affairs, inquiring about delay in McCallum appointment.

Doc. 17341. Sept. 18, 1883. Letter from James S. Delano, Acting Controller, Treasury Dept., to Hon. H. Price, Commissioner of Indian Affairs, concerning McCallum bond.

Doc. 8653. May 3, 1884. Letter from James S. Delano, Acting Comptroller, Treasury Dept., to Hon. H. Price, Commissioner of Indian Affairs, notifying him of receipt of McCallum bond.

Doc. 15407. Aug. 21, 1883. Letter from J. G. McCallum to Hon. H. Price, Commissioner of Indian Affairs, returning corrected bond and necessary affidavits.

Doc. 95. Jan. 3, 1884. Notice from A. Hadley, acting Chief Clerk to Commissioner of Indian Affairs, notifying him of John G. McCallum's appointment as Indian Agent.

Doc. 4b. Executive Appointments 1879-91, vol. 1. Certificate from President Chester A. Arthur appointing John G. McCallum Agent for Mission Indians of California.

Doc. 13243. July 21, 1883. Letter from William Lockwood, chief Clerk to Commissioner of Indian Affairs, transmitting commission for Indian Agent McCallum from President of the United States.

Doc. 6780. April 2, 1884. Letter from J. G. McCallum regarding forwarding of new official bond.

Doc. 7456. April 16, 1884. Letter from U. M. Tell, secretary to Commissioner of Indian Affairs, concerning return of bond application to J. G. McCallum for error corrections.

Doc. 8236. April 23, 1884. Letter from J. G. McCallum to Hon. H. Price, Commissioner of Indian Affairs, returning corrected bond.

Doc. 6130. March 14, 1885. Report from Robert S. Gardner, U. S. Indian Inspector to Secretary of the Interior, regarding his inspection of the Mission Agency, Potrero, California.

Doc. 12582. May 29, 1885. Letter from James Faris, Dep. Marshal, San Bernardino, relative to liquor traffic, Potrero Reservation.

Doc. 17415. July 25, 1885. Letter from S. K. Lankston to Indian Commissioner reporting on conditions at Potrero Reservation.

Doc. 26515A. Nov. 3, 1885. Testimony and deposition regarding wood cutting on the reservation.

Doc. 26515B. J. G. McCallum's response to the charges.

Doc. 23445. Oct. 1, 1885. Letter from John S. Ward, U. S. Indian Agent, to Hon. J.S.C. Atkins, Commissioner of Indian Affairs, taking charge of Potrero Reservation.

Doc. 20050. Aug. 22, 1885. Letter from J. G. McCallum to Hon. J. S. C. Atkins, tendering his resignation as Agent for Mission Indians, Potrero Reservation, Calif.

Doc. 20871. Sept. 8, 1885. Letter to Mr. John G. McCallum accepting his resignation on behalf of the President of the U. S.

Doc. 20321-35A. Appointment Division. Letters sent, vol. 37. Letter from J. S. C. Atkins, Commissioner of Indian Affairs, accepting his resignation as Indian Agent.

MISCELLANEOUS

Affidavit of Publication from San Diego Weekly Union Newspaper. Delinquent notices for Palm Valley Water Co. published on March 5, 1891.

Agreement between J. G. McCallum, D. C. Miller, Thos. W. Scott, attorney for J. G. Hill, dated August 30, 1887, authorizing McCallum to expend certain sums in the final development and promotion of the Palm City Colony.

Agreements between H. Hurley and J. G. McCallum for construction of two sections of the water ditch, dated Feb. 17, 1887, and May 10, 1887.

Bernard, Robert J. "Dedication of Harper East, McManus Hall, and Rosecrans Tower and Court." Speech given on Dec. 9, 1966, Claremont Colleges, Claremont, Calif.

Grant deed by Harry R. Stevens, Los Angeles, to J. G. McCallum, dated Feb. 12, 1891.

Grant deed by James O. Seymour, Los Angeles, Calif., to J. G. McCallum, dated Jan. 5, 1888.

Grant deed by John Stephens to J. G. McCallum, dated April 12, 1887.

Grant deed by M. Byrne to J. G. McCallum, dated Nov. 5, 1887.

Grant deed by Pearl McCallum to Carl Eytel, dated April 30, 1898.

Grant deed by W. E. Van Slyke and M. Byrne to J. G. McCallum, dated March 24, 1885.

Grant deed by Wallace McCallum to J. G. McCallum, Feb. 2, 1889.

Indiana University. Bulletin June 1, 1911. Register of Graduates 1830-1910.

McCallum, Harry F. Contractual agreement with E. J. Jones and O. Pierce, dated August 8, 1896, establishing mining partnership in the Palm Valley Quartz Mine.

McCallum, John Guthrie. Notice dated Feb. 13, 1886, claiming 300 inches of water from Chino Canyon.

McFarland, C. L. "History of water rights controlled by the Palm Springs Water Company." Speech.

McFie, Maynard, "The gay nineties," a paper read at the Sunset Club, Oct. 27, 1944, and published by the Club.

McManus, Pearl McCallum. Letter to Mr. George C. Witter, Los Angeles, outlining her plans for developing Sect. 23 in Palm Springs.

————. Deposition concerning history of McCallum lands and water damage caused by floods and governmental neglect, dated April 4, 1911.

Quit Claim deed by E. H. Thomas to J. G. McCallum and W. E. Van Slyke, dated Jan. 22, 1887.

Report of Commissioner of General Land Office. June 30, 1943. Land grants to Railroads.

Report of Joseph W. Preston, special Indian Agent for the Mission Indians, regarding construction of Whitewater Ditch upon reservation lands, Feb. 7, 1888, and notarized May 10, 1888.

Index

Index

Compiled by Anna Marie and Everett G. Hager

THE McCALLUM SAGA,
*designed by Grant Dahlstrom, has been
composed on the Linotype in
Herman Zapf's Aldus types with Monotype
Bembo chapter heads,
and has been printed on Publisher's
Opaque Text Natural.*